JOHN CANGELOSI

The Improbable Baseball Journey
of the Undersized Kid from Nowhere
to **WORLD SERIES CHAMPION**

JOHN CANGELOSI
AND K.P. WEE

For more information contact:
Riverdale Avenue Books
5676 Riverdale Avenue
Riverdale, NY 10471.

www.riverdaleavebooks.com

Design by www.formatting4U.com
Cover by Scott Carpenter
Digital ISBN: 9781626015135
Print ISBN: 9781626015142
First Edition July 2019

For my parents, John and Gladys, and my children, Alexandra and Austin.
—John Cangelosi

For Rick Ambrozic, Rick Tanton, Adrian Brijbassi, and Nahyun L. Thank you for your unconditional support. Also, for Michael McCormick. You know why.
—K. P. Wee

Table of Contents

Acknowledgments

This idea for this book first came about when I was discussing baseball from the 1980s and 1990s with Michael McCormick, a Chicago-based lawyer. During that conversation, McCormick mentioned his son Matt was taking private lessons to improve his batting technique.

As I resided in Vancouver, Canada, these baseball discussions were being conducted via emails and text messages. Suddenly, John Cangelosi's name came up in the conversation because it just so happened that McCormick's son was receiving his lessons from the former major-league outfielder, who had, following his playing career, founded Cangelosi Baseball, an indoor baseball training facility in Lockport, Illinois.

Being a baseball fan for three decades, I knew of Cangelosi because I watched as many games on TV as I could well in an era before the Internet existed. Back in those days, other than the postseason and World Series games, there were only the usual "Game of the Week" (on ABC, NBC, or CBS over the years) or "ESPN Sunday Night Baseball" that was shown in Canada on TSN. Or Toronto Blue Jays, Montreal Expos and Seattle Mariners games shown on other local stations. And, also TBS (Atlanta Braves), WGN

(Chicago Cubs) and KTLA (Los Angeles Dodgers) games because those "super stations" were part of my TV package. Okay, maybe I did watch a lot of games back then, but this was an era in which not *every* major-league game was televised. You watched whatever was shown on television.

John Cangelosi never played for any of those teams. He wasn't a superstar or even an everyday player on his ball clubs—the Chicago White Sox, Pittsburgh Pirates, Texas Rangers, New York Mets, Houston Astros, Florida Marlins and Colorado Rockies. He was, essentially, a well-traveled journeyman who hit only 12 home runs in the big leagues in an era where "chicks dig the long ball." (That phrase comes from a late 1990s Nike commercial featuring Atlanta Braves pitchers Tom Glavine and Greg Maddux, along with St. Louis Cardinals slugger Mark McGwire, in which actress Heather Locklear is giving McGwire all the attention because he hits home runs and doesn't care about the Cy Young Awards won by Glavine and Maddux. That commercial pretty much sums up that era, where baseball fans cared more about long balls than the small-ball style of play that the light-hitting Cangelosi was proficient at.)

In Cangelosi's case, over his final eight big-league seasons, he hit a total of six home runs… while playing for six different teams. He wasn't a player who made the headlines a lot.

But, as mentioned, I knew of Cangelosi—despite the fact he was a utility player for the majority of his career—because I watched as much baseball on television as I could. (Well, and also because I played Strat-O-Matic and collected baseball cards…) And in the hundreds of games I saw over the years, it seemed that whenever the scrappy, switch-hitting outfielder was in the lineup, he was frequently getting on base and stealing bases against the Braves or Dodgers or Expos. (He got on base a lot against Braves right-hander John Smoltz, a future Hall of Famer.) Or in a nationally-televised ESPN game somewhere (that was shown on TSN in Canada).

Of course, the above comment about fans "digging the long ball" isn't meant to say that that particular era—Cangelosi played in the major leagues from 1986 to 1999 after a brief call-up in 1985—was all about home runs when it came to the offensive side of the game. Exciting players such as Rickey Henderson and Kenny Lofton—and even guys like Otis Nixon, Deion Sanders and Vince Coleman, to name a few—brought fans out of their seats with their incredible—and, at times daring—display of base running. Those were electrifying base stealers who, everyone knew, were going to wreak havoc on the base paths when they got on base.

No, Cangelosi wasn't a Henderson or a Lofton. Because he wasn't an everyday player during the prime of his major-league career, the speedy Cangelosi wasn't in the same category as those base-stealing star outfielders. But when called upon late in the game, he would come off the bench and work the count. He would draw a walk. Steal a base to put himself in scoring position. Not the "sexy" brand of baseball that fans loved in the 1990s—he wasn't going to hit one into the upper deck and he certainly wasn't flashy like a Lofton or a Sanders—but he got the job done in helping his team get a run. And he would do these—get on base and steal the next base—a lot. At least that's what I remembered.

The one thing that both McCormick, who is also an avid baseball memorabilia collector, and I were amazed by was how Cangelosi was able to play 10-plus years in the big leagues despite being an undersized player. At 5'8", Cangelosi wasn't intimidated when stepping into the batter's box to face the likes of Nolan Ryan and Roger Clemens. He must have some good stories about his journey in baseball, we both thought, that he wouldn't mind sharing that could inspire kids. His work ethic, we agreed, must have been off the charts when he was, first, trying to make it to the big leagues, and two, trying to stay there while competing with guys who were bigger than him. In the era in which Cangelosi played, teams seemed to always be looking for bigger and stronger guys who could hit the ball out of the park. The fact that Cangelosi lasted that long in the big leagues must have been a testament to his work ethic and determination, and his will to succeed. Surely, his story would be inspirational to readers. How can anyone who reads his story, we thought, not be inspired by how he overcame the ups and downs in his baseball life?

McCormick and I texted each other back and forth to discuss all these things about the man known as "Cangy." After that lengthy conversation, McCormick sought out Cangelosi, who was interested in discussing his baseball life—and having a book written about it—if it meant being able to inspire others through his stories.

Thank you, obviously, to McCormick for reaching out, and to John Cangelosi for being gracious with his time and willing to share the stories about his improbable baseball journey. Both men were also kind enough to share photos to be used for this book.

Several of his former coaches and managers, along with a rival coach and a former teammate, were more than happy to discuss Cangelosi. These included Harold Baines, John Boles, Terry Collins, Shelly Dunkel, Paul Mainieri, Tommy Sandt and Bobby Valentine. Thank you for spending the time to share your thoughts on John. Thank you too to Jay Horwitz, the PR Director of the New York Mets.

Finally, thank you to Rick Ambrozic, Rick Tanton, Adrian Brijbassi and Nahyun L. Your unconditional support has been inspiring and helped to push me to complete this story. Thank you to you all.

—K. P. Wee
Spring 2019

Introduction

Sunday, October 26, 1997, at Pro Player Stadium.

It was Game Seven of the World Series, with the score 2-2 with one out in the bottom of the 10th inning and two men on for the Florida Marlins. On the mound was Cleveland Indians closer Jose Mesa, one of the best closers in baseball. Two years earlier, in fact, Mesa was the best in the business, as he converted 38 consecutive saves in one stretch—a major-league record at the time—and was instrumental in the Indians' 100-44 regular-season record.

At the plate was a 5'8" pinch-hitter by the name of John Cangelosi, who in his 10th season in the big leagues was in the biggest at-bat of his major-league career. And he was doing it in front of a crowd of 67,204, ready to celebrate if Cangelosi, who grew up in Southern Florida, made contact. A base hit would win the World Series. A walk would load the bases for Moises Alou, one of the hitting stars for the Marlins in the Series.

And the 3-and-2 pitch from Mesa…

* * *

That at-bat had to be the pinnacle of John Cangelosi's career. It had taken him 10 seasons to make an appearance in the Major League Baseball postseason, and there he was, batting in extra innings in the seventh game of the World Series in a stadium a half-hour's drive away from Hialeah, Florida, where he grew up. Even without that World Series appearance, though, the fact that he managed to stay that long in the big leagues was quite a story in itself.

Reaching the major leagues is a difficult accomplishment. When we see a smaller player make it, one who defied all the odds, we tend to root for him because many people cheer for the little guy who makes it big. For an undersized player to be in the big leagues for 10 seasons? It's a remarkable achievement indeed. In today's world of social media, that player automatically becomes a legend.

In the 1980s, the days before social media, however, it was harder for such a player to gain the attention he deserved. Today, we celebrate Jose Altuve, a little guy (5'6") who is an American League Most Valuable Player and a World Champion. Thanks to social media, everything Altuve does on the baseball field is magnified and his accomplishments are celebrated.

In the 1980s, this was impossible. Take Cangelosi, for example, the switch-hitting outfielder who was listed at 5'8"—although some scouts who watched him would insist he was an inch or two shorter than that.

Cangelosi was a little guy labeled "the kid from nowhere"—a phrase the Chicago newspapers of the day were using—who beat out highly-touted prospect Daryl Boston and established veteran Rudy Law (who had stolen a White Sox-record 77 bases just three years earlier) to improbably make the Opening Day lineup as the starting center fielder for the Chicago

White Sox. In his rookie year, he rewarded White Sox manager Tony La Russa for having faith in him by challenging future Hall of Famer Rickey Henderson for the stolen-base lead in the first half of the season. Cangelosi later platooned with Barry Bonds in left field with Pittsburgh—when the future home-run king was in his first few seasons in the big leagues. The undersized Cangelosi would draw walks because of his size—thus compiling solid on-base percentages—and proceed to steal second base to put himself in scoring position.

As Cangelosi himself admits, not all managers liked him on their teams, but the legendary Jim Leyland saw him as one of the missing pieces when building the roster for the 1997 Florida Marlins. Signed as a free agent in the winter of 1996, Cangelosi was a reserve outfielder for Leyland's Marlins and won a World Series ring. "After I left Pittsburgh after the 1990 season, for about five or six years I played for several ball clubs and had a couple of setbacks in the minor leagues," Cangelosi recalls. "But I just never gave up, and good things happened for me in 1995 and 1996 with the Houston Astros and got my career back on track. Then, to play for the Florida Marlins... that was just outstanding. I mean, I believe good things happen to people who work hard. I believe you keep trying to get better, and good things happen."

Such a career is one that should be celebrated. Here was a guy who defied all the odds and not only did he have a 10-year career in Major League Baseball, he also has a World Series ring in his collection. In fact, that ring wasn't even the first one of his pro career. In his first season in pro baseball, he won a ring as a member of the Niagara Falls (New York) Sox, hitting a home run in the 1982 New York-Penn League Championship Series to defeat future Denver Broncos quarterback John Elway's Class-A Oneonta Yankees. And although the feat has been long forgotten, in his rookie year in the big leagues Cangelosi broke a long-standing single-season American League stolen-base record. Cangelosi, because of his work ethic and hustle, was a fan favorite in Chicago and is still recognized in the Midwest because he runs his own baseball school to help kids in the area. Had social media existed during his playing career, it's possible fans would have demanded that his teams start him in the outfield ahead of other teammates. He was a guy that the average fan identified with: a little guy who hustled and had a dream, and made it happen. Fans care about players such as John Cangelosi, who was the proverbial "little engine that could." Fans wanted guys like him to succeed.

In this book, *John Cangelosi: The Improbable Baseball Journey of the Undersized Kid from Nowhere to World Series Champion*, Cangelosi discusses the managers who had the greatest impact in his career, such as Jim Leyland, John Boles and Terry Collins. He discusses what it was like playing with Barry Bonds and Nolan Ryan, as well as his friendship with Bonds, baseball's all-time home run champion. He talks about facing tough pitchers such as John Smoltz and Roger Clemens, and even about how his aggressiveness on the field rubbed legends Clemens, Jack Morris and Sparky Anderson the wrong way. He mentions Toledo, where he played Triple-A ball in 1993. He even discusses his thoughts on performance-enhancing drugs, giving a perspective that is refreshing in that it isn't what you would expect.

Above all, this book tells the story of John Cangelosi's improbable journey in baseball, and it's also a book that we hope will inspire and encourage those who have been told they "can't do it," to keep working hard and have the belief in yourself to succeed.

—K. P. Wee, November 2018

* * *

My Major League Baseball career began in 1985—after a stint in Mexico City earlier that summer—and I became the Opening Day center fielder for the Chicago White Sox the following year. I had a lot of ups and downs during my playing career—and I played for many organizations, including the Pittsburgh Pirates, Texas Rangers, New York Mets, Houston Astros, Florida Marlins and Colorado Rockies—but through hard work and perseverance, I managed to last in the big leagues until 1999.

My career in baseball was an unexpected journey. I mean, a guy my size should not have been in the big leagues. Being a blue-collar guy, I worked hard each and every day even during the times when I was sent down to the minor leagues—whether it was to Buffalo or Vancouver or Toledo—because my goal was always to get back to the big leagues. Every spring training, I had to battle for a job, and my story had a great ending in 1997 when I won the World Series with the Florida Marlins in front of my family.

Essentially, when baseball fans look back at my career, they will remember me as an underdog, an overachiever, a guy who got the most out of his ability. I never gave up. People would tell me I was too short to play in the big leagues. But I ignored them and I kept battling every day. My story, I think, is something that other blue-collar guys can relate to. For the reader, I think it could be an inspirational story in terms of how to get the most out of your ability. Of course, it's not just in baseball. It's something that can be applied to anything you do in life. If you really believe in your abilities and you create a routine, you're going to be successful in the path you're pursuing. That's kind of what my baseball career was about.

I hope that the stories about the ups and downs I encountered in baseball can help to deliver that message to guys who have been told, "You can't get the job"—to not quit, to not give up, to keep fighting. At the end of the day, I hope that my story in baseball can help inspire others to keep knocking doors down, to keep believing, no matter what field they are in. You just have to believe in yourself and keep working towards your goal until you finally achieve it.

—John Cangelosi, November 2018

Chapter One
Growing Up

Johnny never thought so, but he was always one of the best players in Dade County. All the other coaches thought so. Johnny didn't believe it. To this day, there are coaches [whom I run into] that Johnny might've made a play [against] that helped us win a ballgame. They would say, "I'm glad he's gone! I'm glad he's gone! He was a wrecking crew!"

—Shelly Dunkel, Cangelosi's former high
school baseball coach (2018)

"Here's what you need to do… Do you unnnnerstand that? Does that make sense?" the Brooklyn-born hitting coach can be heard year-round yelling in the batting cage. "Practice with a purpose!" and "Practice the right way!" are also often heard when the 5'8" coach is instructing his pupils in the indoor baseball training facility in Lockport, Illinois, some 30 miles southwest of Chicago.

"I was born in Brooklyn, but the neighborhood became drug-infested and so we moved," explains the coach, taking time out of his busy coaching schedule on a Thursday one winter afternoon to reminisce about his baseball life. "My dad bought a small house in a little area in Florida called Hialeah. Moving to Hialeah had a great impact on my life. I was able to play baseball practically year-round. So, my dad was a big influence for being so supportive." And now, the coach wants kids in the Chicago area to be able to practice and play baseball year-round, just like he had during his youth.

The hitting coach is none other than John Cangelosi, founder of Cangelosi Baseball, located inside the Bo Jackson's Elite Sports facility.

Yes, THAT John Cangelosi, the guy who seemingly came out of nowhere to steal a then-American League rookie record 50 bases for the Chicago White Sox in the mid-1980s. (The Chicago papers, in fact, were calling him "the 5-7 Kid from Nowhere" when he became the White Sox's starting center fielder in 1986.) Yes, John Cangelosi, the scrappy former Major League Baseball switch-hitting outfielder who wound up having a 10-year big-league career, winning a World Series ring with the Florida Marlins in 1997. Now, "Cangy," or "Candyman," as he is nicknamed, is back in Chicago helping young kids with the fundamentals, kids who want to someday play in the big leagues as he had from 1985 to 1999.

"My dad taught me a lot about the game at a young age," reflects Cangelosi. "Many of the things he taught me, I use today in my baseball organization." For example, he tells the kids that it's not about winning or losing—or trying to be the best. "It's about loyalty, work ethic, respecting the game and trying to be your best. And if it means you don't win that day, you don't win. But you can't put winning ahead of all those other things. And that's what my dad taught me at a very young age. "That work ethic, along with the knowledge he learned over the years from coaches and other players, is one of the reasons Cangelosi managed to play in the big leagues for 10 seasons, as far as Shelly Dunkel, his former high school coach, is concerned. "I'm not surprised he had that long of a career in the pros," adds Dunkel with a smile today when reflecting on Cangelosi's career. "I still talk to his parents now. They're great people, John and Gladys. Johnny was a great kid too."

* * *

March 10, 1963, was a big day in sports. On that day, future Naismith Memorial Basketball Hall of Famer Wilt Chamberlain scored 70 points—his third-highest point total that season—in the San Francisco Warriors' 163-148 loss to the Syracuse Nationals. Chamberlain, playing in his fourth NBA season, would go on to lead the league in points per game for the fourth consecutive year, at 44.8. In an exhibition baseball game between the Reds and White Sox, meanwhile, 21-year-old rookie Pete Rose went 2-for-2 in his first appearance in a Cincinnati uniform. The future all-time major-league leader in hits would be named the National League's Rookie of the Year that season. On the ice, the National Hockey League's Toronto Maple Leafs extended their undefeated streak to six games with a 1-1 tie in Chicago. The streak would reach 10 before being snapped, and Toronto would go on to win its second straight Stanley Cup—and its 11th overall—a month later. The Maple Leafs would capture two more Stanley Cup championships in the decade—but have never won another.

March 10, 1963, was also the day that John Anthony Cangelosi, the son of an Italian aircraft mechanic, was born. The future Major League Baseball switch-hitter was born to John and Gladys Cangelosi in Brooklyn, New York, five years after the Dodgers had moved from the neighborhood of Flatbush to the City of Angels, Los Angeles. "No, I'm not John Jr. or John the Third or whatever. I'm just John Cangelosi. Well, everyone called me Johnny. My dad is John. I'm just Johnny," Cangelosi explains.

"I hadn't been born yet when the Dodgers were in Brooklyn. My dad was a Brooklyn Dodgers fan. They had some great teams there in the 1950s. But when the team moved west, he said, 'Forget it.' Like a lot of other Brooklyn fans, he never transferred his allegiance to L.A. He became a New York Mets fan instead in the 1960s."

And in fact, the family didn't stay in Brooklyn, either. Cangelosi's father moved the family to Hialeah, Florida, when little Johnny was still in his early childhood years, to get out of their rough neighborhood. "I was born in Brooklyn, but I left there when I was four," says Cangelosi now when asked to reminisce about his childhood in the most populous borough of New York City. "I know I lived in a couple of apartments—and my relatives still lived there—but I really don't recollect much." While he doesn't have a lot of memories about Brooklyn, he does remember going back to New York as a youngster to visit his cousins. "My parents used to take us back to New York once a year to see my [relatives]. One time, we snuck into a game in New York to watch a baseball game," he says now, recalling a time in 1972 when he was at Shea Stadium with one of his cousins. "We were sitting in the stands. I looked at my cousin and said, 'I'm gonna play for the Mets one day.' And I ended up playing for the Mets in '94—so that was kinda a cool little story.

4

"But I wasn't really a Mets fan. Or a Dodgers fan, for that matter. I loved Willie Mays, who, of course, played many years for the Giants! But that day sitting in the stands with my cousin… I remember Jerry Grote was catching, Ed Kranepool was at first base, [Bud] Harrelson was at shortstop, Cleon Jones was in left field, Rusty Staub was in right field, but I can't remember who was their third baseman that day. I think Willie Mays was on that team. Tom Seaver was on that team, also, but he wasn't pitching on that day…"

But he does have a Tom Seaver story. When Cangelosi made it to the White Sox's Opening Day lineup in 1986 as a rookie, the former Mets ace was pitching for Chicago that afternoon. "Everyone has a story about when they met their idol; in my case, I watched Tom Seaver growing up," Cangelosi says now. "He was traded to Boston that year in my rookie year, but he started the season in Chicago."

For Cangelosi, meeting his idol wasn't exactly what he thought it would be like. "Anyway, I had just made the team and everyone was congratulating me, because I wasn't supposed to make the team. So, that was pretty cool. On Opening Day, I was starting in center field and Tom was the starting pitcher. So then, about an hour before the game started, Tom pulled me into the lounge. I thought he was gonna congratulate me too; I was thinking, 'Man, this is great. He's gonna congratulate me! This is Tom Seaver, a guy I watched growing up!' But in the lounge, he was playing with his finger by his thigh. He goes, 'Hey man, I want you to be watching me on the mound. If my thumb goes this way, I want you to move to the left. If my thumb goes that way, I want you to move to the right. You got it?'"

Cangelosi was taken aback by Seaver's instructions. The rookie center fielder, however, wasn't about to let the Hall-of-Famer-to-be intimidate him. "I go, 'Listen, Tom. I'll play center field. You worry about pitching.' I basically let him know that I would do my job, and he could worry about his own!"

He also had some memorable interactions with Pete Rose, the all-time hits king who collected two hits in his first-ever major-league spring-training game the same day Cangelosi was born. "Really? I never knew that," Cangelosi says when told about that piece of trivia. "How cool is that?" The two men first met in 1987, when Cangelosi's Pittsburgh Pirates were playing the Rose-managed Cincinnati Reds at Riverfront Stadium. "Back then at the old Cincinnati stadium, the batting cage was near the Reds' dugout," he recalls. "So, we were in town, and I was hitting in the cage before a game. Pete was sitting nearby and he was watching me hit. After I was done, he came up to me and said, 'Hey man, I like the way you play. You're a really good player.' That's Pete Rose, the all-time hits leader, coming up to talk to me! At the time, I was just in my second year in the big leagues. I said, 'Hey man, I'm not trying to blow smoke up your ass, but I model my game after you. Growing up, you were one of my favorite players…' It was a really good conversation. To me, he was a genuine person. I mean, I wish I'd had 4,000 hits in the big leagues like him.

"Then, years later, when he was out of baseball, I was in Vegas one year. I was in one of the malls… It was the mall at Caesars Palace, I think."

While walking around in that particular mall that summer day during the early 2000s, Cangelosi saw Rose signing autographs for fans in the sporting goods store. He figured he would approach the all-time hits king just to say hello. "As I was walking by, I saw this long lineup, but I decided to walk over. I said, 'Hey, Pete. I know you're busy but I just wanted to say hi.' He said, 'Nah, come sit down!' I sat down and we talked, as he was signing autographs. I believe I'd just retired from baseball at the time. He goes, 'What are you doing now?' He was in the middle of signing autographs and then he got up and said, 'Just stay here. I'm giving stuff away.' He went to the back and brought out a jersey with all his accolades on it—and gave that jersey to me.

"It's great to be able to spend time talking to players you grew up watching… And I mean, I got to play with quite a few Hall of Famers in my career, being teammates with Tom Seaver and also Carlton Fisk and Harold Baines in Chicago… I learned a lot about the game from watching and listening to a lot of these guys."

* * *

There were no Major League Baseball teams in Florida during Cangelosi's youth, but he was nonetheless a big baseball fan because he was able to catch the superstars like Seaver and Rose on television, on the Saturday *Game of the Week* broadcasts. And growing up in Hialeah, like many boys his age, Cangelosi loved all sports and played baseball as well as football and basketball in his youth. He, like the other kids in his neighborhood, also had the advantage of living near a park and playing sports year-round. "I played basketball, football and baseball," he says now. "When I became a little older,

I knew I couldn't play football or basketball, but I did like basketball. But I had a certain talent for baseball and I loved playing the game, so I continued it."

Coming from a middle-class family, the Cangelosis didn't always have a lot of money, and thinking back, John appreciates what his parents did for him so he could play sports, in particular baseball, at a young age. Baseball, he acknowledges today, is an expensive—not to mention time-consuming—sport. As Cangelosi reflects now, his father and mother made huge sacrifices for him—not just monetary but time-wise, too—to have a career in the game of baseball.

"My dad wasn't really around because he worked the night shift," says Cangelosi, recalling the fact that there was a time he and his brother rarely saw their father, an airplane mechanic for Eastern Air Lines, because of that work schedule. "When we got home from school, he would go to work. He would work from 3:00 to 11:00. He worked the night shift. When I came home, he was gone and he was working." Things changed, however, when Cangelosi wanted to play for a baseball league called the Hialeah Accord League—a league started by the father of future big-league umpire Angel Hernandez—and wanted his dad there with him.

"When I started playing for this league, I was a little intimidated and I asked him to be my coach because I didn't know any coaches," Cangelosi recalls. At that time, his father transferred to day shift to accommodate John's baseball schedule. "So, he would go to work at 6:00 or 7:00 in the morning and would be back at 3:00 or 4:00 and take me to practice and be my coach. My dad didn't really have to do that. He was used to a certain schedule. He changed that for me and to be there for me. My dad never really played organized baseball. He grew up in New York and played stick ball on the streets and stuff like that. He taught me a lot of things at a young age, [like] how to respect the game, how to apply myself, [and] how to practice. It's not about winning or losing. It's about playing the game. There are a lot of memories that I have of him, where he taught me value."

One lesson which took a long time for John to truly grasp was controlling his emotions on the field. But he tried his best over the years—because his father had taught him from the time he was in the Hialeah Accord League. "[One] thing that sticks out in my mind came in a game where I had a bad at-bat," Cangelosi says now. "I wore my emotions on my sleeves, so I showed my feelings on the field a lot. If I was mad or pissed off, I didn't really control it all that well when I was younger." One time, Cangelosi made an out in a key part of the game, and frustrated, he threw his helmet, intending to slam it on the ground. "But [the helmet] stuck to my finger and it went over the fence and hit a mom on the shoulder. My dad literally got me by my shoulder, dragged me over to the lady, and made me apologize. 'Never do that again,' he told me. It was a vivid memory. I learned at that time how to still stay mad but control it in a positive way.

"Instead of succumbing to it, I controlled it in a positive way. I channeled my anger when I did something wrong. I used it as a positive, like, 'I'll get 'em next time.' Or 'That ain't gonna happen again,' instead of feeling sorry for myself or taking it out on the field."

That wasn't the only thing his father taught him. Cangelosi also learned, at a young age, to respect the game. And respect the rules. As Shelly Dunkel, his high school coach, remembers, John knew right from wrong by the time he got to Miami Springs. "He had a girlfriend who worked for me as a batgirl at the time," laughs Dunkel, bringing up an example of how Cangelosi followed the rules that were laid out to him. "We had the understanding that business and pleasure don't mix. Let her do her job, he does his job, and stay away. He was good about it. He kept the two separate."

Cangelosi's mother Gladys, of course, was also a big influence early on. "My dad and mom were always there for me," Cangelosi explains. "We were middle-class people; we didn't have much money growing up. Traveling for baseball can be very expensive; they were on every road trip with me. We traveled a lot. My dad took time off work. There were a lot of other kids who would have to go with friends. I don't think my mom and dad ever, ever, missed one game of mine. Never. They were at every game. You take it for granted or you really don't understand the magnitude of it when you're younger, but looking back at it now, I mean, for me, one, it was a security blanket, and two, they got to experience me playing baseball, but it gave me a sense of security or comfort, and it instilled a certain confidence in me that everything was gonna be okay for me."

As Cangelosi himself acknowledges, his mother was there for him in different ways, too. According to him, Gladys had a huge impact in the development of his career, especially during the high school years and in the first years of his professional career. "I don't wanna sound like a softie or anything, but my mom was instrumental in my career," Cangelosi explains now. "The older I got, [the more] I would bounce things off my mom. She was more my security. I liked talking to her. My dad did a great job. But for some reason I had a connection with my mom." When Cangelosi was having a hard time, he would call her and say, "Hey mom, I'm struggling. I'm not seeing the ball." By the time the phone call ended, all the worries had disappeared. "She would have a way of turning it around and making me feel more confident when I got off the phone," he adds.

Cangelosi vividly recalls a specific conversation in his mother's car as she was driving him to a summer tryout. "In high school, you have a high school team and then in the summer time you have a tryout for a Summer League team," he explains. "They normally put three or four high schools in that district together. We would have a tryout and the best players would make that team. I played for this legion team, and this team was by far [the best]. It was an All-Star team. The first year that we played, we went all the way to the Legion World Series. We lost; we came in third place. We lost to [future Mets pitcher] Sid Fernandez; he was pitching for Hawaii and he ended up beating us. We went to the Junior Olympics. Our whole team went when, I wanna say, I was a sophomore or junior in high school, and we went to Colorado Springs. We ended up winning the gold medal. On that team there was me, [future big-league star] Danny Tartabull, Juan Bustabad—he was a shortstop drafted in the first round but never got to the big leagues; he played for Boston in the minor leagues—and a few other guys that got drafted. In fact, 11 of the 12 got drafted, but just me and Danny Tartabull made it to the big leagues.

"So, I'm a sophomore in the 10th grade. My mom's driving me to the tryouts. I go, 'Mom, I'm too small. I'm not gonna make this team.' I was being a little wuss. My mom pretty much kicked me out of the car. 'You get your little ass out there. You're gonna try out, and I'll pick you up in two hours.' I made the team, and the rest was history. It was a great team. A lot of great players came out of there."

His mom was there for him too when he made it to the pros. "When I was in A-ball, I was struggling. I didn't feel good. I called up my mom. She goes, 'Johnny, just go out and have fun. You'll forget about your problems.' She just had a way of defusing my pressure, and I liked talking to her. She made me come out of a lot of slumps and stuff." Even when the Chicago White Sox, who drafted him in the fourth round in 1982, optioned him to Mexico City, his mother was there for him when he was dealing with chicken pox. "We're a small family, very Italian," he adds. "We kinda stick together."

Interestingly, while John Cangelosi went on to play in Major League Baseball, he wasn't the most gifted athlete in the household. According to John himself, it was his brother Vince. "My brother is 18 months older than me," he says now. "My brother was, by far, a better athlete than me. Everything came easy to him. Unfortunately, he had some bad luck early on. But as far as being a pure athlete, my brother could do anything. Football, baseball, basketball. He could do anything he wanted to do, and not really work at it. He was really, really good."

An example of how John Cangelosi wore his emotions on his sleeves came when he had an argument with Vince—right there on the field. It was a quarrel that needed their father to break up. It was an incident which also might have led to Vince's quitting baseball. "I was 12 or 13 years old. My dad was still my coach. He had started coaching me when I was nine or 10.

"So, my dad's the coach. I'm pitching. My brother's the catcher. He finally wanted to play again [after not playing for a year]. My brother would play one year and then not play. That was his downfall. He never stayed with it. I don't know what it was. But he could've had a very promising career in pretty much any sport that he wanted to play.

"So, I'm pitching. I'm wild. I walk the bases loaded. It was 100 degrees in Florida. It's hot and miserable. I'm walking everybody. I think I walk in two or three runs. I'm still on the mound. My brother starts throwing the ball back at me, harder and harder. I told him, 'Stop throwing the ball hard at me. If you do that one more time, I'm gonna let the ball go into center field.' Basically, we start arguing. And I think after that game, it was the last game my brother played. He quit and started doing other things."

In terms of athletics, that was the biggest difference between the brothers. John Cangelosi was determined to play professional baseball; he wouldn't entertain the idea of giving up on his dream. Even if he was having a bad game or things were going tough, he wasn't going to quit. He was going to try to beat you whenever he was on the field, no matter what. Even at a young age, it was clear that Cangelosi had passion for the game.

Those qualities were easily noticeable, even by rival coaches. "And that's how I got recruited to play junior college," Cangelosi reflects now.

Chapter Two
The Road to the Majors

Jim Hendry and I both went to my father, Demie Mainieri. I said, 'Pops, there's this kid at Miami Springs that you've got to get.' We told him all about Johnny Cangelosi, and why we thought that he would be an excellent player. I don't think many schools were recruiting John because of his size. And my dad recruited him just based on Jim's and my recommendation. And Johnny ended up going to Dade-North and having a terrific career.

> —Paul Mainieri, former Columbus High School
> assistant baseball coach (2018)

Paul Mainieri, then an assistant baseball coach with Columbus High School, knew there was something special about John Cangelosi, a short but speedy center fielder for the rival Miami Springs High School. It was apparent watching him play from the opposing dugout and from the coach's box.

Mainieri, now the Head Baseball Coach at Louisiana State University, recalls those days fondly. "I was just a young coach fresh out of playing professional baseball and graduating college," says Mainieri now. "I was coaching at a school called Columbus High School in Miami, Florida. I was actually the assistant coach. The head coach was a guy named Jim Hendry. Jim was only a year older than I am. So, I might have been 22 or 23, and Jim might have been 24. So, we were just young guys. Jim ultimately became the general manager of the Chicago Cubs. [As of 2018, Hendry was a special assistant for New York Yankees general manager Brian Cashman.]

"But at that time, he was just a young high school coach and I was his assistant coach. We were playing Miami Springs High School in a game, and this little guy who was probably 5-foot-8, maybe 170 or 180 pounds or so—just a little guy—and we got beat by Miami Springs High School. It was like a one-man team. This guy was making catches in the outfield. He hit a home run and I think they won 1-0. He was just a really good ballplayer. He basically beat us singlehandedly."

That "little guy" was none other than Cangelosi, who impressed both Mainieri and Hendry enough that the two coaches went to Demie Mainieri, Paul's father and also a head coach in college ball. "A couple of weeks later, we played them again and this time at Columbus High School," explains Paul Mainieri today. "[Cangelosi] would get on base, steal bases and play great defense. He just stood out like a sore thumb even though he was just a little guy. And he threw left-handed and batted right-handed, which was unique in baseball circles. You don't see many people who do that.

"So, I went to my father, who was the coach at Miami Dade-North Community College and had been the coach for many years; when he retired from coaching after a 30-year career, he was generally regarded as the greatest junior college coach in history. He had won a national championship and had five near misses. He was the very first junior college coach to 1,000 career wins. I think he had about 35 of his former players reach the major leagues, including John Cangelosi."

Cangelosi himself remembers those high school days well too. "Paul Mainieri and Jim Hendry both coached at Columbus High School against me—I went to Miami Springs—and they were both coaches on that team. I played very well against them, and then Paul went to his dad, Demie Mainieri, to go recruit me! Paul goes, 'Dad, you've got to see this kid play.' I mean, no one was really coming after me but Paul Mainieri started the ball rolling when he talked to his dad. Demie Mainieri came and saw me play, and I ended up signing with Miami-Dade North."

While Cangelosi dreamed of playing in the major leagues, there were two things working against him despite his hustle and speed on the base paths. One was his height; the other was the fact he batted right-handed while throwing left-handed.

"He was a left-handed thrower and a right-handed hitter," says Paul Mainieri of Cangelosi. "And even though he popped that one out of the ballpark against us and had surprising power for a little guy, his greatest attribute, really, was his speed. He was a tremendous center fielder but he was a great base stealer when he got on base. He was a good hitter batting right-handed. But my father had tremendous foresight that a left-handed throwing/right-handed hitting little guy probably would not have much chance to make it to the major leagues. So, when Johnny got to Dade-North, my dad forced him to learn to switch-hit and bat left-handed as well as right-handed. And even though it was very frustrating at times for Johnny—because he knew he was a better hitter right-handed—my dad forced him to hit left-handed for his own good. And ultimately, that became a very big factor to him making it to the major leagues and having a [ten-year] career in the big leagues."

Cangelosi remembers things a little differently. His becoming a switch-hitter didn't happen until the latter part of his college career. Puzzled that scouts seemingly weren't paying attention to him, he asked Demie Mainieri to talk to them and find out what was going on. And that was when Demie made him hit from the left side in a game, leading to a conversation with Chicago White Sox scout Walt Widmayer. "Demie called me out of class one day to say, 'I want you to hit left-handed today.' He might've done it for Walt, to see if I'd be willing," recalls Cangelosi.

* * *

Unlike today, where only one draft is held each year in June, there were two Major League Baseball drafts per year from the late 1960s up until 1986. The first draft took place in June and involved high-school graduates and college seniors who had just finished their seasons, while the second draft took place in January for high-school and college players who had graduated in December. For John Cangelosi, there were no teams selecting him out of high school, which frustrated him. His patience, however, was rewarded when the White Sox picked him in the fourth round in the 1982 MLB January Draft, after he had played in junior college for a year.

"The way I got drafted was really unique," reflects Cangelosi today. "No one really was recruiting me. Me,

[Rafael] Palmeiro, [Danny] Tartabull, [Jose] Canseco, [and] Lenny Harris would have tryouts. There weren't any showcase camps, so we would have tryouts and there would be scouts there at the University of Miami. We would pretty much take batting practice and do a few things here and there. They always liked what I did, but I never got drafted. Demie Mainieri was my coach; his nickname is 'Doc.' I love this man. He was very pivotal in me getting drafted. I was very close with him. One day, I went into Demie Mainieri's office and said, 'Doc, find out why I didn't get drafted. I mean, I don't get it. Is it because I'm too small? What is it? I wanna play pro ball.'"

Before long, Demie Mainieri found out the answer and immediately relayed it to the anxious Cangelosi. "About a week later, Demie Mainieri pulled me out of class," says Cangelosi now. "Doc said, 'Cangy, hit left-handed today.' So, I was a right-handed hitter and a left-handed thrower. There was really no one in the big leagues that did that except Rickey Henderson. They called us freaks of nature. You know, guys like us where we bat right-handed but throw left-handed. I think there was only Rickey Henderson at the time and Cleon Jones, and maybe one other guy."

Those types of hitters were rare indeed. As ESPN.com senior writer Tim Kurkjian noted in a March 2015 story, only six non-pitchers since 1900 had played at least 500 games in the big leagues batting right-handed and throwing left-handed: Henderson (1979-2003), Jones (1963-1976), Hal Chase (1905-1919), Mark Carreon (1987-1996), Ryan Ludwick (2002-2014) and Cody Ross (2003-2015). Yet, there had been hundreds of players who batted left-handed and threw right-handed, such as Hall of Famers Joe Morgan, George Brett and Carl Yastrzemski.

"Demie Mainieri, my Miami Dade coach, He pulls me out of class and goes, 'You're hitting left-handed today.'"

Cangelosi thought his coach had lost his mind, but as it turned out, there was a method to Mainieri's madness. And as far as Mainieri was concerned, Cangelosi wasn't going to join Henderson, Jones and Chase in the exclusive right-handed hitting/left-handed throwing club in the big leagues.

"So, I hit left-handed and struck out three times," Cangelosi continues. "And I'd never swung left-handed. After the game, Walt Widmayer, the White Sox's main scout, says he was gonna draft me in the fourth round. 'John, if you're willing to learn how to switch-hit... I've been watching you. I love the way you play outfield. You have the ability to play in the big leagues from an outfield standpoint. You're the most mature player I've seen on the bases. You steal bases at will. I love the way you hit right-handed. But if I draft you, you would play A-ball or Double-A ball at best. You can't hit the slider from the right side. But if you're willing to switch hit and learn how to hit left-handed, and just hit ground balls to the shortstop or whatever, you'll be in the big leagues in three years.' God bless his soul. I learned how to hit left-handed."

But Cangelosi made sure that the White Sox knew he would not bat left-handed in games until he was ready. He, in fact, had it written into his first professional contract that he would hit left-handed every day in batting practice—but that he wouldn't have to do it in games until he felt comfortable. "In my contract, it was stated that I didn't have to hit left-handed until I was ready to hit left-handed."

Following the draft, Cangelosi was invited to extended spring training with the White Sox. There, he would take batting practice every day hitting from the left side. "I would take soft tosses," Cangelosi recalls now. "It was a couple of weeks before I went to pro ball. I really didn't have any game situation. I was able to take batting practice. But I didn't have to hit left-handed in a game until I was ready."

John Boles, his manager during extended spring training, saw his left-handed stroke one day and told him, "I don't care if you're comfortable or not. You're ready to hit left-handed." Cangelosi chuckles when thinking back to that day. "So, one day, I was taking batting practice. John Boles goes to me and says, 'You look good hitting left-handed. You're hitting left-handed in the game today.' Basically, I took all the pressure and put it on him. I don't know if I would ever have been ready. It worked out. I put the pressure on the organization like I wanted to blame them if I didn't make it. But it worked out where I was basically hitting left-handed right away."

It was a successful first year in the pros for Cangelosi in 1982. Playing for the Niagara Falls (New York) Sox in the New York-Pennsylvania League in Short-Season A-ball, the 19-year-old Cangelosi batted .289 in 76 games with five home runs and 45 stolen bases (while being caught only seven times). He led the team with a .413 on-base percentage and was easily tops in stolen bases while finishing third on the club in batting average. In fact, he finished second in the league in steals, behind only Geoff Doggett's 66 bags. Doggett, a fellow rookie playing for Geneva in the Cubs organization and also a switch-hitting outfielder, would never make it to the big leagues and would, in fact, be out of professional baseball by the end of the 1985 season.

The following season in 1983, the White Sox sent Cangelosi to their Single-A club in Appleton, Wisconsin, of the Midwest League, reuniting him with manager John Boles. There, Cangelosi again impressed with his bat and his feet. Playing in 128 games, he batted .282 with 87 stolen bases. He was, however, also caught 35 times. He not only led the Midwest League in both stolen bases and caught stealing, but he also finished fifth with a .421 on-base percentage.

While finishing first and second in stolen bases in his first two years was an impressive feat, Cangelosi also accomplished something that not many professional athletes could lay claim to: Winning championship rings in each of his first two professional seasons. Both the 1982 Niagara Falls Sox and 1983 Appleton Foxes won their respective league titles, giving Cangelosi championship rings in his first two professional seasons. "Oh yeah," he reflects today when asked about his championship mementos. "In my first two years, my teams won the league championship. I got a championship ring from 1982. I got one from 1983. I have another one with [the] Triple-A [Denver Zephyrs] with Milwaukee [in 1991]. There's the one with the Marlins in 1997. I have another one when I was coaching with the Cubs; they gave those out to the coaching staff.

"But in 1982, I had a good season in Niagara Falls in the Penn League—and that was the first year that I switch-hit. I was second in the league in stolen bases. We beat the Oneonta Yankees to win the championship in my first year in pro ball. [Pro Football Hall of Famer] John Elway was on that team; he was the right fielder for the Yankees." In that best-of-three New York-Penn League Championship Series, Cangelosi even hit a home run as Niagara Falls denied Elway a championship ring. "In 1983, I played for John Boles, and I think I stole [nearly] 90 bases. We ended up having either the best or second-best record in baseball that year. I don't think we lost more than two games in a row that year. That was the year that we beat the Springfield Cardinals in the championship."

While things couldn't have been better for Cangelosi on the field in those first few seasons of professional baseball, things off the field weren't as easy. "It was hard," he says of life in the minors. "It was a lot of lonely times. Back then, the travel was not too good. A lot of long days. But if you had a dream in mind— mine was getting to the big leagues—you stay focused. And that's what I did. I was just focused. I didn't wanna repeat a league, and I accomplished that. I have a lot of great memories of those years. Just a lot of good memories. I was on some good teams. On a personal level, I put up good numbers, being first or second in stolen bases."

In 1984, Cangelosi, along with Boles, was promoted to Double-A Glens Falls (New York). Cangelosi finished second in the Eastern League with 65 stolen bases, just seven shy of league leader Don Carter of the Buffalo Bisons. Carter, a fleet outfielder, would not make it to the majors, instead toiling in the minors for seven different clubs within three big-league organizations before finishing his playing career in 1986 in the Mexican League. "As a team, we weren't very good, so I didn't go to a championship that year. But in every year that I played, I was either one or two in stolen bases," recalls Cangelosi. Despite not winning the stolen-base crown, he again proved he could reach base, finishing third in the Eastern League in 1984 with a .416 on-base percentage while batting .287. In three minor-league seasons, Cangelosi had batted .286 and had impressed with his hustle and base-stealing. Boles, his manager in two of the three seasons, was definitely impressed by his work ethic and potential.

As far as Cangelosi was concerned, John Boles was the man directly responsible for his being a member of the White Sox's big-league team in 1986. But before that, Boles went to bat for the center fielder while he was toiling away in Mexico in 1985. "In 1985, I got optioned to the Mexico City Reds for Nelson Barrera, who was supposed to be the next Mickey Mantle," recalls Cangelosi. "Roberto Mansur was the owner of the Mexico City Reds; he had seen me play in winter baseball and he liked me. So, when the White Sox wanted Nelson Barrera, Mansur said, 'In exchange, I want cash and I want John Cangelosi to play center field for me.' The White Sox agreed to that, but I didn't agree to it."

The White Sox brass pushed Cangelosi to agree to the assignment. General manager Roland Hemond, assistant general manager Dave Dombrowski, manager Tony La Russa and even owner Jerry Reinsdorf got on the phone to persuade him to change his mind. "When they called me, I said, 'No, I don't wanna go to Mexico. I'm 21 years old. I'm a prospect. I'm not gonna play with

40-year-old men.' I hung up on them, but they called me back," continues Cangelosi. "I believe Roland Hemond was on the phone. Dave Dombrowski and, I believe, Reinsdorf were on the phone too. They all told me, 'If you refuse to go to Mexico, you're gonna be suspended. And you're not gonna be able to play anywhere.'"

Cangelosi was backed into a corner. He had no choice. "[Before I went to Mexico], my friends took me out. We drank a bunch of tequila in Miami. I ended up going to Mexico. It was probably the worst experience in my life because of a couple of things that happened. I have nothing but praise for Roberto Mansur, the owner of the Mexico City Reds. He treated me phenomenally. It was more of a culture shock for me. So, I flew in there and they picked me up in a van. I was sitting on a paint bucket. They drove me to the stadium. It was bad. I mean, the playing conditions were bad. The travel was bad. The first week I was there, the bus that we traveled in had no air-conditioning and no bathroom. We were traveling 16 to 20 hours on the bus."

Feeling frustrated, Cangelosi spoke up. "I went to Roberto Mansur and said, 'Look, I don't wanna sound like I'm better than anybody, but I can't do this. I need to talk to my family back home.' It was expensive back then. If you called collect, it was $700 a month for your phone bill! He told me, 'Don't worry about it; I'll let you use my phone in the office. Don't worry about that. If the travel is more than 10 hours, I'll personally fly you to the game.' He was a tremendous guy. I had a decent apartment. It was a hard place to play. I had a couple of American teammates that made it a bit easier. But then I start playing around with the shortstop's kid. He ended up having chicken pox. I'd never had chicken pox before and I was exposed to it, at the age of 22." When he was taken to the local hospital to get checked out, Cangelosi was frightened by what he saw around him. "The emergency room had mayonnaise jars. I mean, it wasn't sanitary. It was brutal. I didn't feel safe. I was afraid that I would get poked with a needle."

Just prior to his getting the chicken pox, his parents had flown to Mexico to be with him, to watch him play. "They flew back because I wasn't playing," Cangelosi recalls. But his mother had a change of plans. "My mom said, 'You know what? I'm gonna go back to Mexico until Johnny feels better.' She flew all the way back to Mexico. It was the worst four weeks of my life. I didn't leave the house. It was painful. I had chicken pox everywhere—at the bottom of my feet. It was very, very painful. So, my mom took care of me. After I got healthy, she left. I got back on the field."

But there were more problems awaiting Cangelosi. "There was a ball hit in the gap. I'm running after it, I catch it… and that's the last thing I remember. I ran into a brick wall without padding. It knocked me out. I came back to, and then I missed another three or four games."

Incredibly, that wasn't the end of his string of bad luck. "Me, another teammate, we were in a night club. We are having a couple of drinks. We are sitting there and all of a sudden, we hear 'pop, pop, pop, pop!' We're thinking it's balloons over the dance floor. I look at the entrance way, and there were four guys shooting people. I throw the table up to guard us. It felt like an hour. There was nowhere for us to go. There was no doorway. They could've walked toward us. We couldn't do anything. It felt like an hour—but they might've been there for a minute, just shooting randomly at people. Then they left. There were six or seven people who were shot. Nobody died, as far as I remember. The reason they shot up the place was because one of the kids was too young to get in and he was mad. He decided to start shooting at people. Can you believe that?"

On June 1, the White Sox re-acquired Cangelosi and assigned him to Buffalo—thanks to John Boles, then managing the Triple-A Bisons. "John Boles comes to my rescue," Cangelosi, who wound up hitting .353 with 17 stolen bases in 61 games for Mexico City, says now. "He called the White Sox front office and said, 'Hey, I want John Cangelosi back. I need a center fielder. He's the best center fielder in the organization. I want him to play for me.' Within a couple of days, I got optioned back to Buffalo."

Because it's been more than 30 years, Cangelosi has forgotten the dates of the events, but he does remember the devastating earthquake that struck Mexico City that year. On September 19, 1985, the violent trembling of the earth registered a magnitude 8.0, causing severe damage to the Greater Mexico City area and the deaths of at least 10,000 people (although other estimates are higher). According to accounts from major newspapers of the day, the sequence of events included a foreshock of magnitude 5.2 that occurred on May 28, the mainshock on September 19 and two large aftershocks.

Cangelosi seems to recall the major earthquake happening a week after Boles rescued him. In reality, it was about four months later. Regardless, the event was tragic. "When John Boles got me out of there, I think within [four months] after I left, Mexico had an earthquake and those mudslides [that followed]. The earthquake caused mudslides and all kinds of stuff. The stadium where we played was the place where they brought all the dead bodies to be identified. They had no way of identifying them. So, they brought all the dead bodies to the stadium. Where I was living, there was a hospital there. It was eerie. I would've been involved in that devastating event if John Boles didn't get me out of there [and if the earthquake had happened four months earlier]."

Boles, when asked about it today, acknowledges Cangelosi still thanks him every chance he gets. In fact, they discussed that same subject the last time they spoke. "He's always been very grateful that I was able to bring him back to the States to play," Boles says now, insisting he didn't approach the White Sox as a favor. It was because he truly felt Cangelosi could help out in Triple-A Buffalo. "I was with the White Sox [managing in Triple-A] and we had an opening. Because of our past relationship, he was the first guy I thought of who could really come in and help us. And I really believed that he was the guy who was going to be, in the future, able to help our major-league team. And, you know, he [wound up having] a terrific ten-year career."

Things looked up for Cangelosi once he was back in the United States. In late June, with rookie center fielder Daryl Boston struggling (with a .215 average in 64 games with Chicago), the White Sox called Cangelosi up to the big leagues. In his first game on

June 30 at Comiskey Park against the Minnesota Twins, Cangelosi started in center field and went 0-for-2 with a sacrifice bunt against John Butcher, before being pinch-hit for by Jerry Hairston in the eighth. He would be with the White Sox for a week before being sent back to Buffalo, where he would stay for the rest of the year.

While it was a bummer having to finish the season in Buffalo, being called up for the first time to Chicago was amazing, especially since he had begun the year in Mexico City. That 1985 season, for Cangelosi, was an improbable journey indeed. "I came up [to the White Sox] for two weeks and then I got sent back down to Buffalo. When I got called up, it was a dream come true. It's every kid's dream to play in the big leagues. There I was playing in the outfield behind Tom Seaver, who was pitching that day, and Carlton Fisk, who was catching," he reflects fondly about being on the same field with the two future Hall of Famers in his major-league debut. "It was like, 'C'mon. I was like, when I was 10 years old, I was watching them on TV!' I mean, what a great story...

"For me, a guy who wasn't even supposed to be in the big leagues—I mean, my height was supposed to keep me from playing in the major leagues—playing on the same field as Tom Seaver and Carlton Fisk, two of the greatest players in the history of the game... It just goes to show that by working hard and not giving up, anything is possible... If you keep knocking doors down and not give up, regardless of whatever field or profession you're in, you can do it too. You just gotta believe in yourself and keep working hard. And you can succeed too. I know I did."

Chapter Three
The Kid from Nowhere Winds up in Chicago

[When I was the first-base coach with the White Sox from 1982 to 1984] I couldn't give him enough information. He listened and stayed after me. I worked with Daryl Boston the same time, but Daryl didn't pick it up as quickly. John had a great desire to play in the big leagues… He was a little bit frustrated at his size and arm but I told him, 'Your speed is your forte. If you make contact with the bat, you can make it.' It looks like he has. I'm very pleased.

—Davey Nelson, Oakland A's minor-league coordinator (1986)

John Cangelosi, to this day, believes he got his shot at the big leagues in 1986 thanks to John Boles. After a cup of coffee in 1985—five games prior to the All-Star break—he became the White Sox's Opening Day center fielder and leadoff hitter in 1986. In Chicago's second game of the year, Cangelosi would collect his first big-league hit—a home run off Brewers reliever Ray Searage—while adding two stolen bases. In each of his first 21 games, he would reach base safely at least once. For the season, he would hit .235 in 137 games with a pair of home runs and 50 stolen bases, an American League rookie record.

"My first major-league hit was off of Ray Searage, which was a home run," he recalls of the solo shot he hit to left field in the ninth inning of a 4-3 loss to Milwaukee at Comiskey Park on April 9, 1986. "Every at-bat I was trying too hard, I was kinda nervous. Excited. And Ron Kittle threw me his bat. It was like a 35-[ounce], 35-[inch-long] big bat. He goes, 'Take my bat, man! You'll get a hit!' So, I took his bat up there and I ended up hitting that home run."

It was a remarkable journey to the top. Improbable, in fact. Hardly any team wanted him coming out of junior college because of his height. He was unwanted even in the White Sox farm system; he was sent to Mexico in 1985 for Nelson Barrera. He didn't even make the Sox media guide in the spring of 1986, as a major- or minor-leaguer. During spring training, in fact, he was assigned the uniform No. 64, a number normally given to non-rostered players who weren't expected to stay with the big-league club.

As far as Cangelosi is concerned, without Boles, he might have remained unwanted. "In '86, Tony La Russa was our manager," reflects Cangelosi today, crediting Boles for his being in the big leagues that year. "But he got fired, along with [pitching coach] Dave Duncan, [a couple of months] into the season. Then Jim Fregosi took over [as manager]. You go back and you wanna thank people. Certain things that happened in your life are very instrumental to you being successful or moving forward. John Boles was my manager for two years in minor-league baseball. He was my manager in 1983 and 1984, and then a little bit of 1985.

"There was a winter meeting with all the managers and brass, and they go around the room and they ask every minor-league coach. 'Hey, who's the center fielder of the future for the White Sox?' And everybody's raising their hands. 'Daryl Boston.' 'Kenny Williams.' 'Daryl Boston.' 'Kenny Williams.' They were the high draft picks of the organization. And then they got to John Boles. He told me the story himself years later. He was asked who the center fielder of the future was, and he goes, 'John Cangelosi.' He told me, 'You could hear a pin drop—because I thought I'd lost my job.' In hindsight, he had that much confidence in me because I played for him."

"That was a very private organizational meeting so I don't think I should talk about that," Boles, when asked about that meeting, says now. "But, yes, I did say that John Cangelosi was going to be, definitely, a major-league center fielder. I had John for four years. When he was signed, he went to extended spring, where I managed him. Then the next year, the Midwest League, in Appleton, Wisconsin. In 1984, Glens Falls, New York, in the Eastern League in Double-A. And then, 1985, Triple-A in Buffalo, So, I had him four years in a row. And it was very slowly in the process of his development that you just knew that he had the talent and the disposition to make it. Of course, he was one of those guys that, people always say [was too small to play].

"People were still always suspicious, or skeptical, of guys who were small in stature. [You look at] the Jose Altuves of the world that are just great talents [and] Dustin Pedroia with the Red Sox, the same way. And John, of course, was not big in stature. So, when a lot of people are evaluating someone like that, you know, the person really has to stand out and work hard in order to get the same opportunities as maybe some others."

Cangelosi definitely appreciates what Boles told the White Sox brass. "If you don't see me play, you think I'm five-six or whatever and not that impressive, but if you allow me and you see the way I played the game, I could play," adds Cangelosi. "If the ball was in the outfield, I caught it. I knew how to get on first base. I stole 97 bags for him one year [actually, 87]. He knew that I could play. That's pretty much how I got noticed a little bit."

Indeed. When Cangelosi made the '86 team out of spring training, he was referred to in the Chicago papers as "an unknown switch-hitting center fielder of Italian-Puerto Rican descent who's at least an inch shorter than his listed 5-8" and "The Kid from Brooklyn." And "The 5-7 Kid from Nowhere." He wasn't expected to make the team—not when the White Sox also had 6-4 Daryl Boston, a former first-round draft pick who as a 22-year-old in 1985 had seen the most action in center field in Chicago, as well as 29-year-old veteran Rudy Law, who in the club's 1983 AL West championship season had stolen a team-record 77 bases. One Chicago scribe, in fact, acknowledged that Cangelosi was an "out-of-nowhere, switch-hitting sensation," but added he was "too short to play major-league baseball, has no power and can't throw very well." Cangelosi's spring performance, however, made Law expendable and forced Boston, the American Association's Player of the Year in 1984, back to Triple-A Buffalo.

Cangelosi not only credits Boles for his opportunity, but he also points to the previous season when he was assigned to Mexico City. The White Sox, he feels, gave him a token invitation to spring training in 1986 as a way to thank him for accepting the Mexican assignment. "From there, in 1985, they optioned me to Mexico for

Nelson Barrera, a Mexican player," Cangelosi reflects. "I was pissed. I kinda quit. Roland Hemond, Dave Dombrowski and La Russa were on the phone talking to me. They go, 'Hey, look. We're just optioning you out there. We gotta see this guy play.' I go out there for two months and I had the worst time of my life. And then John Boles got me back to Triple-A. And then I got called up to the big leagues for a week. Then I got sent down. In the spring of '86, they gave me a token 'Hey-thanks-for-going-to-Mexico' invitation to big-league camp.

"So, they invited me to big-league camp. I wasn't gonna make the team; I wasn't even on the roster. [One day] Ron Kittle got on base. [La Russa goes], 'Cangy, go pinch-run for him.' I stole second and third. The next day, Carlton Fisk gets on base in the seventh inning on a base hit. They take him out of the game. [La Russa again goes], 'Cangy, go run.' I stole second and third. So, I had six or eight stolen bases before I even had an at-bat. Then, they put me in a 'B' game. I got a couple of hits. To make a long story short, I ended up having a great spring. I was 18-for-18 in stolen bases... I just made it very hard for them to make a decision."

Still, at the time, Cangelosi didn't think he had a shot with Rudy Law and Daryl Boston ahead of him. La Russa, though, kept reassuring him. "Hang in there. You're doing fine," the White Sox skipper told him throughout the spring.

Cangelosi can only smile when thinking back to the final days of that spring. "The very first time that I knew I was gonna make a team was kinda cool. It went down to almost the last game of spring training and I still didn't know if I had made the team or not. We were playing in Fort Lauderdale against the Yankees," he continues. "Ron Guidry's pitching. And I'm playing. And then there's a private plane waiting for after the game because they've got to fly back to Sarasota and then out to Chicago for Opening Day. So, whoever's on that plane makes the team.

"Normally when you're not on the team or you're a non-roster [player], you play the whole game. Or you go in at the end of the game and let the starters go shower first. I started that game, and I think I go 1-for-3 against Guidry. Tony La Russa takes me out of the game in the fourth or fifth inning. 'Go get your sprints in; you're done for the day.' I'm like, 'Why did you take me out of the game? I'm not going anywhere.' But right away, I thought, 'Okay, my name's on that list [of guys who made the team].' So, I run my sprints really quickly, and then I run into the locker room."

A couple of veteran catchers were there, waiting for him. "Nice going! Congratulations!" Carlton Fisk and Marc Hill told a relieved Cangelosi. He looked at the list for himself, and his name, indeed, was on there. Improbably, John Cangelosi, the "Kid from Nowhere," the unknown "Kid from Brooklyn," the kid who had been banished to Mexico City, had cracked the White Sox's 1986 major-league roster. "My name's on that list going back," he recalls fondly. "That's how I found out that I had made the team. Then, when I got on the private jet, the guys on the team congratulated me. Tony La Russa came up and said, 'Congratulations.' That was really exciting. That was the first time I knew I was gonna be in the big leagues for the whole year."

Cangelosi's making the team shouldn't have been a surprise, if the competition for the center-field job between him and Daryl Boston came down to who performed better. While Boston had batted .286 during the spring, Joe Goddard of the *Chicago Sun-Times* called it "a soft .286," referring to the fact Boston had hit only two doubles among his 16 hits. He was only 1-for-4 trying to steal. Cangelosi, meanwhile, batted .333 with those 18 stolen bases. He even led the White Sox in runs, walks and triples. "Tony La Russa told me afterwards that I had made the team," adds Cangelosi. "They sent Daryl Boston back down to the minor leagues. They released Rudy Law, who was guaranteed a million dollars that year. They let him go [in the closing days of spring training], and Tony La Russa gave me my opportunity."

La Russa, in explaining to the *Chicago Sun-Times* then about the decision to keep Cangelosi and send Boston to Triple-A Buffalo, referred to a game against Kansas City on March 21. "Here's where we first began to realize we may have somebody special," the skipper said, pointing to that date on the cardboard calendar on his clubhouse desk. "We were down 1-0 in the ninth inning at Fort Myers against the [defending World Series champion] Royals and Dan Quisenberry was pitching. Quisenberry! This kid gets on, steals second and third, scores on a sacrifice fly and we're in extra innings. So, I started to give him tests: Storm Davis, Ron Guidry, John Tudor. He passed 'em all."

And when Cangelosi started, even against tough pitchers, he passed the tests. In the first inning on April 3 and again on April 4, he created a run, leading off with a walk, stealing second and third, and scoring on a balk on the 3rd and on an infield hit on the 4th. Earlier in the week, he stole second and third against the Cardinals' Mike Heath, who, noted Murray Chass of *The New York Times*, was considered by some to be the best catcher in the game for throwing out runners. "It came down to John fitting our [leadoff] needs," continued La Russa in an April 5th story in the *Chicago Sun-Times*. "As I told Daryl, 'If we had needed someone to drive in runs, it would have been you.'"

For Cangelosi, it all goes back to one man: John Boles. "I was a fourth-round pick—and the organization knew who I was—but I was on the backburner," he says now. "This man just stood up in the room and said, 'Hey, man. I'm sorry. I disagree. I think John Cangelosi is the future center fielder of this team.' From there, they started looking at me a little bit differently."

The rest of the American League began looking at Cangelosi a bit differently by the second week of the 1986 season. As Roger Jackson noted in the May 5th edition of *Sports Illustrated*, "Cangelosi has emerged... as the biggest little surprise in the American League... one of the few Chicago bright spots in an otherwise lackluster season." On April 16, the league took notice when he stole second base against Detroit—with Chicago ahead by six runs in the third inning. "There was an incident and we were playing against the Detroit Tigers," Cangelosi, who also had two hits and scored two runs that day, recalls now. "I didn't know it at the time, but Darnell Coles became my teammate the year after in Pittsburgh and he told me that Sparky Anderson wanted me drilled. We were playing against Detroit and Lance Parrish was the catcher. He was more of an offensive player. He was a good catcher but they really didn't hold runners on back then too well, and he didn't have that good of an arm. So, I stole a lot of bases off Detroit. But he was a great player. I got nothing but respect for him. In the [third inning], I stole second base. It wasn't a blowout game. [Actually, Chicago was ahead 9-3 at the time.] I came up in the fifth inning, and I guess Sparky Anderson told his pitcher, 'I want this kid down, and I want him down NOW!' Like, they were throwing at me on purpose. So, I came up to bat, and Randy O'Neal hit me on the head with a fastball."

When Cangelosi got to first base after being hit by O'Neal, Tigers first baseman Dave Engle told him, "Hey, Cangy, man! That shit was on purpose, man! Steal second and third right now, dude. If I were you, I'd go right now!" Cangelosi, though, wisely stayed put, and two innings later the White Sox retaliated. "Floyd Bannister was on the mound, and La Russa doesn't play that crap," continues Cangelosi. "We threw behind Dave Collins, and there was a big brawl. I mean, a huge brawl. In the midst of it, Jack Morris comes after me and starts yelling at me. I mean, during that brawl, I wasn't fighting or anything. I was just standing there. But Morris looks at me and he goes, 'You know what THAT's about, rookie!' And then Bob James [a 6'4" right-handed reliever with the White Sox] pushed me aside, and goes, 'You mess with him, you mess with me!' He had my back. And then Morris didn't do shit; [instead], he went around to the other side. That was funny."

For his part, O'Neal said at the time that he didn't hit Cangelosi intentionally. "The ball got away from me. I was trying to throw strikes. I never throw at anybody. The ball was slippery because it was cold," O'Neal was quoted as saying in the following day's *Battle Creek (Michigan) Enquirer.* La Russa, naturally, backed his rookie. "I think it's important to understand what the Tigers were trying to do to Cangelosi. It bothers me that our guy got hit first. He stole the base in the third inning. We're struggling and it's hard for me to believe you should shut down your offense in the third inning [even with the six-run lead]," the skipper was quoted as saying in the same newspaper story, referring to the fact Ron Kittle, who'd been 1-for-13; Carlton Fisk, who'd been 0-for-12; and Harold Baines, 0-for-20, had been slumping.

When reflecting back to the incident, Cangelosi can only smile thinking about the fact that, as a rookie, he had rattled the Tigers so much that they wanted to drill him. "Basically, I was embarrassing them, like I was stealing bases at will. Sparky didn't like it."

And it wasn't just Sparky or Morris not liking Cangelosi's exploits on the bases and on the field. In a July 30 victory over Boston, the White Sox handed Roger "Rocket" Clemens just his third loss of the year. In the third inning, Cangelosi bunted for a hit toward second and reached safely, which annoyed the heck out of the Rocket, who would finish 24-4 and capture the AL Cy Young Award that year. "He walked over to me because he had to cover first base," says Cangelosi now. "He looked at me. He was more of an intimidator. Or he tried to be. He goes, 'Hey, you know, that inside plate is mine!' And I said, 'Well, go take it! Hit me! Next time you look at me, I'll be standing on third base.' Left-handed, I was on top of the plate because I couldn't hit the inside pitch. So, I would make that pitch look like a ball all the time. He was pretty much telling me to get off the plate. 'I want that inside plate,' he would say. I said, 'Well, hit me. I ain't going nowhere. Hit me. Next time you look at me, I'll be on third base because you're so frickin' slow.'" Clemens then completely lost his cool two innings later, when Cangelosi reached on a forceout, stole second, advanced to third on a fly ball and scored the go-ahead (and winning) run on Clemens' own two-out error on a Harold Baines ground ball. The Boston ace, who on the error missed first base on Baines' grounder, disagreed with the call and was ejected for bumping first-base umpire Greg Kosc.

Cangelosi also had arguably his best game in Minnesota, collecting four hits and a walk against the Twins on June 18. It would be the first of his six four-hit games in the majors. Three of those hits, including a double, came off future Hall of Famer Bert Blyleven, as he helped Chicago build a 9-5 lead after eight innings. He even scored two runs and stole two bases, giving him 30 steals on the season in just his 58th game. Alas, the White Sox bullpen imploded in the ninth, giving up four runs, and Chicago went on to lose 10-9.

Then, there were the duels with Oakland's Rickey Henderson, the reigning six-time American League base-stealing champion. In a three-game series against Henderson's Yankees in Chicago in early May, the two speedsters put on a show. In the series opener, Henderson singled in the fifth inning and then stole second. Not to be outdone, Cangelosi singled an inning later, and then stole second and third. In the ninth, after Henderson grounded into a force play, he stole second.

The following night, Henderson walked in the fourth and stole second, before singling in the sixth and stealing second and third. In Chicago's half of the sixth, Cangelosi walked and stole both second and third. Cangelosi didn't start the series finale while Henderson didn't reach base, leaving them three steals apart in the AL stolen-base race (22 for Henderson, 19 for Cangelosi). "I had a chance to observe Rickey," Cangelosi reflects. "I wasn't as fast as he was. He had raw speed. Both him and Vince Coleman could steal on raw speed. Their legs were stronger than mine. I stole my bases off the pitcher; my lead was my key asset and my first three steps were very important to me. I probably needed only a couple of innings to read a pitcher and figure out when to run on him. So, the second time I saw a pitcher, I would have an even easier time stealing against him."

Cangelosi would have loved to have had a chance to talk to Henderson about base stealing when they were both in the big leagues, but he never had that opportunity. "Rickey was very—I wouldn't say quiet. I would say he was very to himself. At least that's what I thought. I would love to talk to him, but most of my career I was in the National League and he was in the American League. I really didn't run into him too much. When I did, I asked him a couple of questions. It was toward the end of my career when I saw him [when Rickey was with the Padres]."

Through the White Sox's first 30 games in 1986, Cangelosi already had 19 steals while Henderson, who had averaged 90 stolen bases over the previous six seasons, had stolen 22 for the Yankees. Nobody else in the AL had more than eight. In the NL, the Dodgers'

Mariano Duncan led the circuit with 13 steals. Vince Coleman of the Cardinals, meanwhile, had only nine after leading the majors the previous year with 110. And while Henderson already had 22 in the middle of May in 1986, he didn't reach that same mark until mid-June a year earlier, when he had a Yankees-record 80 steals. Still, Henderson denied to reporters then that Cangelosi had influenced his fast start in '86. "I don't even worry about him," Henderson was quoted as saying in a May 11th story in *The New York Times*. "He's a good base-stealer, but I don't worry about other base-stealers. [The Yankees, as a team, are] not hitting, so I try to make things happen. I might pump him up, make him more aggressive. I can't say he pumps me up."

John Boles wasn't surprised that Cangelosi was among the league leaders in steals in his rookie year. He had that quickness, according to Boles, just as Henderson and Coleman did. "They all were similar insofar as they were very quick," Boles says now, referring to Henderson, Coleman and Cangelosi. "You would call all three of them fast, obviously. But all three had initial 'off-the-mark' quickness. That's essential when you're a base stealer, [when you're talking about] Maury Wills, Rickey Henderson, Vince Coleman, [and] guys like that. Their first two or three steps are so explosive and that's the difference between guys with tremendous quickness and guys who are fast but don't have that quickness. Cangy sure had that quickness. He sure did. He was like lightning. His first two or three steps were really explosive."

In that battle back in early May 1986, Henderson had a slight 5-4 edge over Cangelosi in the stolen-base department. Cangelosi would again lose the second round of the duel at Yankee Stadium later that month, when the Yankees' stolen-base king out-stole him 1-0 over the teams' mini two-game series. In a three-game set in Chicago in early July, Henderson again out-stole Cangelosi 1-0. When the two clubs met for the last time following the All-Star break, Henderson, once again, came out on top, 3-1, in their four-game series. "At that point in the season, we were neck and neck in stolen bases," recalls Cangelosi, referring to the stolen-base race in the American League. "I was second in the league, and I was on pace to steal 80 bags. I could've killed him. I was neck in neck with him." Even NBC was on the Cangelosi bandwagon; in a *Game of the Week* broadcast in late April—less than a month into his first full season—the network had the rookie center fielder read out the White Sox's starting lineup on camera before the game.

"I remember Joe Garagiola interviewing me," he smiles when asked to reflect back to the opening month of that rookie season. "I got interviewed a lot because no one really knew who I was. The South Side of Chicago took a liking to me. I was a small guy, an underdog. It kinda fit well with the blue-collar people of Chicago. They took a great liking to me because I played hard." He even received letters from Little League players who said his arrival in the majors was an inspiration to them. "That made me feel great, knowing that all those kids considered me a hero."

"He was a tremendous 'game player.' He always played to win," adds Boles. "He always played to steal the extra base, and get that extra base either going from first to third—or first to home. He was what we call a 'gamer' in the business. He was just a tough, hard-nosed guy who *always* played to win. Every time—*every* time—he put on the uniform, he played to beat you. And he played a lot. I mean, he very rarely was out. I can't ever remember in the four years that I managed him... I can't ever remember him sitting out a game."

The season, though, would take a dramatic turn for the worse for Cangelosi. Just as he didn't expect to make the Opening Day roster, he didn't expect what would happen in the second half of that 1986 season.

Chapter Four
The AL Rookie Stolen Base King

In my 27 years in baseball, I've never seen a player explode on the scene like this... I figure if this kid walks 80, 90 times and gets 150 hits, he could steal 70, 80 bases. Rickey Henderson will have to extend himself to beat him.

> —Ken "Hawk" Harrelson, Chicago White Sox
> vice-president, as told to *Sports Illustrated*'s
> Roger Jackson (1986)

The 1986 White Sox had several star players—such as slugger Ron Kittle and future Hall of Famers Carlton Fisk and Harold Baines, along with youngsters like Bobby Bonilla and reigning Rookie of the Year Ozzie Guillen—but were a mediocre team, finishing fifth in the American League West with a 72-90 record. On the mound, Hall-of-Famer-to-be Tom Seaver was around, but at the age of 41 he didn't pitch effectively and would be, at his request, traded in late June. Steve Carlton, another future Hall of Famer, arrived late in the season, but his best days were also behind him. While the pitching staff overall posted a 3.93 ERA that was third-best in the American League, no pitcher won more than 11 games. Right-hander Joe Cowley threw a no-hitter in September, but he was only a .500 pitcher on the year. (Cowley, in fact, wouldn't win another major-league game following that no-no.)

One of the bright spots in Chicago was Cangelosi, who had won the starting center-field job out of spring training. Count Joe Goddard of the *Chicago Sun-Times* as one who saw his value to the ball club. "Let's talk about Cangelosi for a minute," opined Goddard two weeks before the All-Star break. "Ownership needs him. He's such a feisty, unaffected little player that without him, the rest of the players seem like heavy-legged plodders... Cangelosi is on pace of 100 walks and 80 stolen bases, and if Fisk-[Greg] Walker-Kittle-Harold Baines ever hit in unison, he'll eclipse 100 runs."

Goddard even compared him to NFL star defensive lineman William Perry, a popular player best known as "The Refrigerator" who, as a rookie, was a key member of the 1985 Chicago Bears defense. "With any kind of team success, the attendance thermometer will rise while Cangelosi's popularity will soar the way The Refrigerator's did with the [defending Super Bowl champion] Bears," the *Chicago Sun-Times* scribe noted in the June 29th piece. "Can't you see them, William Perry carrying Cangelosi to the hamburger counter for another double-cheese? It could happen."

As improbable as that all might have sounded, it certainly seemed that way early on, including the scene in Chicago after Cangelosi's first big-league home run. Those who remained in the crowd of 9,007 at Comiskey Park gave him a large ovation while he circled the bases, he recalls. "The fans really took an immediately liking to me, which was understandable given my background," he says, referring to his Italian-Puerto Rican ethnicity. The bulk of the White Sox's South Side fans, after all, were of Italian and Puerto Rican descent. "I was real popular with the fans there. They really treated me right."

Alas, he wasn't popular enough to make it to the Midsummer Classic. The White Sox had only one representative at the 1986 Major League Baseball All-Star Game: outfielder Harold Baines, who was selected as a reserve. Cangelosi, however, believes he could have been chosen as an All-Star too. For the first two months of the season, he was ranked in the top 10 in on-base percentage. At the break, he was also second in the American League in stolen bases with 39, trailing only Oakland's Rickey Henderson (51). The two players tied for third—Toronto's Lloyd Moseby and Kansas City's Willie Wilson—were not even close, with 21 swipes apiece. "I think I had [around 40] stolen bases at the All-Star break. I was neck in neck with Rickey Henderson. If Harold Baines wasn't on my team, I probably would've made the All-Star team for the White Sox," says Cangelosi, who remains friends with Baines to this day. "But you know, Harold Baines is Harold Baines. He was the one who made the All-Star team."

Baines can't disagree with the idea that Cangelosi deserved to be an All-Star too. "John's a bit on the short side, but he had a lot of energy," Baines says now when asked to recall Cangelosi's rookie year. "I remember him as a scrappy guy. He worked for everything he had. He got a lot out of his talent. Baseball isn't built for guys his size, but the guy who won [the American League] MVP [in 2017, Jose Altuve], was his size."

Although he had a mediocre .243 batting average in the first half, Cangelosi's on-base percentage was a solid .379. (To put things in perspective, future Hall of Famer Tim Raines' career on-base percentage was .385.) And after a slow start to the season in the first two weeks, Cangelosi had hit .281 over a 50-game stretch from April 25 to June 22. While he then had an eight-game hitless streak and struggled in the two weeks leading up to the All-Star break, Cangelosi was still on pace for an outstanding season for a leadoff hitter. He was on pace, if he remained in the lineup in the second half, to finish the season with 96 runs scored, 110 walks and 79 stolen bases. Those would be fine numbers for a leadoff man—and he was doing it in his rookie year. (Again, to put things in perspective, Raines, a National League All-Star for the Montreal Expos in 1986, finished with 91 runs scored, 78 walks and 70 stolen bases.)

But never mind the All-Star Game. The turning point in Cangelosi's season, the way he remembers it, came when manager Tony La Russa was fired in mid-June—just three weeks prior to the All-Star break—with the team struggling at 26-38 through 64 games. Hitting coach Doug Rader was initially named the interim manager, but after two games, the White Sox then named Jim Fregosi as their permanent manager. For Cangelosi, the timing of the managerial change couldn't have come at a worse time. As he recalls, he struggled during a west coast trip to Oakland and Anaheim in Fregosi's first week as the White Sox manager. Although Chicago won four of the six games against the A's and Angels from June 27 to July 2, Cangelosi went 0-for-20 with seven walks. Dating back to the previous series at home against Minnesota, he had gone 0-for-28—and all of this came right on the heels of a 13-game hitting streak from June 10 to June 23. The hitless streak would reach 31 at-bats before Cangelosi smashed an eighth-inning triple off Yankees pitcher Bob Tewksbury on July 4, and it turned out to be a huge hit as he then came home on Ozzie Guillen's fly to center to score the tie-breaking run in Chicago's 2-1 victory.

"[My rookie season] is something that I'm very proud of, but by the same token I feel like I was cheated in the same aspect," Cangelosi, who batted .420 with a .525 on-base percentage during that 13-game streak, reflects today. "I was playing for La Russa, and La Russa got fired. Fregosi took over. For whatever reason, this man just didn't like me. I don't know what it was. Basically, Fregosi takes over, and [from late April up until the time Jim took over] I was hitting .275. [In the series against the A's and Angels], I go [hitless]—they had some really good pitchers [including the Angel's Chuck Finley and Mike Witt]—I didn't have bad at-bats, but I went [hitless]."

The slump dropped his batting average down to .238, from a season-high .268. The new skipper had seen enough. "[Fregosi] calls me into his office after the series. He hands me this big bat, this U1 bat," says Cangelosi, referring to an old-school wood bat model with a thick tapered handle with no knob. "He goes, 'Hey, from now on, you're gonna hit with this bat and you're gonna take a strike.' I'm like, 'Jim, what do you mean take a strike? Sometimes I will, and sometimes I won't. I can't do that. There are advance scouts in the stands.' He goes, 'I'm the manager. You're gonna take a strike.'"

The way Fregosi explained it to the press, Cangelosi needed to work on his swing. His future "will depend on how much he can work on his swing," the skipper was quoted as saying in the *Chicago Sun-Times* on September 15. "I've talked to him about getting a big bat and choking up, about getting a Nellie Fox model and just making contact. Sometimes he has too big a swing for the type of player he is. He needs to hit the ball on the ground. Every time he hits a fly ball, he should slap himself. He's got [nearly 40] stolen bases hitting .240. If he can hit .280, he'd have a chance to steal 70 or 80."

As a rookie, Cangelosi had no choice but to follow the manager's instructions. "So, I'm basically going up there, taking the first pitch all the time. So, it made it very difficult for me to hit. I was 0-and-1, 1-and-1, 0-and-2. He took my bunting game away. I mean, he took a lot of my strengths away. The game's hard enough hitting with three strikes, let alone two. I went on a skid. I think I was 1-for-20-something [actually, 0-for-21 in mid-August]. Then, they call Daryl Boston back up [in late July]. They go out and get [veteran outfielder] George Foster [on August 15, a week after he had been released by the Mets]. Now, he benches me. So now, I'm not even playing. At this point, I was second in the league in stolen bases. I was a rookie. I was 23 years old. We're in last place. We stink. And you're not gonna have this prospect play and learn the game? You put in George Foster—who's 44 years old [actually, 37]—and you're gonna to play him in front of me?

"The whole thing stunk to me. I go about a month without playing. I go into his office, I go, 'Jim, I'm not here to complain about playing time. I just wanna know what's going on. What does my future hold?' He pretty much ripped me. 'You can't play. If it weren't for the people in Chicago that like you so much, I'd send you down. Just keep your mouth shut and get out of here!' He just buried me. Mentally, that took a lot of my confidence away. That was my encounter with him. I would play sporadically."

When Daryl Boston was called up on July 30, Fregosi gave him a full vote of confidence. "Boston will play," the White Sox skipper told the *Chicago Sun-Times* that day, promising to make him the everyday center fielder. "I'm going to give Daryl Boston every opportunity to succeed." Cangelosi, meanwhile, was moved over to left field, a position that during the course of the season would see five other White Sox—Bobby Bonilla, Carlton Fisk, Reid Nichols, Steve Lyons and Ron Kittle—start at least 18 games. Even Ivan Calderon, acquired from Seattle in July, would see some time in left field with the White Sox after being the Mariners' everyday right fielder in the first half of the season. But at least Bonilla, Fisk, Lyons and Kittle were out of the mix at that point. Bonilla, claimed by the White Sox from Pittsburgh in the Rule 5 draft in the off-season, had been traded back to the Pirates on July 23 for pitcher Jose DeLeon. Kittle, meanwhile, was traded to the Yankees the same day Boston was called up, and Lyons, acquired June 29 from Boston in exchange for Tom Seaver, would be benched with Cangelosi taking over left field. As for Fisk, the future Hall-of-Fame catcher had moved back to his familiar position behind the plate by early May after being the Opening Day left fielder.

There were more drastic changes when the 37-year-old Foster, the National League's MVP in 1977, was signed just two weeks later, in mid-August. Lyons was demoted to Triple-A Buffalo while Cangelosi was off to the bench, as Fregosi intended to use Foster in left field against right-handers and as the DH against left-handers. When asked by the local media if it was a difficult decision to play Boston and Foster ahead of Cangelosi, Fregosi simply scoffed. "What's tough about it?" Fregosi said. "You go with the players you think can win for you. If you don't win, you get fired." The George Foster experiment, though, ultimately lasted just three weeks. He batted only .216 in 15 games before being released on September 7.

But with the White Sox going with Foster in mid-August, Cangelosi found himself on the bench. Over the next six weeks, Cangelosi started only 10 of the White Sox's 40 games. In fact, over a two-week stretch beginning in September, he had only one plate appearance (and doubled, off the Royals' Charlie Leibrandt). Alas, when he did get his opportunities, the rookie outfielder would often struggle. During that 40-game stretch from August 14 to September 24 where he was given those 10 starts, Cangelosi batted only .139 with four stolen bases (while being caught three times). Perhaps the pressure of trying to break the American League rookie stolen-base record was getting to him, with the season winding down. At the All-Star break, he had 39 stolen bases, just 11 shy of breaking the AL rookie mark. But now in the season's final month, Cangelosi was running out of games to try and break that record. In the second game of a doubleheader on September 27, he collected two hits in a 4-3 White Sox victory over the visiting Twins but was caught stealing in both of his stolen-base attempts. Fregosi started him in two of the next four games—in series against Minnesota and Seattle—but Cangelosi didn't swipe any bags in either game. At that point, he was stuck at 48 stolen bases with only four games remaining in the season.

* * *

But the story wasn't all that simple. According to Cangelosi, he felt he was cheated out of an opportunity to do something really special as far as the stolen-base record was concerned—even though Fregosi had been made aware of the record well in advance. As far as he was concerned, Fregosi had destroyed his confidence and hadn't given him enough playing time, which wore on Cangelosi. He recalls that in late August, veteran catcher Carlton Fisk put in a good word for him to Fregosi, but nothing happened for weeks.

"I would go three weeks without playing," Cangelosi explains. The White Sox would go into Toronto, and Fregosi would give him a spot start against crafty left-hander Jimmy Key. Or the team would play against Texas, and the skipper would give him another spot start, against knuckleballer Charlie Hough, adds Cangelosi, "because he didn't want someone else to go 0-for-4. You know what I mean?

"I would spot start. And then, finally, we had about a month left in the season. I had 44 stolen bases now [in the final week of August]. If I'd been playing the whole second half, I would've had 75 stolen bases, 80 bases, easily. Carlton Fisk came up to me and said, 'Hey, Cangy, man! You know you can break a stolen base record that hasn't been broken since 1910, man? You should go tell Skip to let you play, man. All you need is six stolen bases!' I'm like, 'Man, I ain't going into that frickin' office to talk to that guy. He can go screw himself.' Fisk goes, 'I'll go talk to him.' He goes into the office. I know for a fact that he said something to Skip."

Fisk was referring to the AL rookie stolen-base record held by Rollie Zeider, a long-forgotten infielder who stole 49 bases for the White Sox in 1910. (In his nine-year major-league career, Zeider would play for all three Chicago teams: the American League's White Sox, the National League's Cubs and the Federal League's Chi-Feds/Whales.) Fregosi might have been told about the record, but still, nothing changed. Cangelosi would only play sporadically—and steal four bags to put himself at 48 on the year—and in the five weeks that Fregosi knew the rookie was chasing the stolen-base record, the manager didn't acknowledge him until the White Sox had just one more series left in the season.

"One week goes by. Two weeks go by," recalls Cangelosi. "Now all of a sudden, we're going to Minnesota. We've got four games left. This man comes back to the plane, sits next to me. He goes, 'Hey man, I heard that you can break a stolen base record. I'm gonna give you an opportunity to do it.' I look at him and I'm like, what I am gonna say? I'm 23 years old. I'm a rookie. 'Oh, thanks.' Inside, I was thinking, 'You knew for a month.' I felt like saying, 'Go screw yourself.' I hadn't played [regularly], and now I had to [break that record in the final] four games. Geez, thanks."

Finally given a chance at the end of the season, Cangelosi was determined to break the mark. And he knew he would have to do it in the first three games of the series, because Frank Viola, the tall left-hander of the Twins with a deadly changeup, was the scheduled starter in the finale and was tough to steal against. "I was just blessed that I was able to get on base. I knew their [catching rotation of Mark Salas-Tim Laudner-Jeff Reed] was not very good. They didn't have any good catch-and-throw [catchers]. I knew their staff wasn't really good at holding runners on. I told myself, 'Let me be aggressive the first couple days'—because I knew the [Twins' starter in the season finale] was gonna be Frank Viola, and he had a good move to first base. [In the third game] Bert Blyleven was pitching. I knew for a fact if I got on against him, he was so slow to the plate I could steal two bases on one pitch!"

He didn't quite do that, but he was definitely aggressive. In the series opener, Cangelosi led off the game with a single up the middle off Neal Heaton and stole second for No. 49. He was now tied with Zeider for the stolen-base mark. Alas, Cangelosi was then gunned down by Jeff Reed (one of three Twins catchers who played in that series) for trying to steal third base and break the record. He didn't reach base again until the 10th inning, when he drew a bases-loaded walk off George Frazier to force home the winning run as the White Sox went on to win 8-4. The following day, Cangelosi was 2-for-4 against Mike Smithson, including another leadoff single. But he didn't have a chance to steal a base as Daryl Boston homered right after his first-inning base hit, and there was no base open when Cangelosi singled in the eighth.

On October 4, in the season's penultimate game, Cangelosi finally broke the rookie stolen-base record. He led off the contest with a single and stole second on Blyleven's first pitch to Boston, his 50th stolen base, breaking the tie with Zeider. He wouldn't steal another base for the rest of the game—or in the regular-season finale—but he found two men waiting for him in the visitors' clubhouse after the contest. Representatives from the National Baseball Hall of Fame, they had come to request, for the museum, the shoes Cangelosi wore to break the record. "I didn't wanna wait for the last day because Frank Viola had one of the best pickoff moves in baseball," Cangelosi recalls. "So, I broke that record against Blyleven, and I gave the Hall of Fame my shoes, but I got to keep the second-base bag."

Imagine that. From being an unknown at the start of the season to breaking a 76-year-old record to having his shoes wanted by the Hall of Fame. It was an improbable journey that began well in the spring before hitting some bumps on the road midseason. The season, at the end of the day, ended in a positive note. And yes, Cangelosi was ecstatic to have broken the stolen-base record. But he felt it could have been more. For starters, while the original record stood for 76 years, Cangelosi's would be in the record books for only six years, as both Milwaukee's Pat Listach (with 54 steals) and Cleveland's Kenny Lofton (with 66) would break the mark in 1992. Then, there was also the rest of his career, which could have gone a different way, according to him, had Jim Fregosi given him a fair shake.

"I ended up with 50 stolen bases. I had the American League rookie stolen-base record. But that's what I was bitter about. I could've had 80 stolen bases. It probably still would be held today. It cost me a lot of money. If I steal 80 bags as a rookie, I could've probably gone anywhere and not become a utility player. [Fregosi] took a lot of value away from me. I never opened my mouth at all, but I had a lot of animosity toward that man. For a couple of years, we went back and forth in the papers. Stupid stuff. But I said something I shouldn't have. He said something he shouldn't have."

Cangelosi does have a point. Even Billy Hamilton, the exciting speedster of the Cincinnati Reds who stole a single-season record 155 bases in the minors in 2012, couldn't match what Cangelosi had accomplished in the first half of his major-league rookie season. Hamilton, in his rookie year in the big leagues in 2014, stole 56 bases in 152 games. His 38 stolen bases, according to the Reds' media guide, were the most ever by a Cincinnati rookie prior to the All-Star Game, but he couldn't surpass the first-half number that was put up by Cangelosi, who had 39 steals in the first half of the 1986 season.

While he might not have reached 80 steals had Fregosi not benched him—it would have been difficult to maintain his first-half pace to begin with—Cangelosi most certainly would have had more than the 54 bags that Listach swiped in 1992. And so, during the early part of his major-league career, Cangelosi blamed Fregosi for the benching. At the time, there was real animosity between the two men. But as Cangelosi says now, he and Fregosi, who passed away in 2014, resolved their differences in the mid-1990s when both were in the National League. "One year, when he was with the Phillies, I was in

Philadelphia," he recalls, likely referring to his time with the Mets in 1994. "I went up to him and said, 'Jim, you got a minute?' I just said, 'Hey look, I just wanna apologize for the things I've been saying. It's water under the bridge. I can't go on like this.' He shook my hand. He said, 'Cangy, man. I'm sorry as well. I treated you wrong. I just wanna apologize to you.' We were both men enough to put it behind us. Let him rest in peace now."

Overall, it was a great season to begin a fine career. Cangelosi, after all, had the opportunity to play with Hall-of-Famers-to-be Carlton Fisk, Harold Baines, Tom Seaver and Steve Carlton in that rookie season. In fact, he was in the same outfield on Opening Day with Fisk, the 38-year-old veteran catcher whom the White Sox asked to move to left field (to allow Joel Skinner to become the regular backstop). Seaver was on the mound, Fisk was in left field and the rookie center fielder was at Fisk's left. "Carlton Fisk was very instrumental in my career," Cangelosi acknowledges now. "I talked to him a lot about the game. After the games we would talk about situations and how to apply myself. From a standpoint like that, he was there for me."

It wasn't just legendary teammates whom Cangelosi had the opportunity to converse with. He even had a picture taken with a former U.S. President. "I even have a picture of myself in a White Sox uniform with Jimmy Carter," Cangelosi says while looking through his photo collection, referring to the man who served as the 39th President of the United States from 1977 to 1981. "It was a good first season for me in the big leagues. I got to meet the President. I broke the stolen-base record. The Hall of Fame came looking for me. I mean, being an underdog, being a 'kid from nowhere,' so to speak, it was a good start to the big leagues... It could've been better and, yes, I did get benched in the second half of the season, but, hey, I stuck with it, and I mean, miracles do happen. It did for me in that rookie season with the White Sox."

Chapter Five
Off to Pittsburgh

Everybody probably just saw him as an extra guy. He had a good year with the White Sox [before coming over to Pittsburgh]… But Cangy was a better player than people probably gave him credit for. John wasn't just some guy that came off the bench. He was a good baseball player. He was gutsy. He had a lot of guts. And he played hard. When he got his chance to get in there, he gave it all he had. He usually played very well. He would play a lot on Sundays, which were day games. Most guys really didn't want to play on Sundays, but he said it was his day to shine and he accepted it. And he went out there and gave it his all. He never cheated you on the field and he gave us everything he had every time he played.

—Tommy Sandt, former Pittsburgh Pirates
first-base coach (2018)

What a difference a year makes. That's what John Cangelosi thought in the spring of 1987. In 1986, it was the best of times with Tony La Russa giving him a shot, naming him the Opening Day center fielder of the White Sox. One year later, it was a different story under skipper Jim Fregosi.

The switch-hitting outfielder was upset being benched when Fregosi took over midseason in 1986 and, to him, it was obvious the manager had no plans to play him moving forward. During the early days of spring training in 1987, Fregosi had already decided on his Opening Day lineup, noted the *Chicago Sun-Times* on March 9th, except for left field. But even so, it became evident that Ivan Calderon, who had led the Puerto Rican winter league in home runs and would be playing in his third big-league season, was the favorite for the job. With Daryl Boston getting another shot to start in center field, Harold Baines once again manning right field and Reid Nichols being the top candidate for the fourth outfielder spot, Cangelosi was at best the White Sox's fifth outfielder. The only spots that were true question marks, remarkably, were the 10th pitcher and utility players—and Opening Day was a full month away. "The rest of the spring will be spent conditioning the pitchers," the manager was quoted as saying in the *Chicago Sun-Times* on the weekend of Chicago's first spring games.

"I don't know what it was with Jim Fregosi," Cangelosi says, recalling the fact that he was pegged for bench duty as the White Sox broke spring-training camp. "He just didn't like me. In '87, I went to spring training, and right from day one I wasn't even gonna make that team. I mean, it was obvious. I guess a trade rumor leaked or something. So, I couldn't afford to get hurt. He basically called me into his office and said, 'Hey look, just report to me every day. We're trying to trade you right now. So, we don't want you being active in case you got hurt.' In '87, I really didn't have a spring training, and that went on for a couple of weeks. Then, toward the end of spring training, I got traded to the Pittsburgh Pirates."

He was dealt to the Pirates for Jim Winn, a right-handed reliever, on March 27. Cangelosi was proven right about Fregosi's obvious disdain toward him; the day before the trade, the White Sox acquired outfielder Gary Redus from Philadelphia, and the Sox skipper had nothing but praise for the newcomer. Redus would "lead off and play an outfield position basically every day," Fregosi told the *Chicago Sun-Times'* Dave van Dyck. Even with Calderon, Boston and Baines already in the outfield? "All I know is that our entire ball club, from top to bottom, is better than at any time last season... We might DH [Redus] and lead him off... I'll try to make use of all of them." (Ironically, Redus would be traded to Pittsburgh late in the 1988 season, where he would be teammates with Cangelosi for two-plus years.)

Cangelosi loved playing in the city of Chicago, but it was time to move on. For him, it was a breath of fresh air in Pittsburgh. "When I got traded over there, [manager] Jimmy Leyland sat me down, and that's just protocol. You get traded to a new team, and he explained my role. It was the obvious. They had Andy Van Slyke in center, Barry Bonds in left and Bobby Bonilla in right. Obviously, my playing time was gonna be diminished, just from a name standpoint."

It should be noted, though, that the 1987 season actually began with Bonds in center, Bonilla in left and Van Slyke in right. Bonilla eventually moved to the infield to become the regular third baseman—while Bonds was moved to left and Van Slyke to center—and R. J. Reynolds also started in right field. The following season, it was indeed Bonds in left and Van Slyke in center, while a trio of outfielders—Reynolds, Darnell Coles and Glenn Wilson—saw playing time in right field. (Coles began the season in Pittsburgh before being traded in July to Seattle for Wilson.) In 1989, Wilson started the season as the everyday right fielder before he was traded to Houston for fellow outfielder Billy Hatcher. As for Bonilla, the switch-hitting power hitter would be the Pirates' everyday third baseman in both 1988 and 1989 before Leyland moved him to right field in 1990.

Cangelosi, meanwhile, would be doing a lot of pinch-running and playing defense, Leyland told him the day he reported to the team. He would get his at-bats, he was assured. "Just be patient; everyone is going to play," Leyland promised. "We don't have nine players on this team. We have 24."

That also meant Cangelosi was going to be sharing time in left field with Bonds, who in his first four big-league seasons from 1986 to 1989 was used primarily as a leadoff man. "When we opened up the season in 1987, Barry was struggling against left-handed pitching, so I kinda fell into a platoon role with Barry Bonds early in his career because he was struggling against lefties," explains Cangelosi. "I had a lot of at-bats. I had a really good season… I think I was second in the league in pinch-hitting, [collecting 10 pinch-hits for the year]. So, I had a quality season as a part-time player in '87."

That, he did. In his first season in Pittsburgh, Cangelosi batted .275 with four homers and 21 stolen bases in 104 games. Improbably, his on-base percentage, over the first two months of the season, was a whopping .524 as he drew 31 walks and was twice hit by pitches in his first 84 plate appearances. In his first start of the year on April 12, he went 4-for-4 in a 7-4 victory over the Cardinals, getting three hits and a walk off St. Louis ace left-hander John Tudor. "That was my first start as a Pittsburgh Pirate. I just saw the ball really well off him." On May 24, Cangelosi frustrated Reds ace Tom Browning, another tough left-hander in the National League. In the first inning, Cangy walked and proceeded to steal both second and third. An inning later, after the Pirates had gotten four runs, Cangelosi again walked and then stole second base. So, that was two walks and three stolen bases in just two innings! The third time Cangelosi came up, Browning drilled him, but the Pirates outfielder got the last laugh as he came home when Barry Bonds, the next hitter, doubled to right.

It was a thrill for Cangelosi having a huge game against the Reds, as the Cincinnati ball club was managed by Pete Rose, baseball's all-time hits leader. "I'm like a Pete Rose on the baseball field," Cangelosi explains. "I had little things about me that [were similar to] him as far as base running and sliding head first. I mean, Willie Mays was my number one idol growing up, but I looked up to guys who had my sort of style of playing, guys like Ralph Garr or Pete Rose. I enjoyed watching them because they stood out—and they were little guys just like me!"

Cangelosi even became the first Pirate in 21 years to steal home, when he accomplished the feat against the Montreal Expos on September 15, breaking a scoreless tie in a game Pittsburgh eventually won 5-1. It happened in the fourth inning, with Cangelosi on third base and Jose Lind on first. "Neal Heaton was the pitcher, and he was actually kinda slow to first base and deliberate. I told my third-base coach, Gene Lamont, 'Hey, if he throws to first base, I'm stealing home next pitch.' I kept creeping off third base. When Heaton showed me that he was going to first base, he was so slow and deliberate that he gave me a lot of time to start home. By the time [Expos first baseman] Andres Galarraga got the ball, I was already at home plate. So, that wasn't the traditional way of stealing home. He went to first base first, and then I stole home that way. Normally, you steal home when the pitcher is throwing home, but I didn't."

When reminded that he also stole second in that inning off Heaton—he didn't steal third because Jose Lind singled him to third base—Cangelosi remembers former White Sox first-base coach Davey Nelson. "Davey Nelson was my mentor, my base-stealing mentor. I got called up briefly in '85, but by then he had left the White Sox. He was more like a minor-league mentor for me. When I was in the minor leagues, he would come down to instructional league and coach. He gave me some tips. He would talk to me. He was more like a base-stealing coach. He was very instrumental in teaching me a few things about base stealing, what to look for and certain things. He also helped me out with coaching when I was done playing. When he was with the Cleveland Indians, he gave me some drills—some base-stealing drills—that I could do with my kids when I was coaching with the Cubs.

"I think there was one record that he always said he had, and I wanted to break it but I could never break it." Cangelosi is referring to Nelson stealing second, third and home in the same inning, which he accomplished as a member of the Texas Rangers on August 30, 1974 against Cleveland. In that game, Nelson led off with a walk against Indians pitcher Dick Bosman, stole second with Cesar Tovar batting, stole third with Jeff Burroughs at the plate and stole home with Mike Hargrove hitting, to give the Rangers their first run. It was one of only two times in which Nelson stole three bases in a major-league game. "And I wanted to do that my whole career—stealing second, third and home in one inning," continues Cangelosi. "But I could never do it. It's hard to do. Sometimes the score dictates the situation because you're showing up the other team. For you to steal second, third and home in the same inning, more than likely it'll have to be in the early innings when it really doesn't mean all that much. The score of the game will dictate you stealing home. I did a lot of second and third in the same inning, but I could never get home. I always wanted to do it because he did it."

Still, Cangelosi did match Nelson in one stat. He would steal three bases in a regular-season game three times in his career, something Nelson accomplished twice. Neither stole four bases in a single game in the big leagues.

And, as far as Pirates first-base coach Tommy Sandt is concerned, Cangelosi did a lot of good things for Pittsburgh. As Sandt recalls today, Cangelosi often came through in the late innings. The numbers support his recollection; in innings seven through nine in 1987, Cangelosi batted .280, including .343 in the eighth innings and .300 in the ninth. "He wasn't a big target," says Sandt. "So, he would walk in the bottom of the ninth—or top of the ninth—and start a rally for us.

And he could run. He got on base a lot for us when it counted. You know, if you're in that role, you're facing a pretty good pitcher. You're facing the other team's closer. So, his at-bats weren't easy."

But Cangelosi sure made them seem easy at times. On June 28, he came on to pinch-hit leading off the eighth inning against Cubs ace (and NL wins leader) Rick Sutcliffe with the Pirates trailing 2-1. In typical Cangelosi fashion, he walked, stole second, came around to score the tying run and even added an RBI single off relief ace Lee Smith in that same inning as Pittsburgh batted around and rallied for a 6-2 victory to complete a three-game sweep of Chicago. In that same month in New York, Cangelosi, facing Mets reliever Roger McDowell in another pinch-hitting assignment, reached base on a bunt single to the right side of the infield, igniting a six-run eighth inning as the Pirates beat the Mets 10-9. On August 18 in Cincinnati, he stunned everybody by leading off the seventh with a pinch-hit home run off lefty Rob Murphy, snapping a 4-4 tie as the Pirates went on to prevail 7-4. For the season, when he was facing a reliever in a game, Cangelosi batted .300 with four extra-base hits and 18 walks—and a .493 on-base percentage—in the first plate appearance against that relief pitcher. In that season alone, he reached base either via walks or base hits in late-inning situations against tough relievers such as Smith, McDowell, Todd Worrell, Ken Dayley, Larry Andersen, Kent Tekulve and Steve Bedrosian. But he was lethal too against starting pitchers when facing them the second time and onwards in the same contest, batting .344, .345 and .357 against the same starter in the second, third and fourth at-bats, respectively. According to Baseball-Reference.com, Cangelosi batted .359 with a .500 on-base percentage when batting in high-leverage situations in 1987.

Leyland was certainly impressed. After all, acquiring Cangelosi had only cost them a pitcher (right-hander Jim Winn) who would appear in just 65 more games in the majors after the trade, none after 1988. "He was a fine addition for us because he was someone we were looking for, a guy who could play the outfield and be a part-time leadoff guy," Leyland told a Chicago sportswriter in mid-April. The Pirates skipper, whom Cangelosi calls a numbers guy, also noted Cangy's value playing on artificial turf, which was the playing surface used at Pittsburgh's Three Rivers Stadium. "We also did some research on his offensive output on turf and it was much better than it was on grass, and we felt that also was a big plus for us."

* * *

The 1987 Pirates were a horrible team. By the All-Star break, they were already 17-and-a-half games out of first place. They spent 93 days in last place in the NL East and were a season-high 18 games under .500 on August 23. But over a three-week stretch, Pittsburgh had two separate seven-game winning streaks.

Pittsburgh also played the defending World Champion New York Mets tough in the final weeks of September. The Mets, trying to win a second consecutive NL East title, were just one-and-a-half games back of first-place St. Louis going into a three-game series against the last-place Pirates in Pittsburgh on September 18. The Pirates took two out of three, winning 10-9 in the opener and 9-8 in a 14-inning thriller in the finale. While Cangelosi didn't do much in that series, he did lead off the opening contest with a home run—off former Pittsburgh ace John Candelaria—to help the Pirates rally from a 3-0 deficit in that one. One week later in New York, the Pirates pounded Mets ace Dwight Gooden in the middle game of another three-game set. As it turned out, the Mets finished three games behind the division-winning Cardinals, and in an era without the wild card, New York missed the postseason despite winning 92 games—a total that was second-best in the National League.

In Pittsburgh, meanwhile, the future seemed bright thanks to a hot streak to end the season. Inspired by the leadership of manager Jim Leyland, the Pirates climbed to fourth by season's end, tied with the Phillies with an 80-82 record. For Cangelosi, the clubhouse in Pittsburgh and the one in Chicago was night and day. "We [the Pirates] are in last place but we have some talent and a positive outlook," he noted that August. "They stick with you here and talk to you. The manager tells you whether he's pleased with you or not. There's a good feeling in the locker room. Over there [in Chicago], it was like the Yankees. If you said something wrong... I lost my confidence and he [Jim Fregosi] got down on me. If I did do good, it seemed like they wanted me to fail... The bottom line is that with Jimmy [Leyland], I know my role. Over there I didn't. I was never appreciated."

And in Pittsburgh, the future was also bright because of the famous outfield trio of Bonds, Bonilla and Van Slyke, while the pitching staff included future NL Cy Young Award winner Doug Drabek (who would win the award in 1990) and future 20-game winner John Smiley. The Pirates were certainly an up-and-coming team, and Cangelosi was happy to be around, even if he wasn't an everyday player. And in Pittsburgh, the other Pirates players loved him. A popular player in the clubhouse, Cangelosi was easily friends with everybody on the team, even the biggest stars like Bonds, who would go on to break baseball's single-season and career home run records, and Bonilla. "With the Pirates, I was really close with John Smiley and R. J. Reynolds," he says. "I was close with them. Smiley was my roommate in Pittsburgh. And Bobby Bonilla. Great guy, great family man."

While some members of the media tend to portray Bonds as a villain, Cangelosi saw a different side of baseball's all-time home-run king when the two were teammates in Pittsburgh. In fact, Cangelosi and Bonds became instant friends when they first met, and they remain friends even today. Cangelosi smiles when recalling how Bonds bought him a motorcycle as a wedding gift during the off-season when he was getting married. "He came to my parents' house in Bradenton, Florida," Cangelosi says. "I was getting married that winter. He showed up at my parents' house and said, 'Hey, I can't make it to your wedding. Come on, jump on the bike.' He and Bobby Bonilla took me to a dealership, and Barry bought me a motorcycle. I'd never been on a motorcycle before. Within 10 minutes, I'd learned how to ride it and then went on the highway going 100 miles per hour. It was me, Barry Bonds and Bobby Bonilla… It was awesome. The workers at the dealership taught me how to ride it; we did it in the parking lot. I learned the gear shifts, and from there I was on the highway within an hour."

For Cangelosi, the visit and the gift were a complete surprise. "I didn't know anything about it. Barry came in and said, 'Come on, jump on the bike. Let's go.' I mean, me and Barry have a great relationship. He's a great guy. He's misunderstood a lot by the public. We have a great relationship. We still talk today, like once a year. Barry's got a good heart."

As for Bonilla, playing with him in Pittsburgh was a reunion of sorts. "Me and Bobby Bonilla played on the same team five times," Cangelosi explains. "We played in Puerto Rico together for eight years; we were on the Mayaguez team in Puerto Rico. That's where I played winter baseball for 13 years. We lived together one year. We both played for the White Sox and the Pirates. Bobby got [selected in the Rule 5 draft by] the White Sox [from Pittsburgh in December 1985]. He was my teammate there and my roommate for a little bit." Then, Bonilla was traded to Pittsburgh in July 1986, and Cangelosi was dealt to the Pirates before the 1987 season. The two were teammates in Pittsburgh until the end of the 1990 playoffs. In 1994, they were reunited in New York with the Mets. "And then we were on the World Series team with the Marlins together [in 1997]. So, me and Bobby played on five different teams together. I go way back with Bobby Bonilla," laughs Cangelosi.

Being reunited with Bonilla brought back fond memories for Cangelosi, especially the days in the Puerto Rican winter league. "My mom was Puerto Rican, so I got to play in Puerto Rico as a native. They call it a 'nativo.' One day in A-ball, I was playing against the Texas Rangers. Orlando Gomez was the coach for the other team. I was playing center field. There was a foul ball down the right-field line and

Kenny Williams lost it because it was twilight. I ran and caught the ball in foul territory in right field. After the game, the coach on the other team says, 'Are you Puerto Rican?' I say, 'Yeah, my mom's Puerto Rican and my dad's Italian.' He goes, 'Please tell me that your mom was born in Puerto Rico.' I said, 'Yes, she was.' And that's how I went into the Puerto Rican draft as a native. I was drafted and they still have the rights to me today. I had the ability to play winter baseball, which at that time was like, Triple-A/Major League Baseball back in the day. That helped me get to the big leagues very quick. I think I was 21 years old, [and] I was playing against guys like [major-league All-Star outfielder Jose] 'Cheo' Cruz.

"Just think about this team: My team the one year that we went to the Caribbean Series, I was the center fielder, Vince Coleman was in left, Bobby Bonilla was in right, Sid Bream was at first base, Harold Reynolds was at second base, Terry Pendleton was at third, [Tom] Pagnozzi was catching. The team that we beat had Sandy Alomar behind the plate, Edgar Martinez at third base, [Carlos] Baerga at shortstop, Roberto Alomar at second base, Carmelo Martinez at first base, Bernie Williams in center field, Ruben Sierra in right field and Juan Gonzalez in left field. Think about those lineups! It was great baseball. We beat them and went to the Caribbean Series. Unfortunately, we never won it. I went to the Caribbean Series five years, but I never won it."

With Cangelosi being an outfielder, you might assume his best friends in the game were fellow outfielders or utility players. Ironically, though, his closest friends in baseball were pitchers, not position players. "For whatever reason, I had a lot of friends everywhere. When I was in Pittsburgh, my best friend was John Smiley, a pitcher. R. J. Reynolds was a close friend of mine as well. When I signed with the Mets, I took a liking to [right-handed pitcher] Pete Smith. We hung out a lot. He was a guy that I went to dinner with. On that team, I hung out with Pete Smith, [closer] John Franco and [starter] Bret Saberhagen. I didn't hang out with any position players on that team. It was weird. With the Marlins, once in a while I hung out with Bobby Bonilla, but I [normally] hung out with Moises Alou, [left-hander] Al Leiter, [right-hander] Alex Fernandez and Darren Daulton."

Cangelosi also admits he learned a lot from sitting beside pitchers and picking their brains on the pitching aspect of the game. The more knowledge he had, the more he was able to succeed at the plate against opposing pitchers. "I had the opportunity to play for a lot of different teams, so I'm gonna have a lot of different friendships. The other thing is, during the game, I really liked sitting next to pitchers versus position players because I would talk to them about what pitches they would throw in that situation if it were me. I mean [I would ask], 'I'm the leadoff hitter. How would you be pitching me right now?' I just wanted to learn more about how a pitcher thought than a position player."

* * *

For Cangelosi, moving to the National League was the ideal situation, particularly since he had become a bench player. In the senior circuit, because the pitcher had to bat, there were pinch-hitting opportunities in the late innings to bat for the starter or reliever, especially when the game was close. If he had still been with the White Sox, or with an American League team, he would not have gotten much playing time at all, since teams in the junior circuit went with set lineups—without the need for pinch-hitting—for the most part.

But still, it was a tough adjustment going from being a starting center fielder to a utility player. He had always been in the everyday lineup, even in the minors, and for the first half of his rookie year in Chicago. By 1987, he had accepted his role and had his routine down pat.

"After the third inning, I would go up and grab a coffee, kinda just tinker around a little bit," he says now, reflecting to the inning-by-inning routine that he had developed in Pittsburgh. "Look at the pitcher from a TV standpoint, to kinda look at location. And then in the fourth inning, I would come out, drink a cup of coffee, watch the game a little bit. After the fifth inning on, I would start mentally preparing myself for that one at-bat. I would see how the game flow was going. If it was a close game, I knew that I might probably pinch-hit in the seventh inning—or eighth inning or ninth inning—depending on who was pitching. If it was a blowout, I probably wouldn't be pinch-hitting. I might go in to play defense and give somebody a rest in the last three innings. Your mindset was dictated on how the game was going for your particular role.

"So, third inning, I would go in and kinda chill out. Have a cup of coffee. Fourth inning, come out. Have another cup of coffee. Watch the game. Fifth inning, I would go in and stretch. I would start to prepare and visualize who I thought I was gonna be facing. While I'm stretching, I'm thinking about who I might be

77

facing. In the sixth inning, I would go down into the tunnel. If they had an indoor batting cage, I would take swings off the machine, left-handed and right-handed. In the seventh inning, I would come back out and see how the game is playing out, understand where that pitcher slot is coming up. After that, I would kinda, like, go back and forth. I would go back and try to get a couple more swings in. I would play it by ear. I would play along with how the lineup is going, and I would be ready when that pitcher came up, just in case Leyland wanted to pinch-hit for him. So, I was always ready even before Leyland came and got me."

"His attitude was pretty upbeat," adds Tommy Sandt. "He obviously wasn't a fourth outfielder behind a bunch of idiots. It was Barry Bonds, Andy Van Slyke [and] Bobby Bonilla ahead of him. He wasn't silly; he knew his role. And he accepted it. Not too many people were going to start over Bonds, Van Slyke and Bonilla. He accepted that, and he was really upbeat. That was part of his job. A good extra guy that at times was a cheerleader. Late in the game he knew when he was going to used, or if he was going to be used. He'd get himself ready mentally and physically, too. Starting about the fifth or sixth inning, he really got into his game mode, because that was his game, late in the game, which is a hard role. You get one at-bat against the other team's closer, and that's a tough chore. He accepted it. It was pretty easy to accept being a backup to those guys. There are a whole lot of guys who would've been backups to them. Any club you're with, the outfield usually has a lot of good players."

Leyland knew Cangelosi was a valuable player to keep around. He certainly knew how difficult

Cangelosi's job was. "I'll make this point about him," the Pirates skipper once told the *Pittsburgh Post-Gazette*'s Gene Collier. "Where do you find a guy that can sit for 10 days or two weeks, come out and bat in the eighth or ninth inning against the other team's toughest reliever, and work a walk, do a pretty decent job?"

Not only did he get himself ready to go in to pinch-hit, Cangelosi also had to be prepared as a pinch-runner. And he had to be extra ready when playing on artificial turf at Pittsburgh's Three Rivers Stadium and at other National League venues such as Houston, Montreal, St. Louis, Philadelphia and Cincinnati. How so? By wearing different shoes. Not to make a fashion statement, of course, but to not get thrown out on the base paths.

"The reason why I wore different shoes [was due to the turf]," he explains. "Back then, the artificial turf was so thin, it was like indoor-outdoor carpet. It wasn't really that good [of a] turf like [today's]. My lead was so big at first base that my front foot was always on the turf and my back foot was on the dirt. On the dirt, I needed a spike to grab hold. On the turf, if I had a spike, it would be very slippery. It would slip. It wouldn't catch. My front foot always had to [have a] turf [shoe]. Then I would have a spike on my back foot. Most of the time, it worked out. Most of the time, I would wear just turf shoes in the outfield. And then I would come back and put my spikes on because the turf was so thin... It hurt my feet to run in the outfield with spikes on. Back then, the turf was really not all that good in most of the parks. That's why I did that. There was really no specific purpose other than comfort and necessity." And the shoes weren't just different; they weren't even from the same shoe company. "I had a contract with Pony at the time. So, I had a Pony spike for my back foot, and I had a Mizuno turf shoe on my front."

He didn't wear different shoes initially when he began his big-league career. But it was when he played at the Metrodome against the Minnesota Twins in his rookie year with Chicago that he realized wearing different shoes made all the difference in terms of not getting picked off versus getting screamed at by the manager. "In Minnesota, there was a design play," Cangelosi explains, referring to a game in June 1986. "Ray Miller [who was the Twins' manager in 1985 and 1986] was my pitching coach in Pittsburgh. He actually tried to get me over there [midway through] my rookie year. When he came over to Pittsburgh, he told me, 'Hey man, I was trying to work out a trade where you came to play for me in Minnesota when the White Sox benched you and didn't wanna get rid of you.' With that being said, he told me that there was one specific game [where] I was on second base with two outs—and I had my spikes on.

"I was going nowhere. Harold Baines was at the plate [with Greg Walker on deck, and both were] left-handed [hitters]. I'm not stealing a base. I'm not doing anything. I had two feet on the turf in a very relaxed position." While the Twins didn't do anything when Baines came up to bat with Cangelosi already on second—Baines ended up reaching base with Cangy staying put—they caught the rookie center fielder by surprise with Walker at the plate. "They put a pickoff play on me, and my feet gave out from under me. I slipped, and so I got thrown out. La Russa was pissed.

He brought me to the runway and started yelling, 'What the hell are you doing?' I said, 'Skip, I wasn't going anywhere, man. I slipped! It was slippery!'

"But anyway, in Minnesota back then, the turf was indoor-outdoor turf. It was very slippery. If I took a lead at first base, my front foot was on the turf all the time. If I had a spike on, I would slip. That's how bad the turf was.

"Fast forward to 1987, when I was with the Pirates. Ray Miller was my pitching coach. He told me that they must have picked off 20 to 30 guys at second base. He goes, 'It was a mandatory pickoff play when a runner at second base had two feet on the carpet, because with spikes on, as soon as you try to pivot to get back, you would slip. So, it was a design play.' That's how the tough the turf was back then." And when Cangelosi went to the National League, he knew, as a base runner, he couldn't wear spikes on turf. So, the front foot had to be a turf shoe while the back foot would be a spike.

For Cangelosi being a fourth or fifth outfielder in Pittsburgh—and later on in his career—it wasn't a matter of simply sitting on the bench. He had to face the opposing team's closer or a tough reliever when he got in. He had to visualize the late-inning at-bat and be ready. And have the proper footwear on. For the most part, he did it well.

Sandt concurs. As far as the Pirates first-base coach is concerned, Cangelosi's contributions with Pittsburgh shouldn't be overlooked. "A lot of times, I think, he faced left-handed pitchers because [the left-handed hitting] Bonds or Van Slyke would need a day off, and against a lefty would be the time to do it, and

Cangy was a switch-hitter. He got some stolen bases for us when it counted," says Sandt.

* * *

In 1988 and 1989, the Pirates missed the postseason—in those days, in the pre-Wild Card era, teams had to win the division in order to qualify for postseason play—and Cangelosi once again didn't see much playing time in Pittsburgh. (Had the Wild Card existed back then, Pittsburgh, which finished second in the NL East in 1988 behind the division champion New York Mets and fourth overall, would have qualified for the playoffs in the National League.) In the two seasons, he had just 278 big-league at-bats and hit .234 with 20 stolen bases. He was also sent down to Triple-A Buffalo in 1988, where he batted .331 in 166 at-bats. (Yes, Cangelosi had also played for the Bisons in 1985, when the club was the Triple-A affiliate of the White Sox. The Bisons then became the Indians' top farm team in 1987 before being Pittsburgh's Triple-A club from 1988 to 1994.)

But 1990 was a different story for the Pirates. Led by the exploits of Barry Bonds and Bobby Bonilla (who finished 1-2 in the National League MVP voting), along with a pitching staff anchored by Cy Young Award winner Doug Drabek, Pittsburgh went 95-67 to capture its first division title since 1979, beating out a star-studded Mets team that featured slugger Darryl Strawberry and fireballer Dwight Gooden. The Pirates, in fact, had the second-best record in all of baseball in 1990, trailing only the American League West champion Oakland Athletics, who went 103-59.

Cangelosi, a fifth outfielder on the team, split the season in Buffalo and Pittsburgh. He was actually waived in spring training but found himself back with the Pirates when the club traded outfielder Billy Hatcher to Cincinnati a week before the start of the season. When Hatcher did well with the Reds as an everyday player—batting .276 with 30 stolen bases in 139 regular-season games before hitting .519 for the entire 1990 postseason as Cincinnati won the World Series—Pirates fans started booing Cangelosi. "I think the fans got hooked up on the Billy Hatcher deal, but they were misinformed on that," Cangelosi told the *Pittsburgh Post-Gazette* that summer. "Billy Hatcher was an everyday player, and with Barry and Andy and Bobby, we couldn't use him. I think [the fact that Hatcher was having a fine year in Cincinnati] is what the fans are thinking. Certainly, I've never said anything or done anything to the Pittsburgh fans, and it's not for lack of hustle or anything like that. They can't expect me to hit .350 playing as little as I do."

They weren't expecting him to fall below the Mendoza Line, though, which was what Cangelosi did in 1990. He batted a career-low .197 in 58 games with the Pirates, contributing only one RBI. But out of his 13 runs scored on the season, one was the game-winner in the division-clinching game in St. Louis on September 30. In the eighth inning of a scoreless game with Drabek, their ace, on the mound, the Pirates loaded the bases against the Cardinals' Joe Magrane. Cangelosi came on to pinch-run for Don Slaught, who'd opened the inning with a single, representing the division-winning run. When Gary Redus flied out to medium center, Cangelosi came home to score the go-ahead run and the Pirates went on to win 2-0, clinching the NL East flag.

It was quite the scene afterward, with Bonds and John Smiley carrying manager Jim Leyland off the field, along with Drabek jumping up and down and hugging first baseman Sid Bream. There was also the traditional champagne spraying in the locker room. "We clinched in St. Louis. I remember the party in the locker room. I don't remember scoring [the winning run]," Cangelosi says now. "That was the first time ever [winning a division title in the big leagues]. It was a great time because it was a bunch of [young players making big contributions to the club]... The first year that I was there, we came in fifth or sixth place. We were just a bunch of young guys. Me, Doug Drabek, Barry Bonds, Bobby Bonilla, Andy Van Slyke. John Smiley. We were all young. We were all in our early 20s. We had Mike LaValliere, Carmelo Martinez, Sid Bream. There were a couple older guys. For us to accomplish something so early, it was a lot of fun, especially on that high stage. It was well rewarding, not only for us but also for Jimmy Leyland and his staff. I mean, they went on to coach together for 15 or 16 years. It was probably one of the better staffs in baseball for a long time."

For Cangelosi, it was also a bittersweet moment as he was later informed by Leyland that he would not be on the postseason roster. The Pirates skipper decided to carry 11 pitchers on his playoff roster, which was unusual because most teams at the time preferred to go with a deeper bench in a short postseason series. The NL West champion Cincinnati Reds, the Pirates' NL Championship Series opponent, carried nine pitchers on their roster, for instance, according to a *Chicago Tribune* story covering the series.

To this day, the decision to leave Cangelosi off the roster still hurts. "That was a very hard decision that he had to make," Cangelosi says of Leyland. "That still doesn't sit well with me. But I understood the business behind it. I wasn't active. He called me into his office. He had a heart-to-heart with me. He said, 'Cangy, I'm gonna put Carmelo Martinez on the roster instead of you. We need more pop off the bench.' He basically went with a different type of player off the bench than me. I'm more of a speed guy, leadoff guy. Get on, if [we're] up or down a run late in the game. He felt like he had enough of that. He felt like in a short [series], Andy, Bobby and Barry would be okay. And that situation wouldn't come up as much as if there was an RBI situation needed. I understood it, but it was very hurtful. [During the playoffs] I did everything with the team. I took batting practice. When the games started, I had to stay in the dugout. But if somebody got hurt, they would've been able to activate me."

As it turned out, Cangelosi wasn't needed at all. The Pirates were ousted by Cincinnati, the eventual World Series champs, in six games. At the time, Leyland was widely criticized for carrying a short bench. "It's as simple as this," Leyland was quoted as saying in the *Chicago Tribune* then. "There's no secret: If the Pirates' starting lineup doesn't do it, then we're in trouble. That's the way it's been all year... Who's the one extra guy? John Cangelosi? They booed him all year. [Third-string catcher] Dann Bilardello? I can't believe that John Cangelosi, [rookie outfielder] Steve Carter [who hit .200 in five at-bats], [reserve outfielder] Mark Ryal [who hit .083 in 12 at-bats] or Dann Bilardello [who batted .054 in 37 at-bats] is going to make a whole lot of difference as compared to having an extra pitcher."

The Pirates would go on to win NL East titles in 1991 and 1992, but once again fall short in the NLCS both times. In those two years, they lost heart-breaking seven-game series to the Atlanta Braves, with John Smoltz blanking them 4-0 in the finale in 1991 and the unheralded Francisco Cabrera driving in the pennant-winning run in the bottom of the ninth in 1992.

Cangelosi's stay in Pittsburgh, meanwhile, would be over following the 1990 NLCS, so he missed out on the other two division championships. "I didn't get tendered a contract after that, but they went to the playoffs two more years in a row. The Atlanta Braves beat them—with Sid Bream [who left Pittsburgh and signed with the Braves following the 1990 season] scoring at home plate [to end the '92 series]—but I wasn't on the team. It was twice that they should've won. But that year in '90, I thought we had the pitching. We definitely had the offense [with] Barry Bonds, Andy Van Slyke [and] Bobby Bonilla. We had Jay Bell, Sid Bream, Chico Lind, Mike LaValliere. We had a great pitching staff with a great bullpen. We were bummed that we got beat. I don't remember if we were favored or not in that series, but Cincinnati ended up beating us. We had a very good team in 1990, but anything can happen in a short series."

The 1990 postseason ended in a sour note for the Pirates. The story with Leyland and Cangelosi would, of course, have a happier ending years later. In 1997, with both men on the Florida Marlins—a club that didn't exist yet in 1990—Leyland, who was the skipper, included Cangelosi on the postseason rosters. Cangelosi had an at-bat in extra innings in Game Seven of the 1997 World Series, and the Marlins won the game an inning later. Both Leyland and Cangelosi would, at last, have their first World Championship rings. It took seven long years after the 1990 loss to Cincinnati, but it all worked out in the end. "Just don't give up," Cangelosi says in reflection. "I ended up being in the minor leagues in 1991 and again in 1993—after spending parts of the 1992 season in Toledo as well—while Jimmy Leyland had some tough years with the Pirates in the mid-1990s, but you don't give up. For me, I just kept grinding and playing hard even in the minors, believing that I would get back to the big leagues. And I won a ring with Jimmy Leyland all those years later.

"I look at it this way… For me, if I didn't get those at-bats in the minors in 1993, I probably wouldn't have gotten a shot back in the big leagues later in my playing career. I mean, it's like, hey, just keep believing in yourself, do the best you can in the situation you're in, give it your best shot and things could work out for you down the road. If you have that blue-collar work ethic and not give up on your dreams, anything can happen. That's what happened for me in those years in the 1990s."

Chapter Six
Back to the Minors

John Cangelosi was one of my favorite guys to ever manage. He's right up there. He's in the top three because his effort and his sincerity about the team was really something that you could count on every day. And I saw it four straight years when I managed him in the minor leagues.

> —John Boles, former Buffalo Bison
> manager (2018)

Throughout Cangelosi's baseball playing career, he heard all the knocks against him. Too small. Too short. No power.

"Have you ever met Cangy?" Tommy Sandt asks rhetorically. "He's probably about 5-8, 5-9, not very tall." Because of his height—he has been listed anywhere from 5-feet-6 to 5-feet-8—there were times when club employees didn't even know Cangelosi was one of the players. Sandt recalls the time when Cangy was acquired by the Pittsburgh Pirates. "He was in Pittsburgh with [me and Jim Leyland's coaching staff]," says Sandt. "That's when I first met him… He got traded from the White Sox to Pittsburgh. The spring training sites are right by each other, Sarasota and

Bradenton. He walked in with his equipment bag, and our clubhouse guy thought he was a shoe salesman. So, [the clubhouse guy] kicked him out. He says, 'I don't want any of you shoe salesmen around!' I guess the guys used to give the clubbies some shoes and I guess one guy didn't or something, and he was upset. He thought Cangy was a shoe rep for Nike or somebody. He told him to get out of the clubhouse. John says, 'No, no, I just got traded from the White Sox!'"

Cangelosi remembers that incident. "He thought I worked for a shoe company. He didn't even think I was a player!" And he gets it. It was his height. Of course, there were other incidents throughout his career. There were jokes his teammates—and even coaches—made about his height. In his rookie year, a White Sox teammate would put a metal exercise ball on the floor, place a cap over it and then give the cap a shove. "Here's Cangy stealing third base!" Sure enough, the cap went scooting across the floor. When asked by sportswriter Roger Jackson in a May 5th edition of *Sports Illustrated* if he could recall playing against someone that little in his many years in the majors, White Sox hitting coach Doug Rader, who had played in the big leagues from 1967 to 1977 and had coached or managed in pro ball since 1979, thought for a moment and quipped, "Billy Barty?" (Barty was an actor who stood three feet and nine inches tall.)

Cangelosi was cool with all the jokes. Near the end of his career, people were still making them. In 1996, for instance, Rockies manager Don Baylor suggested that the ball must have been juiced after Cangelosi smacked a 392-foot homer against Colorado, only the 10th home run of his career. He responded with a 3-for-4 effort the following day, coming within a home run of hitting for the cycle. "You can tell Don Baylor that I've hit homers in both leagues," Cangelosi joked then to a sportswriter from the *Houston Chronicle*. "I don't know if Baylor can say that. I think he hit all of his homers in the American League." There was also the time when, during the nationally-televised 1997 National League Championship Series, NBC broadcaster Bob Costas jokingly compared him to the infamous Eddie Gaedel, the three-foot-seven-inch tiny man who, as a publicity stunt, had a pinch-hitting appearance for Bill Veeck's St. Louis Browns in 1951.

"Yeah, it comes with the territory," Cangelosi says of his height. "[The thing with the baseball cap], that was Ron Kittle. It was when I made the team in spring training. It was only once or twice. He put a cap on the floor and rolled it. He said, 'That was John Cangelosi running after a fly ball.' We all laughed about it. I mean, I was already accustomed to 'short' jokes… that never bothered me. That was just a one-time thing." As for the Eddie Gaedel reference? Cangelosi laughs when told about Costas' comment more than 20 years after the fact. "No, I never heard that one. I didn't really worry about that stuff. I mean, it comes with the territory. I didn't mind it. If they're gonna have fun with it, let them have fun with it."

John Boles, Cangelosi's manager for four straight seasons in the minors, thinks Cangelosi, despite his height, could have been a football player. "He was very aggressive. And he was a leader," says Boles. "He really played each and every game to win. He was a guy that you could count on. He was very dependable. His teammates were all very fond of him because they knew what he was all about. He was a leader. He was a *terrific* leadoff man. When he got on base, he was going to be on second and third because he was going to steal those next two bases. So, he was an ideal leadoff man when I managed him in the minor leagues. He's a type-A personality. He's *aggressive*. You would think he was a wrestler or a football player. He had that type of aggressiveness. He would never back down from anybody. He was *absolutely* fearless."

Boles brings up a great point about Cangelosi's speed. Yes, he already had some sort of advantage at the plate because of his small strike zone, meaning he saw mostly fastballs. And because of Cangelosi's speed, some pitchers, knowing he was going to run, feared him. One time when he was with the Pirates, he led off an inning with a walk after fouling off five pitches. Standing at first base, he drew a total of 14 attempted pickoff throws from Atlanta pitcher Jeff Parrett, according to the game story from the *Pittsburgh Post-Gazette*. "That's amazing," Cangelosi recalls. "But that was part of my job. Everybody knew I was gonna steal a base, and the pitcher's job was to try and keep me close."

And when the thought of him being a football player is brought up, Cangelosi simply laughs. "When I was younger, I really liked football," he recalls fondly of the days when he was a running back in youth football. "But [one day] I was just goofing around playing football and I ended up breaking my wrist. I had to quit the team. So, I didn't play football [anymore after that incident]. After that, my mom and dad said, 'Look, we really don't want you to play football. It's too violent.' I wasn't very big. They kinda made the decision for me to not play football. I was kinda pissed off at the time.

"But we had a league there and we would play flag football. Fast forward to when I was a senior in high school. Demie Mainieri, [who later ended up being] my college [baseball] coach, saw me play in high school and, because he was recruiting at the time, he asked me to come play an exhibition weekend. After the two games, he said, 'Listen, I'm gonna take the team to Venezuela. It's about seven or eight other guys on this team. I want you to come with me to Venezuela. It will be a great experience for you. You'll be my leadoff guy.' I said yes, and my dad said yes. The night before the trip, I was all packed, ready to go."

But Cangelosi also had his flag football commitments that same night. "My dad goes, 'Where are you going?' I'm like, 'I have a championship football game. I have a flag football championship game.' But my dad reminded me that I was going to Venezuela the next day and forbade me to play that night.

"I said, 'Look. You always taught me, once you started something, you don't quit. It's flag football. Nothing's gonna happen to me. I can't let my teammates down in the championship game.'"

Cangelosi won the argument, but going, as it turned out, was a huge mistake. "Two hours later, it was raining, it was muddy. I dove for a pass and I ended up breaking my collarbone. I called [my dad] two hours later from the emergency room. I felt really bad—not because I wasn't going—but because my dad was right. And I felt bad for my mom and dad. They really wanted me to go. I mean, we got through it. But that was another incident where my dad was right."

Eager to get out of the hospital and get back onto the field, Cangelosi pleaded with the doctor to do whatever he could to fix him. "But the doctor goes, 'Man, you're gonna be out for like eight weeks.' It was a very painful injury because they really can't do anything for collarbones. You just have to let it heal… It was very painful."

Whether it was football or baseball, Cangelosi knows he played tough. He played hard. As for baseball, he knows he played tough as well, whether it was in the minor leagues or big leagues. His managers, such as Boles, Jim Leyland and Terry Collins, knew he played tough and played to win. So, it doesn't bother him when others bring up his height or crack jokes about him being the next Eddie Gaedel. "If they're gonna have fun with it, let them have fun with it," he repeats. Instead, he chooses to focus on the positives and recalls comments made by the late Harry Caray, the legendary broadcaster of the Chicago Cubs. "Harry Caray always talked very highly of me. He was complimentary of my play and how I played the game. I actually played well against the Cubs a lot." That, he did. His .337 lifetime average against the Cubs—in 104 at-bats—was the third-highest against any major-league team, trailing only the Pirates (.359) and Rockies (.352). And he even had a career .304 batting average at Wrigley Field. Not counting an 0-for-7 game he had there in 1995, that lifetime Wrigley average would have been .359.

The fact that Cangelosi always played hard made it easy for opponents to root for him, even if he was just a utility player for much of his major-league career. For instance, Doug Dascenzo, an outfielder who played in the majors from 1988 to 1996, idolized him. In his rookie year, Dascenzo told the *Chicago Sun-Times'* Dave van Dyck that he and Cangelosi "[looked] like twins." Others agreed. "Both are 5-7 and about 150 pounds. Both are center fielders who are switch-hitters and have speed," noted van Dyck in a piece that ran on March 13, 1988. Dascenzo was certainly amazed the first time he saw Cangelosi in action when the Cubs were playing in Pittsburgh. "I saw Cangelosi and we do have a resemblance to each other," added Dascenzo, who began his big-league career on the North Side of Chicago. "We play a lot alike. He goes all out, diving for everything and that's what I try to do."

Cangelosi only smiles when thinking back to his interactions with Dascenzo. "Doug Dascenzo and I looked like twins. I mean, you couldn't tell us apart! Our games were very similar. We looked alike. We played the same game."

One spring training, in fact, the two were even on the same ball club, having been signed by the New York Mets. "Me and Doug Dascenzo in 1994 were on the same team with the Mets in spring training," Cangelosi recalls. "After a while, it got aggravating. They would call me 'Doug.' They would call him 'Cangy.' They just kept getting us mixed up all the time. And our lockers were right next to each other, too."

"If I'm sitting in the dugout and I see him in the field, I realize he looks like me," Dascenzo, who wound up not making the Mets' major-league roster, remarked one day that spring to Steve Adamek of *The (New Jersey) Record*. "His size, the color of his hair, he's a left-handed thrower, a switch-hitter, the way he runs… I watched him throw the other day and I kind of wondered if that's what I look like."

Cangelosi eventually figured out a solution. "Finally, one day, I said, 'Dougie, man, screw it. I'm gonna wear your jersey, you wear my jersey… and we're good to go.' That was the whole joke of spring training that year. We actually played against each other in the minor leagues for a couple of years. I had the opportunity to talk to him for a little bit. He's a great guy. He was a great player and I respected him a lot."

Baseball fans in Chicago also respect both Cangelosi and Dascenzo. The two players are still compared to each other even today, long after their playing careers had ended. In 2011, for instance, Cubs blogger Al Yellon discussed the two former outfielders on a post on SBNation.com—and pointed out the two men had another thing in common: their flawless performances on the mound. As Yellon noted, both men had career 0.00 ERAs with Cangelosi working four shutout innings in three appearances and Dascenzo tossing five frames over four appearances. "How odd that the two top names on this list [of top 10 pitching hitters of all-time] are extremely similar players—not-very-tall men (Cangelosi, 5-8; Dascenzo, 5-7) who played good outfield defense, drew a few walks and could steal bases. Dascenzo was often called 'the poor man's Cangelosi' by Cubs fans."

And there's that mention of his height again. Cangelosi didn't get a fair shake, theorizes Mainieri, because of his height. And that stigma carried with him. Long-time manager Terry Collins, who had Cangelosi on his roster with the Houston Astros in 1995 and 1996 (as well as the Triple-A Buffalo Bisons in 1990), offers a different perspective. Collins believes that during Cangelosi's playing career, teams were looking for outfielders who could hit the long ball or drive in runs. "He played a tough position," Collins says. "Even back then, you always looked for guys who had power or guys who produced runs for you. I think John was a little different type of a role player. He could play all three outfield positions. He could give any of those outfielders a night off. In the big leagues, it's hard to play every day, really hard to play every day." Collins, having seen Cangelosi's work ethic in Triple-A Buffalo, had always loved the idea of having the switch-hitting outfielder on his big-league club, but he didn't have a major-league managerial job until 1994 with the Astros. "During the time I had John, I saw him successful in Pittsburgh as a backup player. I knew that was the type of player I wanted when I got to Houston."

Bobby Valentine, who managed Cangelosi in Texas in 1992, acknowledges that undersized players can play in the big leagues, but in the 1990s it was indeed the long-ball era. "They've come back," Valentine says now, referring to players who perform at an elite level despite their size, such as perennial All-Star and 2017 American League MVP Jose Altuve (who is listed at 5 feet 6 inches). "They've come back into vogue, but John's era was getting away from that. You know, it was the big guys. You gotta hit it far, and you gotta hit it far often. You know, I think that was because of the time he played. I think he was negatively viewed—not by me—but by many."

Cangelosi, of course, was more of a base stealer; he could pinch-run for a ball club or be a valuable fourth outfielder. He could draw walks. He could pinch-hit when you needed someone to get on base to start a rally. But he just wasn't an everyday outfielder in the big leagues because of his lack of power.

Then how do you explain Cangelosi, a valuable switch-hitting, base-stealing outfielder, not having a job in the big leagues following the 1990 season?

True, he was coming off a season in Pittsburgh where, as a fifth outfielder (behind Bobby Bonilla, Barry Bonds, Andy Van Slyke and R. J. Reynolds), he hit just .197 in 58 games. (As Cangelosi himself acknowledges now, Reynolds, a close friend of his, was the best fourth outfielder in the league, meaning there weren't a lot of opportunities for the team's fifth outfielder to play.) It got so bad that the home crowd routinely booed him at Three Rivers Stadium. Critics opined that Cangelosi didn't get on base enough. "… For a guy so intent on a walk," noted Gene Collier from the *Pittsburgh Post-Gazette* in August 1990, "he doesn't have an especially good appreciation of the strike zone, often fouling off ball four, ball five, ball six, and taking strike three." But Cangelosi, who split the season between Triple-A Buffalo and the Pirates, had only 76 at-bats with Pittsburgh and was used primarily in defensive and pinch-hitting roles. While he fared better in Triple-A—in his 24 games with Buffalo, he hit .348, scored 17 runs and stole 15 bases—his production at the big-league level simply wasn't enough for the Pirates to re-sign him, and the switch-hitting outfielder wound up signing a minor-league contract with the Chicago White Sox in February.

By then, after being just four years away from Chicago, things had changed in the White Sox organization. Catcher Carlton Fisk and shortstop Ozzie Guillen were still around, but Jim Fregosi was long gone, having been fired following the 1988 season. Gone too was Daryl Boston, waived by the White Sox in April 1990 after appearing in only five games that season. Expected to become a major-league star, Boston instead would mainly be a role player for the remainder of his big-league career. He played for the Mets, Rockies and Yankees, and he never appeared in another major-league game following the 1994 players' strike. As for Ivan Calderon, who'd won the left-field job in 1987, he'd been dealt to Montreal (along with pitcher Barry Jones, one of Cangelosi's teammates in Pittsburgh) for future Hall of Famer Tim Raines and two other players. And Harold Baines? He'd been dealt to Texas in 1989 in a trade that sent outfielder Sammy Sosa and left-hander Wilson Alvarez to Chicago—and was now playing in Oakland for the three-time defending AL champion A's. The White Sox, meanwhile, now had a starting outfield of Raines in left, Lance Johnson in center and Sosa in right.

Cangelosi believed at the time he could make the team as a utility outfielder. And it was a young ball club on the rise, unlike the 1986 team that finished last in the AL in hitting. (The '86 White Sox were last in runs, hits, doubles, home runs, batting average and total bases.) The 1991 club was led by young sluggers Frank Thomas and Robin Ventura, and featured an up-and-coming pitching staff that included Alvarez, Jack McDowell, Alex Fernandez, Melido Perez, Greg Hibbard and record-setting stopper Bobby Thigpen, who'd notched 57 saves the previous year to break the single-season record. Not only that, the White Sox would be playing in a brand new ballpark in 1991, New Comiskey Park, after calling the original Comiskey

Park home from 1910 to 1990. (Renamed U.S. Cellular Field in 2003, the new ballpark would become known as Guaranteed Rate Field beginning in 2017.)

While the ballpark, along with the manager and core players, was new, there was a familiar face back on the South Side. Ken "Hawk" Harrelson, the Sox general manager for one season in 1986 when Cangelosi was a rookie, was back as the White Sox's main play-by-play announcer for television broadcasts, after doing Yankees games on SportsChannel New York and *Game of the Week* broadcasts on NBC during the time he was away from Chicago. "Hawk Harrelson, when he took over, he was the one—[along with] Tony La Russa—[who] gave me an opportunity to play in the big leagues," Cangelosi recalls fondly. "Hawk said, 'Keep doing the things you're doing; we're gonna find room for you.' He stayed in my corner. He definitely was in my corner. I have nothing but nice things to say about Hawk Harrelson."

Plus, Cangelosi loved playing in Chicago, so signing with the organization was a no-brainer. "In 1991 as a free agent, I decided to try and come back to the White Sox. My agent thought it was a good fit," he explains. "I came back to the White Sox, and Timmy Raines got hurt early in the spring. So, I had a lot of at-bats, like 40-something at-bats, and Walt Hriniak was the hitting coach. I had a great spring. I hit over .400. I had some stolen bases. Obviously, I should've made the team."

At least one member of the Chicago media thought so. With the start of the regular season just days away, Dave van Dyck of the *Chicago Sun-Times* thought that Cangelosi would make the ball club. With "one spot open [on the 25-man roster]… the nod probably will go to veteran base stealer Cangelosi, who is hitting .421 with four stolen bases in five attempts this spring," the sportswriter opined in a piece on April 5. At the time, skipper Jeff Torborg seemed to indicate that was his choice, too. "He's been real good; he hasn't done anything wrong," Torborg said just five days before Opening Day. "… He's a professional."

It was hard to argue that Cangelosi, with his productive spring, didn't belong in the majors. His final spring stats: a .429 batting average (18-for-42), three RBIs and four stolen bases. "But I got screwed by numbers," says Cangelosi. "We had [utility infielder] Steve Lyons at the time and he was guaranteed $650,000. Jeff Torborg called me into the office and they were trying to trade Steve Lyons so they wouldn't have to pay him that salary—because they would have to eat that salary. So, it went all the way to midnight. They told me they couldn't trade Lyons. 'Why don't you go to Vancouver? Don't get an apartment. Don't get settled in. As soon as we trade Steve Lyons, we will call you up or activate you.' I'm like, 'Okay, that's fine.' Obviously, they didn't hold up their end of the deal. I don't know what happened. Walt Hriniak came up to me and said, 'Hey, they screwed you.' I go to Vancouver, and a month into it they released Steve Lyons and then they just made a different transaction."

Lyons, as it turned out, was released on April 13—on the opening weekend of the season—and picked up as a free agent by the Boston Red Sox the following week. The release was necessitated when Chicago activated veteran knuckleball pitcher Charlie

Hough from the disabled list. Cangelosi, meanwhile, never got called up by the White Sox. Unhappy playing in Triple-A, he struggled in his 30 games with Vancouver, hitting .245 with nine steals but only one extra-base hit. "I was stuck in Vancouver, and that was when I asked to be traded. That's one of the times it didn't fall my way."

The White Sox granted him his wish, trading him to the Milwaukee Brewers for minor-league infielder Esteban Beltre on May 23. (By being dealt to the Brewers, Cangelosi missed witnessing Vancouver outfielder Rodney McCray crashing through an outfield fence attempting to make a catch at Portland's Civic Stadium. "That was actually on the next road trip in Portland," Cangelosi says when asked about McCray's infamous play from May 27, 1991, "after I'd been traded.") Cangelosi finished the 1991 season with Triple-A Denver in the American Association, where he hit .294 in 83 games with 26 stolen bases. He never played a game for the major-league club in Milwaukee, which already had Darryl Hamilton as a utility outfielder behind the starting trio of Greg Vaughn, Robin Yount and Dante Bichette. But even when Candy Maldonado, another outfielder, was traded to Toronto in August, the Brewers didn't call Cangelosi up. "That season, really, was one of the times things didn't fall my way," Cangelosi acknowledges now.

While it might have been hard to be in the minor leagues for a full season—especially for a guy who'd been in the majors for parts of five seasons—Cangelosi never quit. He never lost sight of his goal of wanting to get back to the big leagues, and he knew he had to continue to play hard every day. And take care of his body. "Each league that I played in, I wanted to play with the maturity that I didn't wanna repeat a league," Cangelosi says now. "I kept my goals very simple. I went out there every day to try and make management and my manager understand that there was nothing more I could do in that league. Off the field, it was very hard back then taking care of yourself, as far as from the standpoint of the bus rides. That was pretty difficult. I pretty much tried to take care of myself the best way I could. But at the end of the day, some kids get homesick. Some guys quit because they wanted to go home."

And the food in the minors was nothing compared to what they served in the big leagues. "Man, everything's different in the majors and minors!" Cangelosi says with a laugh. "In the major leagues, everything got better toward the end of my career. But there are some stadiums where the clubhouse guys don't do a very good job, but there are clubbies that do a really outstanding job. And the food is phenomenal. I don't know how they do it today. I'm sure most of them catered it. They would make relationships with really nice restaurants. After the game, we had a full spread—we didn't even have to go out and eat if we didn't want to. It was great food. We had snacks all day. I mean, we would have ice cream, tuna sandwiches, luncheon meat. You name it, we had it in the big leagues. In the minor leagues, you were lucky if you had peanut butter and jelly sandwiches! And you had to make your own. There was no food in the minor leagues! We had no food. Maybe the clubhouse guy got hotdogs from the concessions stands after the game. Toward the end of my career, when I got sent down a couple times, some clubhouse guys had luncheon meat available. [Basically, they had] very bare minimal stuff in the minor leagues, compared to the big leagues."

Some players quit along the way because they became homesick or they simply couldn't get adjusted to those long bus rides, according to Cangelosi. For him, though, it was different. Believing he could still play in the big leagues, he never wanted to quit. "I always wanted to be a Major League Baseball player. I had my blinders on. I had no other game plan. I didn't know what else to do. So, it was very easy for me to stay focused on those bus trips. I had a game plan; I wanted to get to the big leagues. You do a lot of reminiscing. You dream. You have a lot of ups and downs. I just tried to stay positive through the ups and downs—and tried to stay even keel. Like, when you had great games, don't get too high. When you had bad games, don't get too low. Learn how to talk to yourself. Remain positive. Sometimes you had a bad tournament and you get on the bus, you had eight hours to think about it. Learn how to talk to yourself when you have bad games or bad months. There's always someone out there that has a worse scenario than you."

He then gives an example of what he's referring to, one he remembers vividly. "In 1992, it was probably the easiest team I had to make with the Rangers. In the last game of spring training, I had the worst game of my life. I struck out three times and made an error in the outfield. I don't think I made an error in the outfield for 10 years in my career. I had a really bad game. And I brought the game home with me. I was upset. I was mad. I probably didn't make the team. Now instead of making more money, I was gonna make less money in Triple-A. It just really affected me that day."

Still upset, Cangelosi went to a local mall, walking around aimlessly. "I was walking in the mall, and this handicapped child was walking towards me. And she had this big smile on her face. At that moment, it was one of those light-bulb-goes-off moment. I said, 'You know what? She has this handicap thing that she has to deal with. And she's happy, no worries, no nothing. And I'm worried about this, about that.' From that day on, whenever a baseball situation got that heavy for me or I started doubting myself, I just put my mind somewhere where someone else's situation was worse than me, and that kinda subsided the pressure."

As it turned out, he didn't have to worry about not making the Rangers' big-league club.

Chapter Seven
Hello, Arlington… and Holy, Toledo!

He played the game right. Everyone thinks leaders have to speak up. Sometimes you lead by example. That's what John did. He led by example. Here's a guy who was a major-league player at one time, a good big-league player. He got sent down [to Triple-A in 1990], didn't pout, didn't mope or go, 'Woe is me. I'm being screwed.' He said, 'No, I'm going back! I'm gonna work hard to get back up there!' He put forth the effort in the way he played, and he got back to the big leagues. You salute guys like that. And that's why with the younger players, you just tell them, 'Hey, look. You wanna try to get to the big leagues? Do what he does. Show up, and play hard every night.'
—Terry Collins, former Buffalo Bisons manager
and Houston Astros manager (2018)

Following the 1991 season, Cangelosi signed with the Texas Rangers and made the team out of spring training as a reserve outfielder. "It was a big-league invite," says Cangelosi now. "Me and my agent sat down. We go, 'Okay, these guys only have three or five outfielders.' It was a good fit for me at the time. I liked Bobby Valentine as a manager. I was there to make a team in '92."

Just three days prior to Opening Day, the Rangers decided to keep Cangelosi as their fifth outfielder, releasing veteran Gary Pettis to open a roster spot for him. While Cangy didn't hit well that spring—he batted .255 with 10 stolen bases in 11 attempts—Pettis fared even worse, hitting just .156 with six stolen bases and 15 strikeouts in 45 at-bats. Although both players offered the Rangers the same thing—both were switch-hitting outfielders with little power who could run and play defense—Valentine preferred Cangelosi. "John has a real good feel for the game," Valentine was quoted as saying in the *Fort Worth (Texas) Star-Telegram* then. "He has a baseball attitude a little different than Gary's."

The 1992 Rangers had a hard-hitting lineup which included major-league home-run leader Juan Gonzalez (43 homers), Dean Palmer (26), Rafael Palmeiro (22), Kevin Reimer (16), Ruben Sierra (14) and Brian Downing (10)—all of whom slugged at least 10 homers. (Sierra, though, was traded late in the season, along with pitchers Bobby Witt and Jeff Russell, to the Oakland A's for Jose Canseco .) They also had veteran infielder Julio Franco and future Hall-of-Fame catcher Ivan Rodriguez, who would go on to win the Gold Glove that season at the age of 20. On the mound, the Rangers had a pair of workhorses in Kevin Brown (21-11, 3.32) and Jose Guzman (16-11, 3.66) as well as veteran closer Jeff Russell (28 saves, 1.91) and relievers Kenny Rogers (3.09) and Matt Whiteside (1.93), but the rest of the staff, for the most part, struggled. Fireballer Nolan Ryan, at the age of 45, was nearing the end of his Hall-of-Fame career, posting an uncharacteristic 3.72 ERA while going 5-9.

Led by manager Valentine, the Rangers were expected to contend for the American League West title—and they did, until the bottom fell out midseason. Heading into a three-game series in Oakland on June 12, the Rangers were just one game behind the division-leading Athletics. Alas, the A's swept the Rangers in the series, beating them 6-5 in 14 innings in the opener before stunning Texas with six runs in the bottom of the eighth to break open a tie game in the second contest. The shell-shocked Rangers then lost the finale 6-1, despite having Kevin Brown on the mound. To make matters worse, Texas then lost two of three in Anaheim against the California Angels immediately following the Oakland series, dropping a pair of close games to Bert Blyleven and Mark Langston. "I remember we went into Oakland for a big series, but the A's had great pitching— Bob Welch, Dave Stewart, [and Mike Moore]," Cangelosi recalls. "They were really tough on us."

For Cangelosi, it was a tough year in Texas. Up to that point in the season, including the road trip to California, he'd appeared in 52 of the Rangers' first 68 games, but only 16 of them were starts. While he homered in his first at-bat of the season—off Mariners lefty Kevin Brown at the Kingdome in Seattle—and delivered a game-winning, pinch-hit ninth-inning single off Jeff Reardon in Boston on April 26, Cangelosi normally came into the game in the late innings for defensive purposes or as a pinch-runner. (Not to be confused with the Rangers' Kevin Brown, the Seattle pitcher was a left-hander—and that game in which Cangelosi homered turned out to be Brown's last appearance in the major leagues. As for Reardon, the right-handed Red Sox reliever went on to break baseball's all-time saves record later that summer, surpassing Rollie Fingers' 341 career saves.) In 21 of those appearances, he didn't even have an official plate appearance. In 62 at-bats, he was hitting just .177 with six stolen bases.

When he did get a rare start, there would be some weird plays. Against the Yankees early in the season, for instance, he walked twice and scored two runs while starting in left field but looked helpless on a pop fly in the late innings, allowing New York to plate the winning run.

On June 10 against Seattle, television cameras showed him reacting angrily when a young fan reached over the railing and touched a ball with a glove as Cangelosi, playing left field, was trying to field the ball in foul territory. The fan lost the glove on the field and Cangelosi flung it into the stands, hitting him. "I didn't throw the glove at the kid; I threw it on the stairs," Cangelosi later explained. "It was just the heat of the moment. I was busting my butt to get the ball. Parents should know better. They should tell their kids to leave the ball alone. But what the TV isn't going to show is that I made it up to the kid. I gave him batting gloves and shook his hand and apologized... I should not have shown my anger."

Of course, Cangelosi did make some spectacular plays along the way. In Minnesota, for instance, he leaped into the Metrodome Plexiglas in center field to catch a deep drive struck by Kirby Puckett, stealing an extra-base hit away from the Twins' future Hall of Famer.

Following the disastrous West Coast trip which saw Texas lose five of six, the Rangers returned home, where Cangelosi saw more playing time over a two-week stretch. Valentine started him in six of the Rangers' next 13 games beginning on June 19—all in the No. 9 hole—but Cangy batted just .222 with no stolen bases while facing some of the toughest pitchers in the league in the Blue Jays' trio of Jack Morris, David Wells and Juan Guzman, and the Yankees' Melido Perez. Clearly frustrated with his role, Cangelosi finally voiced his concerns to the skipper at the end of a home series against Milwaukee on July 8.

"Being a utility player in the American League is very hard because my role really is more suited for the National League," Cangelosi laments now. "In the National League, at least you got to pinch-hit. You got an at-bat here and there. In the American League, you really hardly ever pinch-hit. You just kinda played defense. There are no transitions or anything. There's no moving things around. I was in 90 games with the Rangers and I had only 50 or 60 at-bats. [Actually, it was 73 games and 85 at-bats.] Basically, I would go in to play defense in the seventh or eighth inning and not even get an at-bat. So, I was in 90 games but I wouldn't even hit. I was hitting like .150 and I go into Bobby Valentine's office. I go, 'Bobby, it's just hard for me to get something going. I don't have any at-bats. What can I do? Can I get a little more playing time so I can get feel better about myself?' Bobby answers, 'Cangy, as long as I'm here, you're here.'"

But with the Rangers six-and-a-half games out of first place on the morning of July 9, the organization fired Valentine and named coach Toby Harrah the new manager. Cangelosi was stunned. His time in Texas was coming to an end too; he got the official word on

July 19 when the Rangers released him. "So, I asked Bobby for more playing time, and he said, 'Cangy, as long as I'm here, you're here.' The next day, they fired him. That was an ongoing joke between him and me. Whenever I saw him again, he would go, 'Man, you got me fired!' We would joke and laugh about it. As soon as he got fired, they called me into the office the next day and they wanted to send me down. But I had five years or more [of major-league service time] and I could refuse an assignment, and that's what I did. I didn't wanna go to Triple-A. [Rangers general manager] Tom Grieve and Toby Harrah wanted to send me down and call somebody else up. But I just refused the assignment." And so, 10 days after Valentine was fired, Cangelosi was gone too, as the club released him after not being able to work out a trade.

Valentine laughs when reminded now about that ongoing joke between him and Cangelosi. "There was a number one draft choice that they wanted to play," Valentine says, referring to Rangers outfielder Donald Harris. "I thought that John was a better player than Donald Harris, and I was sticking to my guns. I wanted John on the team, and that became a little bit of a situation." As it turned out, Valentine knew what he was talking about. The first-round pick (fifth overall) by the Rangers in the 1989 MLB Draft, Harris wound up appearing in only 82 major-league games, hitting .205. During that 1992 season, Harris batted only .182 in 24 games. While he would go on to play professional baseball until the year 2000—on eight other teams in Triple-A and various independent leagues—he was out of the major leagues by the end of the 1993 season. "But that's far from the reason that I was no longer employed," Valentine adds with a laugh, referring to the fact that his preference of Cangelosi over Harris wasn't why he was let go in Texas. "I think John left the team soon after I was gone, so we might've had a little connection at the hip." The two men would cross paths again in 1994 at the Mets' spring-training camp, when Valentine was the manager of the club's Triple-A affiliate and Cangelosi was a non-roster invitee.

Though he spent just half the season in Texas, Cangelosi enjoyed his time in Arlington and especially appreciated the opportunity to play with teammates such as Ruben Sierra, Juan Gonzalez and Nolan Ryan. Playing on a team with All-Star caliber players Sierra and Gonzalez in the outfield presented a similar situation to his time in Pittsburgh, where Cangelosi was a utility man behind Barry Bonds, Bobby Bonilla and Andy Van Slyke. He knew he wasn't going to be playing too much behind Sierra and Gonzalez, and he had no bitter feelings. "I played against Ruben in Puerto Rico," says Cangelosi, who also played against Gonzalez in winter ball. "Ruben was a very quiet guy. I love him. I played with him in 1992 with the Rangers. Great guy. Very quiet. He came over from Puerto Rico and didn't really learn how to speak English all that well. So, he was kinda to himself. But other than that, just a class act. A nice guy. A gentleman. Great player."

His history with Ryan went back to the days when Cangelosi was with Pittsburgh and the Hall-of-Famer-to-be was in Houston. But Cangelosi pointed to a game on May 27, 1992, that showed just what kind of a positive teammate Ryan was. In an eventual 4-3, 11-inning victory against Chicago, Cangelosi came on in the eighth inning to pinch-run for Brian Downing, who'd led off with a single. White Sox pitcher Alex Fernandez immediately picked Cangelosi off first base, but Cangy made it to second base when Fernandez's throw eluded first baseman Frank Thomas. Cangy's luck, however, ran out moments later.

On the next pitch, when Dean Palmer hit a comebacker to Fernandez, Cangelosi took off for third and was thrown out easily. The Rangers didn't score in that inning, and when Cangelosi returned to the dugout, he was upset at himself. After the game, which Texas won a Kevin Reimer walk-off double three innings later, Cangelosi was still miffed at himself for his base running gaffes. But Ryan, the Rangers starter in that game, told him to keep his chin up.

"Nolan Ryan was there for me in different ways," Cangelosi says now. "But what a class act. I have nothing but great things to say about him. When I was with the Pirates, Jimmy Leyland used to play me against Nolan Ryan all the time because he was slow to the plate." Cangelosi is referring to the 1987 season, when Ryan went 8-16 despite a league-leading 2.76 ERA. Going into a game in Houston that September, Cangelosi had already frustrated Ryan with three walks and a stolen base in two previous contests that year. "One game, I got on base. I took a couple of close pitches, fouled some balls off. Full count, could've been strike three, but the guy called ball four," recalls Cangelosi. "So, I went to first base, and I stole second and [was thrown out trying to steal] third. My second at-bat, I took a couple of borderline pitches that could've been strikes, I fouled a pitch off, they called ball four. I steal second [again]." So, in what already had been a frustrating year for Ryan, here was Cangelosi walking five times and stealing three bases off of the future Hall of Famer.

"I come up in the [sixth inning], took some close pitches, had a good at-bat, 3-and-2... and Nolan Ryan struts over, 'If you wanna walk that bad, I'll walk you.' In other words, he was gonna drill me the next time I came up." Cangelosi took the payoff pitch, which was called strike three. "Thank God they took him out of the game [before my next at-bat]." Of course, the following year, Cangelosi was at it again, costing Ryan a win. In a game in May 1988, Cangelosi came on in the bottom of the seventh inning to pinch-hit for Pirates pitcher Doug Drabek with Ryan's Astros ahead 3-2. Cangelosi drew a leadoff walk, stole second, went to third on a single and scored the tying run on Bobby Bonilla's RBI single to center, and Ryan wound up with a no-decision. In 10 career plate appearances against Nolan Ryan, Cangelosi never got a hit—going 0-for-4—but drew six walks with only two strikeouts. And, oh, there were those four big stolen bases too.

"In '92, I'm his teammate and also his locker mate," continues Cangelosi. "What a great guy. He'd go out there and sign autographs. Just a total gentleman. I didn't really get too many at-bats with Texas. I came in for defense a lot. One game we were playing against the White Sox [in that May 1992 contest against Alex Fernandez] and I'm on second base. I made a big running mistake [on that Dean Palmer comebacker to Fernandez]. I was really upset. I was mad at myself after the game. Nolan goes, 'Hey. Don't worry about it.' He was there for me. I shower and come back. He's still there. We start talking. Then I lean over at him and go, 'Nolan. Do you remember…' 'Yeah, I was gonna drill you right in the ribs!'

"He [then] goes, 'You were doing your job, and I had to do my job.' He was just a very genuine person. If Nolan Ryan could be like that and give time to people that he doesn't know… That's the standard for me. Everyone should stop and sign autographs and treat people equal. I just love the man, to be honest with you."

And while Cangelosi got chewed out as a rookie in Chicago by Tony La Russa for his misadventures on the base paths, it was a different story in Texas. Valentine trusted him during their brief time with the Rangers and recalls he never had to address those base running blunders with Cangelosi. "He was very hard on himself, so I never had to be hard on him, that's for sure," the long-time big-league manager says now. "I think I tried to reach out and, you know, improve his belief system. But he was trying, he was emotional and, like I said, he was hard on himself. There's no doubt about that."

Nine days after his release on July 28 by the Rangers, Cangelosi signed with the Detroit Tigers, who were set in right field with Rob Deer and in center with the tandem of Milt Cuyler and Gary Pettis. The Tigers, who were second-to-last in the American League East at the time, were also set in left with veterans Dan Gladden and Mark Carreon. As if that wasn't enough, utility man Tony Phillips also started a handful of games in each outfield position. For Cangelosi, he knew if he could get some at-bats in Triple-A and get into a groove, he could make the team easily late in the season in time for the

September call-ups. Sure, the Tigers were an American League team and had enough outfielders, but Cangelosi knew he was the type of player that manager Sparky Anderson loved—a guy who drew walks and hustled at all times. And even if he wasn't called up that year, Cangelosi believed, the at-bats in the minor leagues would certainly help in terms of attracting interest from other ball clubs in 1993.

In Triple-A Toledo in 1992, Cangelosi appeared in 27 games and batted .270 in 74 at-bats with 10 stolen bases. As it turned out, he didn't get called up by the Tigers at all. But Cangelosi chose to re-sign with the Tigers for the 1993 season, and he spent the entire year in Toledo, batting .292 in 439 at-bats with 39 steals. He even hit six home runs, the most he ever hit in a single season in professional ball.

Cangelosi knows in his heart that he should have played for the Tigers in 1993. But an injury during spring training changed the way Anderson looked at him. "[Following the release from Texas] I signed with Detroit, and I finished the last month-and-a-half in Toledo," reflects Cangelosi. "I ended up signing back with them in 1993, and it was probably the easiest team that I ever had to make. Sparky Anderson loved me. He liked older players. Sparky, at the time, really liked me. Sparky liked veteran players. It was the easiest team that I had to make. One game early in the spring, I hit a ground ball and tried to beat out an infield hit. But I blew my lower abdominal muscle and my groin at the same time. It was very painful and a very aggravating injury. When it first happened, I thought it would be just a week or so. I went into the training room and told them, 'Give me any drugs that you have. Just get me back on the field!' But there's nothing quick about healing for those two muscles."

Wanting to make the team, Cangelosi realized he needed to be out there playing, but he couldn't do anything because the injury hampered his mobility. Anderson, meanwhile, became impatient waiting for him to heal. "Basically, Sparky kept asking me, 'Hey, when are you gonna be ready? When are you gonna be ready?' So, I tried my hardest. About two weeks later, I knew I wasn't ready but I said, 'I'm good. I'm good.' I tried to play in a game and I couldn't play. I went into center field. I knew I wasn't good. Somebody hit the ball to me. I think I had to go five feet [to make the play], but I could barely get there. Two days later, Sparky called me into his office. 'Hey man, I gotta send you down.' He totally lost confidence in me. I ended up not making the team. I go to the Triple-A minor-league camp. But I don't even play. I'm just there to get treatments. And I would go home.

"So, anyway, I report to Toledo. I started the season on the disabled list in Triple-A for a month-and-a-half. All I'm doing is walking along the outfield track. That's pretty much my rehab. There's nothing else I can do. I finally start playing a month-and-a-half into the season. I'm playing well. I got my swing back. I had a 28-game hitting streak in Toledo. I had six or seven home runs. I mean, I was locked in. I was playing really good. In the middle of that 28-game hitting streak, I'm thinking, 'I'm gonna get called up!' And then, I called my agent and said, 'Am I ever gonna get called up? What else do I have to do? I've got this long hitting streak. I've got 27 stolen bases. And I missed the first month of the season!'"

Cangelosi never got a straight answer until Jerry Walker, the Tigers' general manager, made a trip out to Ned Skeldon Stadium, the Triple-A ballpark. "In the middle of that hitting streak, the general manager comes into Toledo," recalls Cangelosi. "I said, 'Hey man, I'm playing well. Can you tell Sparky I'm healthy? I mean, look at my numbers. I missed the first month of the season, but I've got 20 stolen bases.' Here I was, thinking I was gonna be called up." The response, however, was devastating. "The general manager goes, 'To be honest with you, Cangy, once Sparky gets on a certain side of you, then it's over. You know what I mean?' Basically, he was saying that once you're on the bad side of Sparky Anderson, he doesn't value you anymore."

Cangelosi took the news hard, realizing his major-league career was probably over. "I go, 'So, I'm never gonna get called up? Well, then try and trade me or something.' But [Walker] said, 'I'll try to do my best, but that's part of the game.' I'm like, 'Whatever.' I was ready to quit, to be honest with you, because I didn't like Toledo... I was actually gonna retire that year. I just said, 'You know what? My daughter, Alexandra, was just born. Let me stick it out. I've got two months left and then I'll quit. I'll finish my season.'"

Wait. He didn't like Toledo? Surely, that couldn't be right. After all, the Toledo Mud Hens have been referred to as minor-league baseball's second-most famous team (right behind the Durham Bulls), and professional baseball had been played off and on in that city since 1883. Surely, it must have been a treat to play in a city with such a rich baseball history. Cangelosi, though, has a different view, explaining that no ballplayer who had been in the majors would ever enjoy being demoted. "First of all, when you've been in the big leagues for a while and you then get sent down to Triple-A, you really don't like it," he says.

"I didn't like Toledo. I mean, I know it's famous for the guy on *M*A*S*H*," Cangelosi continues, referring to actor Jamie Farr from the famous CBS television sitcom which aired from 1972 to 1983. "I think that's [why] they sold so many hats and so much memorabilia there… It's because of the guy on *M*A*S*H*. That's why Toledo was famous—it's because of him. He used to wear the jersey and the hat on the show. But the stadium was old. It was brutal. I hated going to the ballpark every day. We took batting practice sometimes in a shed, where they cooked food. It was terrible. I really didn't like going to the ballpark. The only bright side of it is that's where my daughter, Alexandra, was born. She was born in Toledo, [where they had] the best hospital for prenatal [care] and all that stuff. That was the only bright side [of being there]. That's probably the only reason why I ended up staying—because I had, like, an outlet. And where I lived, I didn't live in Toledo. I actually lived in Perrysburg, Ohio, which is across the river. And it's a beautiful town. It's like a Mayberry town. Ironically, that's where Jimmy Leyland was born. That's where he's from.

"I basically said, 'You know what? I'm just gonna stay. And then at the end of the year, I'll re-evaluate it.' But I was ready to give it up at that particular time. I didn't like going to the ballpark. On the professional side, here you are, you're playing and it's really hard to play knowing that you're not gonna get called up to the big leagues with that team. So, it's hard to stay motivated. I would rather [Walker] had said nothing to me. The unknown is better than saying, 'Hey man, Sparky Anderson isn't gonna give you a September call-up either.' Then, it was like, 'What am I playing for, then?' So, that was difficult, but I got through that. It was fun to go home to my daughter. I stayed up with her late. It was just a good time that way. But I didn't like Toledo at all."

Cangelosi recounts his time in Toledo matter-of-factly, without any hint of resentment. He felt, with his Triple-A numbers, he deserved a call-up. He still feels that way today. "But I didn't like Toledo at all. I mean, it was a very old stadium. The conditions were really bad. It was just an old stadium. Now, they've got a brand new, beautiful stadium. But Perrysburg, the town I lived in, was really nice. But other than that, the teammates were great. Joe Sparks, the manager, was really good to me. The coaches were really good to me. I have nothing bad to say about my team or the organization. It was more like, I couldn't get back to the big leagues."

While he is no fan of Toledo, it's no question which National League city he loved. "I loved Pittsburgh," Cangelosi says now. "When I first got traded to Pittsburgh, I'm like, 'Oh damn. Steel mill… God. Great. I'm going to one of the horseshit cities in the world, right?'" Instead, he was proven wrong. "But it turned out to be beautiful, man. Great people. Beautiful city. I was in an Italian community. I was well-received there. I ended up buying a place there. That was my first purchase of a home. Going to the ballpark every day, going through the Fort Pitt Tunnel, and then as soon as you come out of the Fort Pitt Tunnel, you see Three Rivers Stadium. You see the football stadium. I mean, it's beautiful. I loved it there. That small-market town, I got nothing but praise for. I loved it."

New York, on the other hand, was a little different. "I was born in New York and raised in Miami. I really did not like playing in New York. It was a hassle getting to the ballpark. I mean, it was expensive. It was just hard. You know what I mean? I didn't like playing for a big city like that. A lot of guys like playing there, but it was very expensive. You had to plan for traffic. There was just a lot of stress on me. Plus, my family was there. I would leave 30 or 40 tickets. They didn't bother me too much. There were a lot of distractions with New York, let's just say that. But some guys like it. Some guys love playing in New York. I really didn't. I didn't care for it.

"With Pittsburgh, my longest tenure was there; I played there four years. That's probably my top city. Places that I liked to visit when I played—I liked Atlanta, and I actually liked Montreal. Montreal was a nice place. I really liked playing in Montreal. I really didn't like L.A. I liked 'Frisco because of the people and the city. I liked San Diego. Denver was really nice."

Then there was Chicago, too. While he had family in New York, he also had family in the Windy City. That's why when Cangelosi was in town to play the Cubs, he would be spending time with family instead of goofing off at the site of the famous Sheridan horse statue near Wrigley Field. "I never did it because I was in the American League, but that was a tradition where if you were a rookie, they [played this joke on you with the horse]. Then, when I got traded to the National League, I already had a year in, so I wasn't considered a rookie. They would all meet at the hotel. They would go to this famous horse, wherever it was. For good luck, they would make the rookies paint the balls on the horse!"

Indeed. The veteran players didn't want to get involved with defacing public property, so the rookies were put up to doing it instead. After all, nothing says, "I'm in the majors now," like climbing up to a horse statue's manly parts and spray painting them. The Pirates' veterans, for instance, would send the rookies out into the night with spray cans—or even paint cans and brushes—to do the deed using the Pirates' bright yellow color. For the Dodgers, it was Dodger Blue. For the Giants, it was orange; for the Reds and Cardinals, it was some shade of red; and so on. "I never went, but I heard about it," adds Cangelosi, "because the next morning what they would do to the rookie, unbeknownst to him, [was that] they had a cop come into the locker room and pretty much say, 'Hey, we've got it on footage. We saw so-and-so. We've got to take him in.'

"They would do this whole spiel where they would turn him around and handcuff him. The rookie would be shitting in his pants. It was actually quite funny. Then at the end, we would start laughing and the rookie would know it was a joke. That was a tradition. That one night, [Pirates rookie] Barry Jones was doing it—he was one of our pitchers—and because the horse is fairly big, I guess he jumped off and sprained his ankle real bad. He had to go on the D.L.

"They only did it to rookies. For me, it was hard [to be involved] because my family was in Chicago. Anytime I came into Chicago, it wasn't a road trip for me. I was more with my family. It was hard for me to say, 'Hey, I'm gonna be gone for a couple of hours,' and that kinda stuff."

There were other rookie-hazing pranks the veteran players did at the time, too. Interestingly, though, Cangelosi was never on the receiving end. "I don't know if other teams did it. They also did, if you were a rookie, sometimes the last road trip, we used to take the guy's clothes away from them during the game. We used to make them dress up in girl outfits or clown outfits. This was when we had to go through the airports back in the day, when it wasn't chartered. Basically, if you had four or five rookies on the team, you would take their personal clothes and belongings. We would give them a funny outfit to wear. Most of the time it would be, like, a girl outfit. That was pretty funny. It didn't happen to me, again, because I broke in not in the National League but in the American League. I guess the American League really didn't do much! I was a rookie in 1986 and they really didn't haze me or anything. I don't know if this was more of a National League thing. But in the American League, they didn't do anything to me."

For Cangelosi, being on the road in NL cities meant going out with teammates. "Back then, there was no technology like what we have today. It wasn't the tech world yet. There weren't cell phones or light computers that you could carry around. Basically, there was really nothing to do in your hotel room. Today, you have cell phones, iPods, iPads, computers that you could bring with you and all that. Back then, there was really none of that. And I wasn't one who stayed in the hotel room because I was all wired up from the game." So, he went out with teammates. "We went out all the time and enjoyed the town. It was an experience. It was almost like, you know, being a college kid. You don't have to study or whatever; you're gonna go out. Any team that I ever played for, there were six or seven of us that would go out all the time. We would go out to dinner all the time, go out for some drinks and then call it a night. Some guys could go back to the hotel room and watch TV, order a pizza and then go to bed. I couldn't do that. I wasn't wired up that way."

But he was far away from the big leagues in 1993. Being stuck in Toledo, he truly did think about retiring at that point. Now 30 years of age during the 1993 season and with no big-league job on the horizon, Cangelosi was ready to start a family. "Again, I was in Toledo and I had a 28-game hitting streak. I had 27 stolen bases. I missed the first month of the season. [The Tigers] weren't calling me up. I was thinking, 'I've got five years in. I'm gonna retire.' My daughter was born in Toledo that year. I have two kids, and she's my oldest. My son, Austin, was born [the following year in 1994], and he played baseball at Indiana University in Indiana. Great player. Didn't get drafted. Had a great college career. Now, he's at a military school in Carolina. Again, sometimes you have to have a little luck. He definitely had the ability to play pro ball. He's in a good place now and hopefully he can be a great college coach. My daughter's doing well. She's in college…

"Like I said, she was born in Toledo in 1993. And I got to come home every night to her, which was precious. I stayed up with her late. I mean, coming home every night to her was one of the things that got me through that summer. I ended up sticking out the season. If I wasn't gonna be playing in the big leagues again, I was gonna retire."

As it turned out, Cangelosi's big-league career wasn't over just yet. Just like how Paul Mainieri and Jim Hendry were impressed by him in high school, and just like how John Boles vouched for him in the White Sox organization, there was someone on the Mets who recommended Cangelosi for a job.

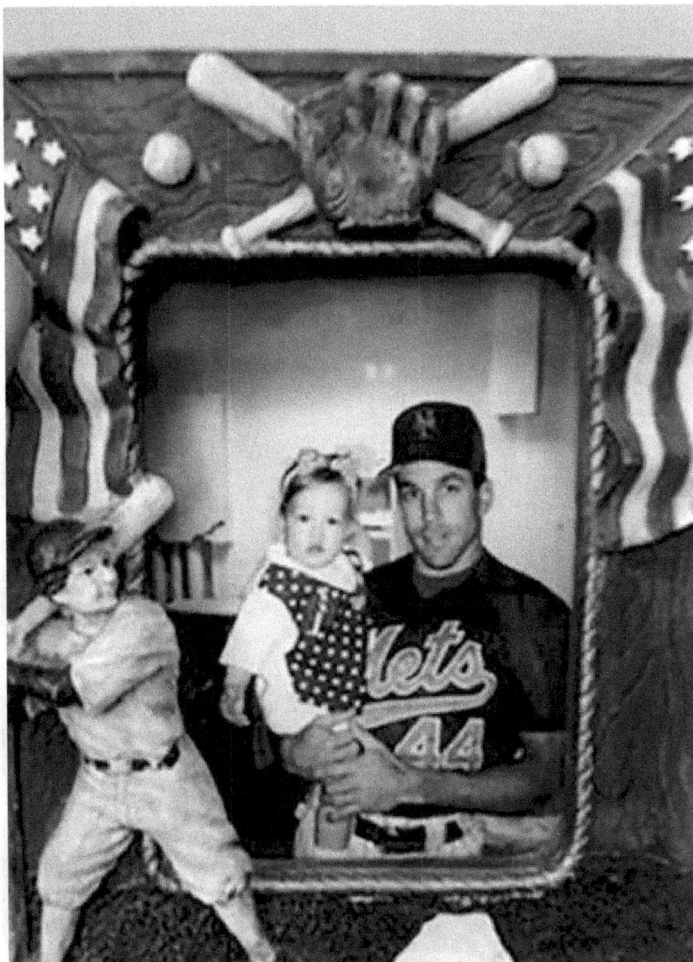

While Cangelosi didn't enjoy his brief stint with the New York Mets, coming home every night to baby daughter Alexandra was a highlight during the 1994 season (John Cangelosi).

This is the actual base that John Cangelosi swiped to break the AL rookie stolen-base record on October 4, 1986, against the Minnesota Twins. Cangelosi broke a record that had stood for 76 years (John Cangelosi).

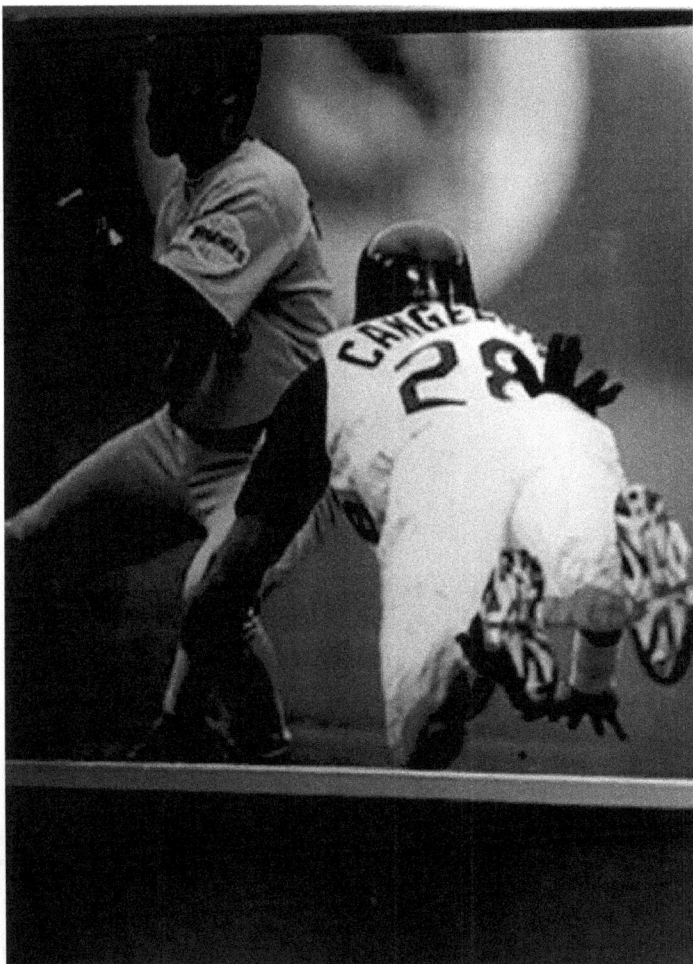

Cangelosi didn't get much playing time with the Florida Marlins in 1997-98, but he showed his hustle every time he was in the lineup. Here, Cangelosi attempts a steal against the San Diego Padres (John Cangelosi).

Cangelosi leaps to congratulate his Marlins teammates following a walk-off victory over the San Francisco Giants in Game Two of the 1997 NL Division Series (John Cangelosi).

Cangelosi and his two children, Alexandra and Austin, hang out with Billy the Marlin, the official mascot of the Marlins baseball franchise (John Cangelosi).

Cangelosi preaches his catchphrase "Practice with a purpose" to all of his students at Cangelosi Baseball (John Cangelosi).

Cangelosi takes time out of his coaching schedule to pose with one of his students, Matt McCormick (Michael McCormick)

Cangelosi today where he can be found working with kids at Cangelosi Baseball on a regular basis, even during the off-season. "It's not just my name and face on the building," he says. "When I put my name behind something, I'm actually there working. People appreciate that." (Michael McCormick)

Chapter Eight

Back in the Bigs… and onto the Cover of SI

John was a joy [to have on the team]. I didn't have him for a long time. He was there for a while in Texas. You know, his effort was better than 99 percent of his teammates and his opposition, and his desire to get better was uncanny. He was there early, working. You know, for an undersized player, he never played as though he was undersized. He always played as though he was a big guy. He played with great enthusiasm and self-confidence. I loved everything about him.

—Bobby Valentine, former Texas
Rangers manager (2018)

John Cangelosi's major-league career seemed over when he spent the entire 1993 season in Triple-A and was then released by the Tigers on October 15. But, as it turned out, he didn't retire. After receiving offers from the San Diego Padres, New York Mets and St. Louis Cardinals, Cangelosi ultimately signed a one-year minor-league deal in November with the Mets, a ball club in need of a leadoff hitter following the departure of left fielder Vince Coleman. (The Mets had announced in August of 1993 that Coleman would not return to the club in 1994; he would be traded to the Kansas City Royals for fellow outfielder Kevin McReynolds in January 1994.)

What made the Mets interested in signing him? As Cangelosi recalls, it was because he had hit well against the Mets' Triple-A club in 1992 and 1993 when he was in Toledo. "I happened to play against Tidewater, the affiliate of the Mets. [The team was known as the Tidewater Tides in 1992 and became the Norfolk Tides the following year.] Clint Hurdle was the manager at the time," he explains. "And I just wore them out. I would get three hits one game, four hits the other game. I just played really well against them. And then that winter when I came home, that's where everything started over again. [During a meeting within the Mets organization], Clint Hurdle and his pitching coach [were there to give their input]. And the only reason I know that is Clint told me. The [Mets' brass] go, 'We need an extra outfielder. Anyone got any stats or numbers on anybody?' Clint Hurdle spoke up on my behalf and said, 'Hey man, Cangelosi wore us out. He could be a good fourth or fifth outfielder for us in the big leagues.'" Although Hurdle would leave the New York organization in September 1993 and then land a roving minor-league hitting instructor job with the Rockies the following month, he spoke up on behalf of Cangelosi prior to leaving the Mets. "And the rest was history," adds Cangelosi. "That winter I signed with the Mets. I went to spring training in '94 and I made the team."

"Even though I didn't wanna be in Triple-A [in 1993], that was probably the best thing for me because I ended up getting five more years in the big leagues and a World Series ring. In '93, I didn't make the team [in

Detroit] and had to go to Toledo. But at least I played every day in Toledo. I got back in shape, from a baseball standpoint. I started seeing the ball better. I started getting my confidence back. My legs were in shape. So, basically, I got 300 or 400 at-bats in Triple-A, but at least I got my stock back up as well. That way, when I got back to the big leagues, I became a utility player again. But if I don't go down in '93, in my opinion, maybe I never play in the big leagues again... But I played that time, and then I ended up getting back in shape."

A non-roster camp invitee with the Mets in 1994, Cangelosi went on a tear during spring training, batting .429 with an on-base percentage of .571 at one point. In a B squad game in mid-March against the Indians, Cangelosi went 3-for-5—giving him an incredible nine hits over his last 12 at-bats—while making an over-the-shoulder catch at the left-field fence to thwart a Cleveland scoring threat in the third inning. A few days earlier, he had gone 4-for-4 in a split-squad game against Houston. With Vince Coleman having been dealt to Kansas City—following a disappointing three years with the Mets which culminated with him suspended in August '93 after he, as a practical joke, threw a firecracker into a crowd of people in a Dodger Stadium parking lot—New York didn't seem to have a capable leadoff hitter. "We just don't have a typical leadoff guy," Mets skipper Dallas Green acknowledged to *The New York Times* that spring. "Let's face it, we're just not going to have that kind of guy, in all probability."

"Who led off for us that year?" Cangelosi asks rhetorically now, trying to remember what happened on the '94 Mets during spring training. "Jeff Kent led off for us a couple of times. And we had Fernando Vina, who would lead off for a little bit. When Fernando Vina made the team, then he was more leading off for us. He was part-time or something. And then Ryan Thompson sometimes would lead off. We really didn't have a solidified leadoff guy."

Once again, Cangelosi had hit well in the spring to warrant a starting job on a major-league roster. The Mets needed a capable leadoff hitter, and Cangelosi seemed perfect for the job. But once again, similar to what happened with the White Sox in 1991, it didn't turn out that way. Despite the Mets' lack of a leadoff man and Cangelosi's stellar spring, Green decided against having Cangy be that guy, opting instead for an outfield of Kevin McReynolds (in left field), Ryan Thompson (in center) and Jeromy Burnitz (in right). Alas, Cangelosi wasn't even the club's fourth outfielder, as that role went to Joe Orsulak, a left-handed hitting veteran who had a lifetime .279 average over his eight full major-league seasons through 1993. What should have been a happy homecoming—Cangelosi was born in Brooklyn and his family rooted for the Mets—was instead another setback along the switch-hitting outfielder's improbable major-league journey.

From the Mets' perspective, the plan made sense. McReynolds, despite being on the downside of his career, was a former first-round pick and had finished third in NL MVP voting six years earlier on the 1988 division-winning Mets (while receiving several first-place votes). Although he'd had two disappointing seasons in Kansas City following a December 1991 trade to the Royals that brought pitcher Bret

Saberhagen to New York, McReynolds, reacquired by the Mets in the Coleman deal in January 1994, was expected to be a contributor. "This is a trade to help us be competitive right now in 1994 and hopefully beyond. He plays hard, he plays hurt, and he lets his glove and his bat do the talking," general manager Joe McIlvaine said of McReynolds the day the trade was announced.

Thompson, meanwhile, had been acquired as one of the key players in a trade that sent former ace David Cone to the Blue Jays in August 1992. A 26-year-old in his second full season in the majors, the athletic Thompson, projected to be an impact player in the big leagues, wasn't going to lose his job to Cangelosi. Then, there was Burnitz, another former first-round pick who had smacked 13 home runs as a 24-year-old rookie in 1993. He wasn't going to lose his job to Cangelosi either. (Burnitz, expected to be the club's everyday right fielder in his second big-league season, would hit just .192 through the first month of the year and be sent back to Triple-A Norfolk in May before being called back up later in the season. When Burnitz was sent down, Orsulak took over as the everyday right fielder.)

Then, just days before the regular season began, the club also traded right-handed pitcher Anthony Young and minor-league left-hander Ottis Smith to the Cubs for shortstop Jose Vizcaino, who was promptly penciled in as the Mets' leadoff man. (Vizcaino, who went on to play for eight teams in the major leagues, including all four former and current New York clubs, is most known by New York baseball fans for his game-winning RBI single in the bottom of the 12th inning in Game One of the 2000 World Series for the Yankees against the Mets. Vizcaino also played for the Dodgers and Giants during his 18-year big-league career.) Although Cangelosi made the team—ahead of fellow non-roster outfielders Doug Dascenzo, Patrick Howell and Rick Parker—he would be relegated to bench duties. "I know they brought in Vizcaino just before the season started," Cangelosi recalls. "But again, during the whole spring, there were a few guys they were trying out for that role, to bat leadoff. I knew I had the ability to play in the big leagues as a leadoff hitter. They decided to go in a different direction."

The Mets' decision to acquire Vizcaino paid immediate dividends, as the shortstop homered, tripled, and delivered a sacrifice fly on Opening Day in Chicago. (In that same game, the Cubs' leadoff man, Tuffy Rhodes, homered three times off Dwight Gooden.) Other than hitting in the No. 2 hole for 15 games, Vizcaino kept the leadoff job for the duration of the season until the players' strike in August forced the eventual cancelation of the 1994 campaign. It should be noted, though, that while the shortstop's batting average was .291 in mid-June, he would bat just .214 over the next five weeks and wind up with a .256 average when the strike hit.

Cangelosi, meanwhile, would start only 21 games for the Mets, nine of them in the leadoff spot, while appearing in 62 games overall. Although he batted .350 in the month of April, things would go south after that. In his 111 at-bats, the switch-hitting outfielder batted .252 with only five stolen bases.

And while Cangelosi didn't play much—or hit

much—there were some memorable moments that summer. On May 10 in Montreal, with Thompson sidelined with an injured hand, Cangelosi started and batted leadoff, collecting four hits with two RBIs as the Mets rallied past the Expos, 3-2 in 10 innings.

Three days later on May 13 at Shea Stadium against Atlanta, Cangelosi went 0-for-3 with two strikeouts against Braves lefty Tom Glavine, but he was happy to see umpire Angel Hernandez behind the plate. It was the first time that Hernandez, who'd begun his big-league umpiring career in the National League in 1991, was involved in a game with Cangelosi's team. For Cangelosi, seeing Hernandez in the big leagues brought back some fond childhood memories.

"Angel Hernandez's dad started this league named Hialeah Accord League, where I grew up in Miami," explains Cangelosi. "It's a little area called Hialeah, Florida. He started this league, and throughout the years, I think 15 kids—maybe even more—that played in that league ended up becoming major-league players. When I played, my dad coached me at 10, and for a couple games, there was myself, [Rafael] Palmeiro and Danny Tartabull on the same team. Guys like Rickey Gutierrez played in that league. So did Alex Ochoa. [Jose] Canseco played against us a lot. Basically, in that one area, there was me, Canseco, Oddibe McDowell, Lenny Harris, Palmeiro, Danny Tartabull, Alex Ochoa, Alex Fernandez... The list goes on. And I know I'm leaving people out.

"Hialeah, Florida, was really, really good baseball. And that's not even including the guys who were drafted that didn't make it. We were all from that little area. It was like, within a 20-mile radius, there were probably about 20 [future] major-league ballplayers who grew up in that area. We played Little League against each other, we played high school ball against each other, and some of us played college ball. I went to Miami-Dade North. Alex Fernandez and Palmeiro and those guys went to Dade-South... Well, Alex Fernandez went to University of Miami, left there, went to Dade-South, and got drafted. Palmeiro did it opposite; he went to Dade-South first, then he went on to Mississippi State. And then he got drafted there. But I mean, there was a tremendous number of major-league ballplayers in that one little area.

"But Angel Hernandez's dad started and founded this league, and it got us off the streets at a very young age. I thank that man every day of my life because there was a lot of corruption and a lot of stuff going on in Miami when we were growing up. But every weekend we were out there all day long. It was a very competitive league, but it also kept us out of trouble. When we saw each other in the big leagues [all these years later], we talked about how we grew up and where we grew up. We all pulled for each other. It was just like a small fraternity. The guys that were from Miami and played in Hialeah, it was a fraternity. Whenever I saw Lenny Harris or Alex Fernandez— obviously, Alex was my teammate on the Marlins in 1997 and 1998—it was kinda cool because, you know, we grew up in a bad time. It was a great time for sports. But there was a lot of stuff going on. And we managed to get out of the neighborhood. You know, our only outlet was sports. And for us to be successful, and then going back to that area years later, it was awesome. So, whenever we saw each other, it was a great bond. It was a great privilege."

Seeing Angel Hernandez behind home plate brought back those memories. "I would talk to Angel Hernandez," Cangelosi continues. "You try not to talk before the game, but during the game we would joke around, whatever. Once it's business, it's business. A couple times, I met him after the game—but not too much because you can't kinda hang out with an umpire. But a couple of times we hooked up. I have a baseball school now—Cangelosi Baseball—and Angel lives in West Palm Beach. So, during the winter time, whenever I go to that area in Jupiter, Florida, he comes out and we have dinner, and catch up with everybody. Great guy, great family."

And if Hernandez called him out on strikes? "The umpire always has the last call, right?" laughs Cangelosi. "Let me put it this way. Even though he's my friend, if he makes a call, I'm not really gonna argue. I'm hoping the umpire makes the call my way. I took a lot of pitches. I worked the count a lot. I took a lot of close pitches to get on base. So, I wanted the umpires to respect me, and I respected them. We had a good relationship. I didn't wanna yell at them, treat them like crap, and then all of a sudden it comes down to a call. Instinctively, they ring you up on a ball call."

Then, there was also the John Smoltz incident—which took place the following afternoon on Saturday, May 14. With the game scoreless, Cangelosi led off the third inning with a single on a 1-2 pitch, which ignited a three-run inning to put the Mets ahead 3-0. The following inning, Smoltz drilled Cangelosi with two outs and nobody on base on the second pitch. In the fifth, Mets outfielder Ryan Thompson hit a grand slam with two outs, putting the Mets up 7-0. For Thompson, who'd been dealing with a hand injury, it was a relief as he had struck out in each of his previous six at-bats; in fact, he had been hitless in his previous eight at-bats and had gone 2-for-35 over the past 13 games. Because it was his first career grand slam—and his first hit after those six consecutive strikeouts—Thompson was naturally ecstatic but, as far as the Braves were concerned, was also overly demonstrative as he rounded the bases. "I guess Thompson wanted to savor the experience because he pimped his way around the bases," Charlie O'Brien, who was catching for the Braves that day, recalled years later in his 2015 autobiography *The Cy Young Catcher*. "Took him forever to get to home plate [and Smoltz] was pissed."

The next hitter was none other than Cangelosi, and on the very first pitch Smoltz plunked him on the lower back. Cangelosi immediately charged the mound, precipitating a bench-clearing brawl. After the game, Smoltz said he didn't hit Cangelosi on purpose after the Thompson grand slam. "The intent was to throw inside. This one happened to hit him," Smoltz told the *Associated Press*. "He was on top of the plate. The circumstances looked bad."

The way O'Brien explained it years later, he didn't call for the pitch and Smoltz never acknowledged if he'd thrown at Cangelosi on purpose. The veteran catcher, though, did admit it probably wasn't the right way to handle things; it might have been better if Smoltz took care of Thompson in a later at-bat. "Cangelosi had always hit John well, and John, I guess, took advantage of the situation. Two birds with one stone," O'Brien opined. "First pitch, he drilled Cangelosi dead square in the back. John never said if he did this intentionally, and I didn't call for it, but where the pitch was and how Thompson took his time around the bases, it was pretty clear that Smoltz knew what he was doing. You knew something was coming. It was going to be either Thompson next time up or this dude, one of the two."

"[This] was in 1994 and I was on the cover of *Sports Illustrated* because they were doing a story about brawls," recalls Cangelosi. On that cover, there was O'Brien on Cangelosi's back, the catcher's fist cocked, pounding him. Terry Pendleton, the Braves' third baseman, was in the cover too with his hands up, attempting to play peacemaker.

"He was having a rough day on the mound, and a guy just hit a grand slam off him," noted O'Brien of Smoltz years later. "He took his frustration out on the next guy who happened to have a history of wearing him out. Cangelosi would fight balls off and battle, then Smoltz would leave a pitch in the middle of the plate, and Cangelosi would drill him."

Cangelosi and Smoltz did have a good laugh about the incident that winter. In fact, the two men even shook hands. "My best friend was Pete Smith, an old Atlanta Braves pitcher [who was with the Mets in 1994]. He was getting married that winter. When I was going to his wedding, it was [going to be] all the Atlanta Braves [in attendance], and John Smoltz was gonna be there." Smith, of course, gave Smoltz a ribbing. "Smith was going, 'Cangy's coming to the wedding to kick your ass,' and all that kinda stuff. We had fun with that. We shook hands, we took pictures; it was all good."

As for O'Brien, Cangelosi does acknowledge the catcher's right in protecting his catcher. But he does refute something that is mentioned in O'Brien's 2015 autobiography. "The bottom line is that I don't know why hitters run out to the mound," O'Brien opined, referring to how hitters who charge the mound hardly ever get a good blow in, and in fact, they are the ones who get pummeled. "…Like Cangelosi. Think he had a black eye the next day. My buddy, Billy Spiers, played with the Mets then, and later on he told me that Cangelosi said he'd never charge the mound again. He took a thumping for doing it."

"But Billy Spiers wasn't even on my team in New York," Cangelosi clarifies. "That's incorrect. Billy Spiers was a teammate of mine in Houston, and we got into a brawl with the Montreal Expos, with Danny Darwin and Henry Rodriguez. That's when I got into a fight with Jeff Juden." In that 1996 incident at Olympic Stadium, Darwin, then with the Astros, hit the Expos' Rodriguez with a pitch an inning after Rodriguez stood at home plate admiring a home run, leading to the heated bench-clearing brawl. During the brawl, Juden, the Expos' six-foot-seven, 265-pound pitcher, was pulled down from behind by Cangelosi, before Juden body slammed him. Cangelosi, listed at 165 pounds, ended up landing several punches on the pitcher.

"Danny Darwin was a good pitcher, and a great guy," continues Cangelosi. "He pitched more than 15 years in the big leagues. Just a class teammate. He was a great guy. I wouldn't cross him because he would drop you in a minute as well! We got into [that] big brawl in Montreal. He drilled Henry Rodriguez and we had mayhem for 20 minutes. There were a couple fights here and there. Jeff Juden had Craig Biggio by the neck, and I said, 'Let him go! Let him go!' He wouldn't let him go, so I grabbed Juden by the shirt and knocked him to the ground. He charged me. I punched him, like, 20 times. Basically, me and him got into a fight."

For that 1996 fight, Cangelosi received a four-game suspension. "When you get suspended, it's like being on the disabled list. You don't feel like you're part of the team. You come out and get your work in, but you can't help the team. It's hard when you're in a pennant race [as the '96 Astros were] and you can't help the team… But I didn't regret [the incident with Juden]. Baseball is a team sport, and sometimes things like that are gonna happen. But you've got to defend your teammates when you see something like that [Juden going after Biggio] going on. Juden's a big guy; he should've been trying to pull people off instead of going after them. I'm not saying fighting is right, but I don't regret what I did. I do regret not playing [for four games].

"But I never had a conversation with Billy Spiers about Charlie O'Brien and John Smoltz. I didn't even feel Charlie hitting me. I never talked to the guy after that. If I'd mentioned anything about not charging the mound again, it was not because of the fight. That had nothing to do with it. It had to do with, after the fact, when everyone's piling up on you and you're at the bottom of the pile, it's claustrophobic, man. My knees are all twisted. The pile keeps getting heavier. I mean, Charlie O'Brien had nothing to do with me deciding [whether] to charge or not. But he is supposed to protect his pitcher. Every catcher does that. I just reacted. But I just charged when it happened. It was more of a spontaneous reaction. And then, it kinda worked out for me. From there, I got on the cover of *Sports Illustrated*. So, it benefited me more than anything!"

By midseason, manager Dallas Green saw that having Cangelosi on the roster didn't provide any benefit to the Mets. The team, which lost 10 of 12 beginning at the end of May, had sunk to last place. The clubhouse, meanwhile, had become an unhappy room with star players either complaining about the pitching rotation (staff ace Bret Saberhagen) or criticizing ownership and management (closer John Franco). Or cursing the manager's name (slugger Bobby Bonilla)—due to the way Green would, according to a July 12th piece by Jennifer Frey in *The New York Times*, constantly rip players to the media for their mistakes. Then, there was also Dwight Gooden's suspension; the former Cy Young Award winner, after making just seven starts in 1994, was banned for 60 days for violating his drug aftercare program and had pitched his last game for the Mets.

Green certainly didn't make himself any more popular amongst the veteran players when on July 8, the manager decided he no longer wanted Cangelosi on the team, releasing the switch-hitting outfielder. "Around the All-Star break, Dallas Green wanted to send me down, and I refused the assignment," Cangelosi recalls. "Two things, I knew that Dallas Green didn't like me and I didn't care much for him either. I knew the strike was going to hit, so I just assumed just get off the major-league roster, and I ended up playing [for the Astros' minor-league team in] Triple-A [Tucson] for a little bit [in 1995 after the strike ended]."

The Mets skipper, meanwhile, told the press Cangelosi was never a part of the club's future to begin with. "What we want to do is make some changes and try to move forward," Green was quoted as saying in *The New York Times* on July 12, the day of the All-Star Game. "We don't want to be stuck where we are." He was, however, singing the praises of rookie Rico Brogna. "You can never have enough quality people in your clubhouse and on the field. What the Mets are trying to do right now is upgrade our personnel and see what some kids can do. Rico is a perfect example of that."

While nobody thought John Cangelosi fit into the Mets' long-term plans, some were still puzzled by his release. Jennifer Frey of *The New York Times*, for instance, thought the move seemed difficult to justify. "At 31, Cangelosi is neither an integral fixture in the Mets' system or a young player expected to blossom," Frey opined the day after Cangelosi was released. "But he is a better-than-average utility outfielder who has done what the Mets have asked this season, particularly in situations when the outfield has been stretched thin." In addition, Cangelosi "played flawless defense," and "save for [Kevin] McReynolds, Cangelosi is the only member of the Mets to play more than a smattering of innings without incurring an error," noted Frey.

When pressed for more details on the release, Green pointed to the stats. Cangelosi had only one RBI in his final 30 games as a Met and went the entire season without hitting a home run. For the year, the switch-hitting outfielder had only four doubles while driving in just four runs, numbers Green wasn't pleased with. "Offensively, we've sputtered so much that I've got to find ways to get the offense going, and in my estimation, Cangelosi is not one that can do that for me," the Mets skipper told the press, citing the club's need for power and RBIs. Interestingly, the Mets opted to keep three reserve infielders—Tim Bogar (.143, 1 HR, 3 RBIs up to that point), Luis Rivera (.237, 3 HR, 4 RBIs), and rookie Fernando Vina (.252, 0 HR, 4 RBIs)—who also had shown little offensive production. Green, though, argued he needed late-inning defensive replacements in the infield and not the outfield. And because the Mets had only four outfielders following Cangelosi's release—with Ryan Thompson, Joe Orsulak, Jim Lindeman and Kevin McReynolds still on the roster—Green had even made first baseman David Segui play the outfield sometimes, a move that Segui himself, according to a report in *The New York Times*, was unhappy about.

Several of the Mets players, including Bonilla, Franco, Saberhagen and right-hander Pete Smith, were shocked and unhappy about the club's decision to release the popular Cangelosi. "Bret Saberhagen was another great teammate of mine with New York," says Cangelosi, who was 0-for-8 lifetime in regular-season play against Saberhagen, without ever reaching base against the right-hander. "Back in the day when I was with the White Sox in my rookie year, going into Kansas City and facing that staff, they had the best staff ever. You would go there and hope you don't go 0-for-20 in a four-game set. I mean, you had to face Bret Saberhagen; he was 21 years old at the time and he was throwing 96, 97 [miles per hour], and he had a sinker, slider, changeup. Then you had [to face] Mark Gubicza [and] Danny Jackson [in that same series]. I mean, they were phenomenal together, that staff.

"And Pete Smith was also my teammate in New York. [When I was going to face him in a game], he would joke around and say, 'Hey, I'm gonna give you a pitch to hit.' When I got a hit [in spring training] off Bret Saberhagen, he would say, 'Hey, this doesn't mean anything.' We had good relationships. I got along with everybody. I had a lot of friendships because I played on many teams. But once you get between the lines, you're competing and you forget about them. After the game, you can hang out with them. But when you're playing the game, you compete."

His situation in New York was not unlike the one he had encountered in Chicago with Jim Fregosi. On the White Sox, he had a strong rookie season. On the Mets, Cangelosi could have contributed. He could, after all, play all three outfield positions. He could provide speed off the bench. He could be used in double switches. He hadn't lost a step; he could still run and play good defense. Still, the situation with Green, says Cangelosi, was different from that with Fregosi. While Cangelosi and Fregosi shook hands and moved on, the diminutive outfielder didn't have a chance to do so with Green. "My thing with Dallas Green wasn't as publicized," he says matter-of-factly today. "Between me and Jim, there was more like we went back and forth in the paper a little bit. With Dallas Green, it was more my own personal opinion of what he did to me. Once I refused assignment and went to a different team, I really never talked about it anymore. That situation I shouldn't have been sent down. I really didn't have any drama with Dallas Green. There was no drama that went the next level."

While he doesn't care to talk much about Green, Cangelosi has plenty to say about—and nothing but praise for—his next big-league manager, Houston's Terry Collins. "You talk about people who are very pivotal in your career. I had Jimmy Leyland. I had John Boles. Terry Collins was, by far, most pivotal in me getting my extra four years and getting my stock and value back up. In 1988, when I got sent down to Buffalo, he was my manager in Triple-A when Leyland sent me down to get some at-bats. Terry told me this story years later, so this came directly from him. Terry thought I was gonna go down there and big-league it, you know, just kinda half-ass it or don't play hard. That's just not me. When I went down there, not only did I work the younger players with the base running, but when I played, I played hard. Once you're between the lines, you forget about where you're at. I love the game."

Former first-base coach Tommy Sandt, who got to know the switch-hitting outfielder during their time with the Pirates and Marlins, lost touch with him for several years after Cangelosi left Pittsburgh at the end of the 1990 season. Sandt, however, isn't surprised Cangelosi continued to play hard each time he was demoted. "I mean, I managed in Triple-A, and when guys get sent down, some of them would come down and pout," says the first-base coach today. "[But then], some [other players] would come down and say, 'I don't wanna be here. I'm gonna play, play well, and get called back up. I'm not gonna be here forever. I'm getting outta here.' I'm sure that was Cangy's attitude. Some guys just don't accept it, and they don't play well. Knowing John, I'm sure he did well, because he would always get called back up [during his time in the Pirates organization]. I'm sure that's how he took it. I don't know that for a fact, because I wasn't there. Once a guy gets sent down, you lose contact with them. You get reports, but you don't really stay in contact. I'm sure he took it the right way. John's a fighter. There's no doubt about that."

"[When] I got called back up, Terry called me to his office," says Cangelosi, continuing the story about his interaction with Collins, "and said, 'I gotta be honest with you. At first, when you came down here, I thought you were gonna be a pain in the ass. But man, you came down here and not only were you a good teammate, you played hard. And I appreciate everything you did. If I'm ever in a position to help you out, you can count on me. If I'm ever in a position to give you a job, I'll do it. I appreciate everything you did here. I love the way you play. I'll help you out whichever way I can.'

"After that, I pretty much lost touch with him. Then, years later, he got the [managerial] job with Houston. In '94, when I refused assignment, now I'm at home before the strike. I had no job. I'm not home for even two days, and Terry Collins calls me. Terry Collins calls me up personally and says, 'Hey, what happened in New York? Are you retiring? Why did you quit or refuse assignment?'

"I go, 'I'm on a guaranteed contract. I didn't wanna make minor-league money. [Dallas Green] wasn't gonna call me back up. Terry, I didn't like him. He didn't like me. I just need to go somewhere else to play. I wanna play. I wasn't supposed to be sent down.'

"'Alright. Cool. If the strike doesn't hit, I'm gonna sign you. I'm gonna offer you a contract.'

"'Alright, where's your Triple-A team?'

"'No, you're coming to Houston. I'm gonna offer you a big-league job.'

"So, this guy, Terry Collins, remembered what I did for him, and he was gonna give me another opportunity [in the big leagues]. So, obviously, the strike hit, and he called back. Terry goes, 'Just stay in shape. Go to Puerto Rico. Go to winter ball, stay in shape, do whatever you got to do, and next year we'll sign you.'"

Collins, whose first big-league managerial job was in Houston from 1994 to 1996, remembers that phone call. "I didn't really know if I had a job available," Collins, who also managed the New York Mets from 2011 to 2017 and is currently the special assistant to the general manager, says today. "I just wanted to make sure he was okay, if everything was all right. I tried to create a spot because guys like him, they set examples. He's the kind of guy you want on your team if you're going to be successful. I've said this when I took over here in New York with the Mets. This guy gave you the best pinch-hitting at-bat you could ask for. I can't tell you how many nights I put John Cangelosi to lead the inning off. The count was going to be 3-and-2. He was going to grind out an at-bat like nobody else did. The rest of the team saw how the pitcher's going to pitch, how he's going to get you out.

"A couple of my pinch-hitters here in New York, I told them the same story. 'Look, I had a guy in Houston. This guy's job was to get on base. That's all he was trying to do. He wasn't trying to hit a three-run home run. His thinking was, his job is to get on base, to make the team successful.' That's why I wanted him on my team. You talk about guys' roles. You have guys on every team that are basically bench players, guys that come off the bench to help. I used John's example with my guys in New York. 'Hey, I had a guy in Houston. That's what he did. He was a successful major-league player. We won games because of him.'"

During that 1994 phone call, Collins' message to Cangelosi was simple: stay in shape, and the following year, the Astros would sign him. "We all know what happened the next year," continues Cangelosi, referring to the use of so-called replacement players, the non-union players brought in by owners during the 1994-95 Major League Baseball players' strike, for spring-training games in 1995. That April, the strike, the fourth in-season work stoppage in baseball in 22 years, finally ended, after 232 days.

Prior to the end of the strike, Cangelosi, along with free-agent infielder Mike Brumley and catcher Jerry Goff, had signed with the Astros in the spring. When asked to work out with the replacement players, though, Cangelosi, like Brumley and Goff, didn't want to be involved with them. "The next year [1995], there wasn't any spring training because the [strike] was still going on," Cangelosi, who signed his minor-league deal with Houston in February 1995, continues. (It should be noted that while Baseball-Reference.com states Cangelosi signed with the Astros on March 23, 1995, other sources, including the July 21, 1995 edition of the *Houston Chronicle*, say that he signed the deal in February.) "I had to go to minor-league camp. There was no spring training for me in the big leagues. To make a long story short, [the Astros] kept asking me to be a replacement player. I refused, obviously. But the union called me and said that I had to go because I was under minor-league contract at the time, and Major League Baseball could suspend me if I didn't show up to the replacement camp. So, I went there and told [Astros general manager Bob]

Watson, 'Look, I'm coming here because I had to. I'm not a replacement player, nor will I ever be a replacement player.' There was me, Jerry Goff, Mike Brumley, and a few other guys. There was Craig McMurtry, a pitcher, who ended up crossing. He was an Atlanta Braves pitcher and they kept going after him. McMurtry was a great guy, a gentleman. I have no ill feelings of what he did. He was a great guy.

"But we had six or seven guys that had big-league time that they were trying to attack. I refused it, refused it, refused it. There was no spring training for us. They kicked us out, so I had no spring training. I ended up starting the season in Tucson because there was no major-league camp at the time. So, I was in Triple-A with Tucson, playing two or three weeks. Maybe a month."

In that one month, Cangelosi tore up the Pacific Coast League, batting .368 in 30 games. Unlike his stints in Triple-A Toledo in 1992 and 1993, however, when Tigers manager Sparky Anderson never called him up, this time Collins promoted him when a spot opened up on the major-league roster. "Phil Plantier got hurt," Cangelosi explains, referring to the Astros left fielder who'd been acquired by Houston as part of an 11-player trade with San Diego back in December 1994. "Terry Collins called me up to the big leagues, and then the rest was history. [In one of my first games], I faced John Smoltz. I went 4-for-4. And whenever Terry played me, I just saw the ball really well right away. I was hitting .357 the first two weeks I was up. When Phil Plantier came off the disabled list, they traded him and kept me in the big leagues. That trade kinda helped both myself and Plantier. He went over to the Padres to have a chance to play every day, and I was gonna get more at-bats in Houston."

Not only did the Astros trade Plantier back to San Diego (for pitchers Rich Loiselle and Jeff Tabaka), they also dealt outfielder Luis Gonzalez (along with catcher Scott Servais) to the Cubs midseason (for catcher Rick Wilkins) as the ball club shifted from its long-ball philosophy back to the speed-defense-pitching formula. While Houston also called up speedy rookie Brian Hunter from Triple-A in June to be the everyday center fielder and leadoff hitter—and then acquired outfielder Derrick May from Milwaukee—Collins still managed to keep Cangelosi in the lineup. "Terry Collins played me," continues Cangelosi, thankful his manager didn't keep him on the bench. "I hit over .300 that year in [201] at-bats. I kept getting on base, and that's what I was supposed to do, with [Craig] Biggio, [Jeff] Bagwell and [Derek] Bell coming up and driving runs home. I was one of the top three in on-base percentage that year. [Actually, he had a .457 on-base percentage but didn't have enough plate appearances to qualify for the league lead. Barry Bonds, with a .431 on-base percentage, was the official National League leader.]

"I had 21 stolen bases. He just got my value back up because he played me. Not only did he keep me, but he also played me. I thank him every day. I played the next year with them in 1996. Because I started playing and doing my thing again, that's when Jimmy Leyland called me and gave me a two-year deal in 1997 [to play for the Florida Marlins]. Basically, he gave me a chance to play five more years in the big leagues—and win a World Series ring in 1997—because I probably wouldn't have gotten back to the big leagues [if not for him]."

Collins, recalling the way Cangelosi hustled and

played the game the right way during his stint in Triple-A Buffalo in 1990, knew the switch-hitting outfielder belonged in the big leagues. He also knew Cangelosi was a good fit on the Astros ball club. "He earned it," Collins says now of Cangelosi's spot in Houston. "You just don't hand out chances. He earned everything he got. That's why I loved him. I thought he played the game the way it's supposed to be played. He gave you every ounce every day. That's why when he played for me in Buffalo, I thought, 'If I ever get a chance to get a big-league managing job, I'm gonna try to get him.' I was lucky enough, and it worked out. But he earned it. It wasn't any gift."

Cangelosi thanks Terry Collins for giving him a shot. But he also recalls how former Pirates teammate Barry Bonds, who'd moved on to the Giants, had his back—even though they were on opposing ball clubs. "Barry Bonds is misunderstood," Cangelosi says of baseball's home-run king. "He really is a good guy. He was a really good teammate. He was really, really good to me. We're still friends today. He definitely had my back in a lot of situations. The one that comes to mind—there's a couple—[occurred] in 1989 or 1990 [when] I was on the fence of maybe being sent down or not making the club for a little bit. Leyland, I guess, was talking to Barry, Bobby Bonilla, and a few other guys. Barry stood up for me and said, 'No, you know what? We got him. Let's keep Cangy. He's part of this team. He's been with us for a while...' That was one occasion where he stood up for me."

Fast forward to Houston in 1995. "I get called up. There is where Terry Collins took care of me. At the time, I had two little kids; my son was probably five or six months old, and my daughter was almost two. I was in Tucson first. I had an apartment in Tucson. I got called up. Phil Plantier was on the disabled list. I ended up staying there longer than they expected. I was killing it; I [had an on-base percentage] over .400. We would go on the road, and my family would have to fly back to Tucson. Every homestand, they would fly back to Houston. We would have to stay in a hotel room because I wasn't allowed to get an apartment yet because they didn't know if I was gonna stay or not."

By late July, Cangelosi was still on the team and his situation hadn't changed. By then, outfielders Gonzalez and Plantier were both gone. The Astros had Hunter, the electrifying rookie, in center field and Derek Bell in right. May and James Mouton platooned in left, with Cangelosi getting a few starts there as well. Collins also had Brumley and veteran Milt Thompson to put in the outfield, but Cangelosi knew he was staying put. Yet, he still wasn't allowed to get an apartment in Houston.

But things changed when the San Francisco Giants came into town for a series in late July. "Barry Bonds comes into town with the Giants. I'd been up for [over] a month now, and I'm [playing] well. Terry Collins is playing me. It was getting very expensive for me, paying for the hotel and paying for the apartment in Tucson. Just a lot of stress with not having a place to live, with two young kids. Then all of a sudden, I was talking to Barry. 'Bob Watson doesn't wanna let me get an apartment. I don't know what his deal is…'

"After batting practice, Barry Bonds went into Bob Watson's office and said, 'Hey man, Cangy's on this team! Get him an apartment! Let him frickin' bring his family here… Look, he's on the roster!' I swear to God, after the game Watson calls me into his office to say, 'All right, Cangy. Go ahead. You can get an apartment. You're good to go.' That was really nice of Barry."

Perhaps it was because of his conversation with Bonds. Or maybe it was simply a load off of his shoulders after hearing Watson's news. But whatever the reason, Cangelosi absolutely killed the Giants in that home series. He hit safely in all four games while getting the start in three of them, as Houston took three of four against San Francisco. Cangelosi batted .643 in the four games (9-for-14), going 3-for-4 with three runs scored in the opener and 4-for-4 with three more runs in the third contest. In the finale, with the Astros trailing 2-1 in the ninth against Giants ace William VanLandingham, he came on to pinch-hit for catcher Jerry Goff and led off with a double. (In his first two major-league seasons in 1994 and 1995, VanLandingham was the Giants' top pitcher. The right-hander was 14-5 with a 3.61 ERA in 34 appearances (32 starts) while striking out 151 batters over 206.2 innings.) Cangelosi would come home to score on a sacrifice fly, and the Astros won the game off Scott Service an inning later. "Getting four hits in a game is a nice personal achievement," Cangelosi says, "but it's only nice when the team wins. My job was to get on base, whether it was with hits or with four errors. I just wanted to go out there and get on base two or three times a game, no matter how, with Craig Biggio, Jeff Bagwell and Derek Bell coming up. And if I did that, chances were good that I could score and help the team win the game."

That Giants series wasn't the only highlight of Cangelosi's summer in 1995. He also had a memorable 10-day stretch from June 16 to June 25, where he appeared in six games including a stint on the mound in a blowout loss against the Chicago Cubs. "My ERA in the major leagues is 0.00. It was actually on *This Week in Baseball*. One week I had a really crazy week. It all started in New York [on June 16]. It was an extra-inning game. I think it was the 16th inning or whatever it was."

After both teams scored once in the 12th and twice in the 15th, Houston won it in the 16th with the help of Cangelosi's bizarre hit. "I [was at the plate] and with two strikes, the guy, [Mets left-handed reliever Eric] Gunderson, threw a breaking ball," says Cangelosi, who had entered that night as a pinch-hitter back in the 13th inning and stayed in the game. "I kinda checked my swing. I fouled it off. It was going foul down the first-base line and it must have hit a sewer pipe or a sprinkler head. And it trickled fair."

Cangelosi, who hadn't been running, sped up as the ball trickled between Gunderson and first baseman Rico Brogna. Nobody could make a play, and Cangelosi was safe. "I ended up getting a base hit. I stole second. Then Bagwell got a base hit. We win the game.

"Then we come back to Houston. We're playing against the Cubs [on June 22, and] we're getting our ass kicked. We were short on pitching. We were playing a lot of games. Terry Collins asked me if I wanted to pitch. 'I know you pitched before. You wanna pitch?' I said yes, and I ended up pitching an inning." After issuing a leadoff walk to Todd Pratt, Cangelosi managed to get the next three outs on only 10 pitches, getting two groundouts and a lineout to right. "I got Sammy Sosa out, Todd Zeile out, and Rick Wilkins," Cangelosi recalls. As for his career pitching appearances, he's proud he got guys out without giving up much. The first time came with Pittsburgh in 1988 against the Dodgers, when he gave up a double to Mike Marshall but retired the other six batters he faced—Franklin Stubbs, Jeff Hamilton, Mike Devereaux, Rick Dempsey, Dave Anderson and pitcher Brad Havens. "Then, the last time I pitched was with the Marlins [in 1997] against San Diego."

Three nights after his pitching performance, there was more wackiness for Cangelosi against Chicago. With Houston ahead 10-6, he came up to pinch-hit and drew a walk. "We ended up batting around the order in that inning. I come up again for the second time in that inning and I hit a three-run homer [off Bryan Hickerson]. So, I started with a walk, and I hit a three-run homer. And then we win the game. That was kinda cool. It was a wacky week."

But what was truly wacky was the way the pennant race played out in 1995.

Chapter Nine
Houston: Close but No Cigar

John is a welcome addition to our ball club. He's got speed, he can play center field, and he can get on base. It's a movement for us to help our depth.
> —Dave Dombrowski, Florida Marlins general manager, upon signing Cangelosi as a free agent (November 1996)

Following the 1993 season, Major League Baseball had realigned, moving Houston and Cincinnati out of the NL West into the newly-created Central Division. Pittsburgh, Chicago and St. Louis also joined the Central, moving over from the East. Atlanta, meanwhile, moved out of the West to join the NL East. In the AL, it was the White Sox, Royals and Twins moving out of the West into the new Central Division, while Milwaukee and Cleveland also left the AL East to join the Central. With three divisions in each league, Major League Baseball's playoff format was adjusted to include all three division winners plus a wild card. The players' strike, however, ended the 1994 season in August, wiping out the postseason as well.

So, 1995 was the first year everybody—the teams, the media and the fans—experienced the pennant race with the wild card as well as the new playoff format. Things were wild in the AL West, with California owning an 11-game lead over second-place Texas and a 13-game advantage over third-place Seattle on August 2, with less than two months remaining. One week later, the Angels still owned an 11-game cushion over both the Rangers and Mariners. As late as August 24, California was still ahead of Texas by eight-and-a-half games and Seattle by 11-and-a-half games.

On that same day, it seemed all of the races in the AL had been decided, with Boston owning a 15-and-a-half-game advantage in the East and Cleveland running away with the Central with an 18-and-a-half-game cushion. But that's where the wild card came in. On September 1, just three games separated six teams vying for one wild-card spot, with Kansas City and Seattle tied atop the wild-card standings, and Texas, the Yankees, Milwaukee and Oakland no more than three games back.

As it turned out, though, the AL West race wasn't over. The Mariners mounted a late-season comeback while the Angels suffered through a late-season collapse, forcing a tie-breaker for the division crown (which was won by Seattle). The Yankees, meanwhile, won the AL wild card on the final weekend of the season, allowing long-time team captain Don Mattingly to reach the postseason for the only time in his playing career. (Mattingly never appeared in the World Series in his playing career; the Yankees made the Series the year prior to Mattingly's rookie year, 1981, and the year after his last with the club, 1996.)

In the National League, Houston was one of the teams involved in the pennant chase in the second half of the season, and for a while, the 1995 Astros looked like they would reach the postseason by being the senior circuit's first wild-card team. On August 4, after sweeping a doubleheader in Pittsburgh, Houston was 54-38 and enjoyed a six-game cushion over the Philadelphia Phillies (and a six-and-a-half-game lead on the Los Angeles Dodgers) in the wild-card standings. While the Astros were ahead of the pack in the wild-card race, they were also only four-and-a-half games back of the NL Central-leading Cincinnati Reds.

Cangelosi, for one, doesn't mind the wild card. It allows more teams to be involved in the pennant race down the stretch. "Having the wild card helped us out on the Marlins in 1997. Or else we wouldn't have made it. That was the first year [a wild-card team won a World Series]. Thank God for the wild card, or else we would've never made it. [And 1995] was the first year of the wild card, wasn't it?"

But disaster struck for Houston. The Astros proceeded to lose their next six games in a row before sophomore left-hander Mike Hampton defeated the Mets 3-1 to end the streak. Alas, later in the month, the Astros dropped 11 straight games, a skid that included three-game sweeps at the hands of the Reds and Braves, along with a four-game sweep in Florida to a Marlins ball club that was among the worst in the National League. The Astros would go 9-20 in the month of August before rebounding to win 17 of their final 28 games. Cangelosi, however, wasn't one of the problems during Houston's ugly slide. Whenever Terry Collins called upon him, he produced; in 45 at-bats in August he batted .356, and this came after he hit .462 during the month of July in 26 at-bats.

"For two months this season," Collins was quoted as saying in the *Houston Chronicle* late in the 1995 campaign of Cangelosi, "I don't know where we'd have been without him. He does nothing but get on base and create runs, and when he comes to the ballpark, you know exactly what you're going to get every day... An ideal situation is to have John pinch-hitting leading off the eighth or ninth. I bet he's been on base 75 to 80 percent of the time in that situation. And when Brian [Hunter] went down, he made the leadoff guy."

But because of that August slump, the Astros had no shot to catch Cincinnati, which wound up winning the NL Central by nine games. Amazingly, though, Houston still had a shot at the wild card. On September 1, Houston and Colorado were tied atop the wild-card standings, with Philadelphia, the Cubs, San Diego and Montreal no more than three games back. (The Giants, seven games below .500 with a 55-62 record, were only five games out.)

Thanks in part to a hot streak that saw the Astros win nine of 12 beginning in mid-September, Houston was still alive in the final week of the regular season. For the lone NL wild-card spot, it was down to the Astros and the loser of the NL West—Colorado or Los Angeles. In what was a truly wacky final weekend of the season, even the Cubs still had a shot going into their final series—a four-game set at home against the Astros.

Houston trailed Colorado by a game in the wild-card standings heading into that final weekend—and desperately needed San Francisco to play spoilers. The Rockies, in just their third year of existence, clearly had the advantage as they would be playing their final four games at home, while the Astros had to play on the road. To make things even more complicated, the Rockies still had a shot to overtake the Dodgers atop the NL West standings, as Colorado was only a half-game out of first place in the divisional race.

Cangelosi, whose previous experience with a pennant race in the big leagues came in 1990 with Pittsburgh, admits now that he, along with the rest of the '95 Astros teammates, paid attention to what was happening in the other games. "We had to win one or two games and that would've forced a playoff [with Colorado]," he says now. "We were scoreboard watching and kinda involved in that."

In the series opener, the Astros lost 12-11 in 11 innings—blowing five separate leads from the sixth inning on—while the Rockies were walloped 12-4 by the Giants. Remarkably, in the game at Wrigley, a contest that saw both Houston and Chicago combine for 36 hits, 17 by the Astros, none belonged to Cangelosi, who went 0-for-7.

When asked now about that final weekend, Cangelosi laments the team blew its chances. "But I hit the ball good that game," he says, referring to his hitless afternoon. "My at-bats really were irrelevant in terms of winning or losing that game. I didn't come up in a key situation that would've won or lost the game; it was more like I just had a bad day, a very boring day… Not to put blame on anybody—it was all our fault—but we just happened to struggle all at once."

Actually, for Cangelosi, it was just that one game where he struggled. Because Derek Bell was sidelined with an injury—and missed the entire month of

September—Cangelosi would appear in 27 games in September, starting 20 of them. Other than the 0-for-7 afternoon, he would prove he was more than capable of producing in meaningful games in an everyday role. In 88 at-bats from September 1 until the end of the season, Cangelosi would bat .284 with five extra-base hits, 23 walks and 10 stolen bases.

For that one day, he just didn't get any breaks— even when he hit the ball hard. "I mean, I hit the ball good. A couple of times I didn't," he adds. "It was [an extra-inning] game, so I just happened to get a lot of at-bats but I didn't do anything that day."

The following afternoon, with Cangelosi getting the day off (and Derrick May in his place in left field and Milt Thompson in the lineup in right), Houston lost 4-3 in 10 innings—with Astros relievers Mike Henneman and Dean Hartgraves blowing a 3-0 lead in the ninth—while Colorado was outslugged 10-7 by the Giants. (At this point, the Cubs, thanks to their two victories and the two losses by the Rockies, were still alive in the wild-card race.)

In the season's penultimate game, Cangelosi was back in the lineup and contributed two run-scoring base hits in five at-bats out of the leadoff spot, and the Astros finally beat the Cubs 9-8 (and eliminated Chicago from wild-card contention). Cangy started things off by drawing a leadoff walk against Frank Castillo and coming home on Craig Biggio's homer. He then singled home Ricky Gutierrez in the fifth for a two-run Houston lead, before driving in Gutierrez again on another RBI single two innings later, breaking the 8-8 tie. But alas, the Rockies won too by hammering the Giants 9-3.

"I'm glad to be a big part of this," Cangelosi said then, "but it's not the do-or-die that's so stressful. It's this damned series. We go up by two; they go up by two. I've caught myself getting real pumped up. I'm always up, but I've been on an adrenalin high here, like this is the World Series." Because of his knack of coming up huge all season, the Houston press wasn't surprised at Cangelosi's two hits. "The big-money boys certainly did their part," noted sportswriter Ed Fowler in the *Houston Chronicle* on October 1st, referring to the exploits of Biggio and Jeff Bagwell. "But no one showed up bigger than the 5-8, 160-pound Cangelosi, who drove in the last two runs in a 9-8 win that sustained the heartbeat going into the final game of the season. If only for this one game, he represented a whopping return on a minimum-wage investment. Actually, he made less, for Cangelosi opened this season in the minors. Over the last six years, he has visited Buffalo, Vancouver, Denver, Toledo and Tucson, mixed in with short stints with the Pirates, Rangers and Mets." Cangelosi, added Fowler, "produces as usual."

"I mean, who would've thunk it?" smiles Cangelosi now. "To be released by the Mets the year before and then starting the season in the minors, going to Houston and being in the everyday lineup in the middle of the season, and going into the final weekend playing for a playoff spot... I mean, I didn't get a hit in that extra-inning game to open that series. But you forget about it and try to help the team the next game. That's what I did the rest of that series. We were in the wild-card race. You had to forget about it and try to win that next game to stay alive. For me, as a guy that came in to pinch-hit for the most of my career, that's what you have to do. You get your one at-bat or whatever, and you hit the ball hard but it doesn't go your way, then you get ready for your next opportunity. That's the way I prepared myself. That's how I was able to stay in the big leagues as long as I did. That year in 1995, I just happened to be more of an everyday player in September."

The race came down to the season's final day, with Houston beating Chicago 8-7—with Cangelosi again going 2-for-5—and needing a Rockies loss to force a tie in the wild-card standings. Colorado, however, refused to cooperate, rallying from an 8-2 deficit to stun the Giants 10-9 and capture the National League's final playoff spot.

Critics pointed to manager Terry Collins as part of the problem in Houston. Hall of Famer and baseball analyst Joe Morgan was one. "Adversity is part of baseball; if a manager can't cope with it, his team will suffer," Morgan opined in his 1999 book *Long Balls, No Strikes*, adding that Collins "learned this lesson when he was with Houston.

"The Astros were a talented team when Collins was there [from 1994 to 1996]. They finished second three times but failed to make the playoffs because the manager exerted too much pressure on them. He was so uptight, his players thought each pitch was life-and-death. It wasn't anything Terry said; it was his demeanor. Collins was edgy in the dugout during the games, always looking like someone who was just waiting for disaster to strike. And the moment anything actually went wrong, you could smell the panic on him. Players pick up on that. To alleviate the tension the manager is bringing to the clubhouse, they put added pressure on themselves to perform well, which invariably chokes off their natural abilities so that they can't play their best… By the way, I've been watching Collins since he joined the Angels [in 1997], and he's a much more laid-back skipper. When I complimented him on this change, he said former Angel infielder-outfielder Tony Phillips had talked to him about relaxing more and that it had really made an impression."

Cangelosi, though, doesn't blame Collins for the Astros' collapse. In fact, he has nothing but praise for the Houston skipper. Instead, he feels the players didn't perform and let the season get away. "In the month of [August], we lost, like, 20 games. We had a lot of closed door meetings," Cangelosi recalls now. "Terry Collins was trying to do everything positive to get us going. But at the end of the day, I think we just, collectively as a group, put too much pressure to do better instead of just going out there one game at a time. Individually, I think we all put pressure on ourselves and we didn't play up to our capabilities. And that happens."

While Houston missed the 1995 postseason, it was a good year for Cangelosi individually. After not being wanted by the Rangers, Brewers, Tigers and Mets organizations following his four seasons in Pittsburgh, he had found a home in Houston. Signed for just one year, he became a free agent after the 1995 season and received offers from Atlanta and San Francisco—but he chose to re-sign with the Astros for the 1996 campaign. In fact, it was Collins who convinced him to re-sign—although Cangelosi had to accept a minor-league contract with oral assurances that he would be on the team. "I felt like I owed it to Terry. He gave me an opportunity to play in 1995. With the strike, it was hard for me to get on anywhere. But Terry said, 'Come on in and do your job, and we'll find a place for you.'

"That year [1995], I proved to Terry I could play. I wasn't really a platoon player. It was more about matchups. A platoon player would platoon with one person, where you play against a lefty and I play against a righty. For us, it was more like matchups and trying to get everybody playing time. I guess we platooned together but I played a lot that year. When Derek Bell went down with an injury, Brian Hunter got called up, and I pretty much became somewhat of an everyday player. This was midseason in '95. So, Hunter became the center fielder when Bell was hurt, and then in '96 he was the everyday center fielder. That year in '95, I was the left fielder. Then when Derek Bell came back from his injury, he was the right fielder.

"But Terry Collins tried to get everybody playing time. If there was a tough righty, Derek Bell would get some action. I think Collins was playing percentages. He would probably look at stats and think, 'Derek Bell hit well against this guy, so I'm gonna play him today.' Or 'Cangy hit well against this guy, so I'm gonna play him today.'"

Or James Mouton versus a certain pitcher. And Derrick May. Collins had no shortage of outfielders, but the Astros skipper managed to find enough playing time for Mouton, May and Cangelosi. "With the three of us on the bench, it was more of a roving rotation [among] all three of us to get the best matchups. I believe what Terry was doing there was to get the right matchups. Terry gave me an opportunity to play, but also it was about getting the right matchups," adds Cangelosi.

"Milt Thompson was also on our team but it was toward the end of his career. He was more like a left-handed bat off the bench. Me and Derrick May still kinda had some years left. Derrick May is a totally different player than I am. He would play when we had a certain type of matchup... Derrick May was more of an RBI guy, gap hitter, doubles guy, home run once in a while. I was more of a leadoff guy. When Derek Bell went down, Terry Collins would go back and forth between Biggio and me batting first."

The way the season ended—just short of a playoff berth—was a bitter pill for Cangelosi and the Astros to swallow. But in 1996, it was a similar script. Entering play on September 1, the Astros were the NL Central leaders. A four-game losing streak, capped by a three-game sweep in St. Louis, however, dropped Houston to second place. The wild card that year was likely not an option, as both Montreal and Los Angeles, the second-place teams in the East and West, respectively, had better records than Houston. On September 12, after completing a seven-game homestand which saw the Astros go 4-3, they were still only one-and-a-half games out of first place in the Central. But a nine-game losing streak—including an 0-8 road trip which saw the Astros get broomed in Colorado, Atlanta and Florida—followed. By the time the streak was snapped, Houston had already been eliminated from both the division and wild-card races. The Astros' sorry September record in 1996? A dismal 8-17.

"That sucked, to be honest with you. It was two years in a row, we handed it to them. I think we lost a

[six]-game lead [over a period of] three weeks [in 1995]...," says Cangelosi. "It was crazy. We lost something like 18 out of 24 games in [August], it was something stupid. We couldn't do anything right. In '95, it went down to the last day in Chicago. If we would've won that game and someone would've lost, we would've been [tied for] the wild card [and forced a one-game playoff]. But we choked. We put a lot of pressure on ourselves."

Then, in 1996, it was the same story. "[Craig] Biggio and [Derek] Bell struggled at the time [in the final month of 1996, and] we did nothing right the last month. We should've gone to the playoffs in 1995 and 1996. We had a great team. We had a great offensive team, good pitching. We just choked."

Upon further reflection, Cangelosi believes the '95 collapse was on the players' minds in 1996, and the pressure just snowballed with every loss. The players, it seemed, put more pressure on themselves— and it backfired. "In my opinion, in the last month of '96, it seemed like the year before, it happened where everyone kinda struggled at once. We would get good pitching, but then we wouldn't hit. They called them the 'Killer B's.'... Biggio and Bell struggled at once. We lost our RBI, run-producing threat."

Indeed. Cangelosi is referring to the trio of Jeff Bagwell, Biggio and Bell. In 1996, third baseman Sean Berry, acquired from Montreal in the off-season, was part of the "Killer B's" too. With two-thirds of the "Killer B's" struggling in September, it was tough for Houston to challenge for a playoff spot. Bell, who batted just .229 in the second half of the 1996 season, hit .200 in the month of September with no homers and seven

RBIs. Biggio, meanwhile, batted .172 with no homers and nine RBIs in September. Both players had hit at least one home run and collected double digits in RBIs in each of the other months during the season. Bagwell, however, rose to the occasion by hitting .302 in the month of September. Alas, his two homers and 16 RBIs weren't enough to offset the slumps of Bell and Biggio. As for Berry, his September numbers were .296 with four homers and 14 RBIs.

"And then everyone else started putting pressure on themselves to offset that," continues Cangelosi, who was part of the September problem with a .190 batting average and .277 on-base percentage—and no steals. His own slump came after he'd batted .297 in the first half, including .328 with 10 stolen bases in June when he started 15 games and appeared in 21 contests overall that month. "It's a team effort, but in '95 we just, for whatever reason, put a lot of pressure on ourselves and didn't get it done. Then in 1996, I feel like the month of September we remembered what we did and we kinda just put pressure on ourselves again. Again, that's my opinion—because if you look back at it, both years [down the stretch] we played terrible. Terrible."

Both near misses were tough to swallow. The collapse in 1995, though, probably hurt Cangelosi more, career-wise. "At the time, I was playing every day because Derek Bell got hurt." With Bell sidelined for the remainder of the season after surgery to remove a blood clot in mid-September revealed he had a muscle tear in his left thigh, Cangelosi had become the Astros' starting left fielder. "I would've been a starter in the playoffs," Cangelosi says now. "Me on that stage, I would've probably got paid more money the following year because my role would've been more important."

While that was true, one key for Cangelosi during his two years in Houston was the fact that he, for the most part, avoided significant injuries. Back in 1993, when he became injured during spring training with the Tigers, he ended up not making the team at all. With Houston, he remained healthy and productive. Of course, there were some freak things that were outside of his control. He remembers specifically being hit by a pitch against the Cardinals in 1996—and also being hit by a bat swung by his own Astros teammate in 1995!

He acknowledges, though, that for a little guy who played hard every time he was in the lineup, he was fortunate to have avoided serious injuries during his big-league career. "I really didn't get hurt all that bad," he says now, trying to list all of the memorable ones he suffered. "But there was one with Jimmy Leyland [in Pittsburgh]." One time, Cangelosi dove and caught a ball, but he badly hyperextended his thumb. "So, [the trainers] gave me a cortisone shot in my thumb. I didn't tell Jimmy Leyland. I wasn't on the D.L. or anything. He asked me to pinch-hit the next day, and I'm like, 'Shit.' I really couldn't swing the bat all that well. I'm going up there knowing I'm trying to get a walk. I'm not gonna swing the bat. I go up there. Ball one, ball two, strike one, ball three, strike two… And then I'm like, 'Shit! I've gotta swing the bat!' [The pitcher] throws me a 3-and-2 fastball. I popped it up. It was a bad swing. [Back in the dugout] Leyland goes, 'What's wrong with you?'

"I go, 'Skip, I had a cortisone shot last night. I can't even feel my finger. I can't move it.'

"He frickin' goes, 'What the fuck is going on here?' He got the trainers involved. He was like, 'Whenever one of my players can't play, blah blah blah…' It was like he was getting mad at the trainers. I said, 'Skip, man, just blame me. It's not their fault. I'll tell you next time.'

"Also, in my rookie year with the White Sox, I was facing Dickie Noles. He was pitching for Cleveland. I'm hitting lefty, and he hits me in the front part of my knee. [Three nights earlier], the Yankees [had] come into town. [Dennis] Rasmussen, who's left-handed, [had hit] me on the same knee, but on the other side. So now, my knee was really bad. [White Sox head athletic trainer] Herm Schneider gets all the swelling out. I missed only one game, which was incredible. Herm was probably one of the best trainers I ever had. To make a long story short, 15 years go by. Now, I'm coaching with the Chicago Cubs. Dickie Noles happens to be in spring training somewhere. This guy comes up to me, and I guess, through his recovery, because he was an alcoholic, it was therapy for him to apologize. Or whatever you wanna call it. He comes up to me and goes, 'Cangy, I just wanna let you know. I wanna apologize for hitting you in the knee in 1986. I wasn't right back then. I just wanna apologize.' I'm like, 'Dickie, don't even worry about it.' I guess that was therapy for him—or whatever the case it was—but I thought that was kinda weird."

Finally, he recalls those two specific injuries with Houston in 1995 and 1996. "There was another injury that I had. I'm having a great year for Terry Collins in 1995 with the Astros. I'm killing it, man. I'm playing every day. It was frickin' awesome, man. Then Rick Wilkins, the catcher, had this habit of swinging a bat in the dugout all the time. He was just swinging bats where you shouldn't be swinging bats." One day, Cangelosi was the victim of one of Wilkins' careless swings. "I was in his hitting group. I'm standing right next to him. He basically takes a full swing and hits me in my ribcage with the bat. Then, I'm playing. I hit a ground ball to short, and now I can't frickin' run. So, I didn't play for, like, six or seven games. It was painful."

It was even more painful in the first inning of a game in late August 1996 against St. Louis. (That injury might have explained why he struggled that September, although Cangelosi refuses to attribute his slump to it.) "The only time I had a serious injury was when [pitcher Alan] Benes drilled me in the back of the knee. I went to first base, but I couldn't run." He had to be replaced by James Mouton in the second inning. "I went on the [15-day] disabled list. [The trainers] had to drain blood twice. I mean, it swelled up so bad that they actually drained my knee twice. That was, really, the only serious injury that I had."

And really, Cangelosi's stint in Houston didn't end well. A .297 hitter in the first half of the 1996 season, he hit poorly when the calendar turned to September. For whatever reason, he had a hard time coming off the bench the entire year. While he hit .286 as the Astros' leadoff man, he also went just 1-for-28 (.036) with three walks and no RBIs as a pinch-hitter in 1996. (As a defensive replacement, though, he was 6-for-16—a .375 average—when he also batted later in that same game.) Even today, he remembers those frustrating outs he made as a pinch-hitter that year.

"It's a lot easier to play every day than it is to do what I did," Cangelosi reflects. "One, you faced the top closers in the league. You get one at-bat. And then you are either Billy the Kid or Billy the Goat. It's a situation where everyone wants me on first base because it's late in the game and we're up a run or down a run. Everyone knows that I'm up there trying to work the count too. I need to get on base. That was very difficult. You've been sitting there the whole game. You get one at-bat. And now the closer is throwing 98, 99 miles an hour. You get one at-bat. You're stiff. You've been sitting the whole game. You're not warmed up.

"The other thing is, when I did get on base, now everyone in the ballpark knows that I'm gonna try and steal a base, which makes it even harder. There's no surprise. There's no 'Oh, is he gonna go or not go?' Everybody in the ballpark knows I'm gonna run. Here, late in the game, I can't get thrown out. So, it was a very difficult role that I had, and I accepted it. I tried to do the best that I could do in that role.

"It was trying at times because sometimes you sit there and you doubt yourself. It's easy to get 500 or 600 at-bats and be in some sort of rhythm. When you do that, you're seeing the ball better. I mean, it's different if you're a utility guy. You get 200 at-bats as a utility player. A hundred of them are pinch-hitting. It's very difficult. I took that as a challenge. A couple years, if I recall correctly, I was either in the top three in pinch-hitting or on-base percentage. I was, if I remember correctly, always pretty good with on-base percentages. I got on base a lot."

In 1996, Cangelosi just had one of those bad years as a pinch-hitter. But it wasn't because he wasn't prepared. It was just one of those years. "You had your good years and you had your bad years," he adds. "In the first year with Houston, I hit .320. I had a good year off the bench. Then the following year, I think I hit over .300 as a starter. I hit .100 as a pinch-hitter. I had nothing to show for it. I was 1-for-25 or something. It was crazy. I got on base on walks. But I was very good at what I did. Managers knew that, one, I was a switch-hitter, and two, they could count on me being ready in those certain situations."

Cangelosi had re-signed with the Astros in 1996 because of Terry Collins, and would have wanted to stay in Houston had the manager remained. But following yet another disappointing season for a team expected to contend for a division title, it was the manager who ultimately paid the price for the ball club's failure to reach the postseason. After the 1996 season, Collins was let go despite his 224-197 record in three seasons as the Astros' manager. He wouldn't be out of a job long, though, as he would be hired by the Anaheim Angels for the 1997 season.

Cangelosi, meanwhile, had also played his last game for the Astros. He, too, wouldn't be out of a job long. In November, he would receive a phone call from a familiar voice recruiting him to return home and play for a team in South Florida.

Chapter Ten
Going Home to Florida

I wanted Cangelosi. Having a guy like him is almost a necessity. People don't realize it's a tough role and when you can get a veteran player with a track record... He's got a great attitude for the role he plays on the ball club. That's why we wanted him. He was one of the guys I really wanted. That sounds like a small signing after Bobby [Bonilla] and Moises [Alou] and Alex [Fernandez], but Cangelosi was a pretty important signing for this club.
    —Jim Leyland, Florida Marlins manager, as told to
        USA Today and *The Palm Beach Post* (1997)

Cangelosi always wanted to play again for Jim Leyland, a man he considers the best manager he played for. And when Leyland phoned him up in November of 1996, Cangelosi was ecstatic.
    Leyland, who had won three straight division titles in Pittsburgh (1990-1992), had then gone through some lean years with the club as the Pirates couldn't afford to re-sign their star players such as Bobby Bonilla, Doug Drabek and Barry Bonds. Tired of the rebuilding process in Pittsburgh—the team was a last-place outfit in back-to-back years in 1995 and 1996—

Leyland had resigned as manager of the low-budget Pirates in mid-September. The week after the regular season ended, he had agreed to a five-year deal to manage the Florida Marlins, a ball club that had not had a winning season since it began play in 1993. Why the Marlins? Billionaire owner H. Wayne Huizenga had promised Leyland he would spend the money to make the ball club a contender. It was unlike the past four seasons Leyland had experienced in Pittsburgh, where the small-market Pirates wouldn't spend money to bring in high-priced free agents to improve the club.

And now, Leyland, who had a chance to lure free agents to his new ball club, was recruiting Cangelosi to play for the Marlins. Yes, to be a utility outfielder—but also a piece to the puzzle of a potential championship club. Cangelosi, who at times was an everyday player in Houston under Terry Collins, would be a reserve player once again under Leyland in Florida, but he didn't mind one bit.

"Jimmy Leyland is a class act," Cangelosi, who batted .284 as a starter in 1996 with Houston but went just 1-for-28 as a pinch-hitter, says. "We have a very good relationship. He's very smart man. He always out-managed the other team. He always had a strong bench. He knew that I would prepare myself. He knew that I was good at my role. So, whenever there was an opportunity to get me, he got me. I was blessed to play for him on four different teams. There were some good times and some hard times. In Pittsburgh, he sent me down a couple times to the minor leagues. We were both in tears but, I mean, it was the right thing to do. I wasn't playing much. I had to get some at-bats and get back into shape. He says, 'Cangy, I gotta send you down. It hurts me, but you gotta get some at-bats and you gotta play.' Through all the turmoil and everything, he was very, very good to me. Not because I didn't deserve it. But he was just very good to me.

"Then, with the Marlins, the year that we won the World Series, I was the first one that he signed. He called me up personally, because I would always joke with him throughout the years. 'Hey man, get me back on your team.' He would go, 'But Cangy, you can't play no more.' And all that joking around. Then all of a sudden in 1997, he calls me, and he goes, 'Hey man, this is the year.' He always wanted to win a World Series. Obviously, everybody does. But he goes, 'This is the year, and you're the first one.' That was the year they signed Alex Fernandez, Moises Alou, Bobby Bonilla, [Jim] Eisenreich. I think there were seven free agents. I was the first one he signed. I wish I would've signed for the other guys' money, but I'll take it."

There were actually six free agents, and while Cangelosi might have been the first player Leyland called, officially he was the second one signed. The signings began a week before Thanksgiving, with Bonilla being the first. The Marlins signed Bonilla to a four-year deal for $23.3 million on November 22, and inked Cangelosi four days later to a two-year contract worth $1.075 million. On December 3, the club signed Jim Eisenreich for two years at $3 million. A week later, right-hander Alex Fernandez, one of the top pitchers in the American League when he was with the White Sox, signed a five-year deal for $35, giving the Marlins a strong starting staff that already included aces Kevin Brown and Al Leiter. Over the next three days, Florida also signed reliever Dennis Cook ($1.7 million, two years) and outfielder Moises Alou ($25 million, five years).

The signings, totaling $89 million, were met with criticism. The consensus was the Marlins, in their attempt to overtake Atlanta in the NL East, overspent on the players they signed. "It adds up to the biggest holiday shopping spree ever," opined Michael Farber in the December 23, 1996, edition of *Sports Illustrated*. "In a three-week binge that began on November 22 and ended last Thursday [on December 12] when the MasterCard people started getting suspicious, the Marlins committed $89,075,000 to those six free agents...

"They overspent for Bobby Bonilla, who hits plenty but who hasn't found a home either in the field or with a team since leaving the Pittsburgh Pirates after the 1991 season. They made journeyman left-handed reliever Dennis Cook an offer so generous that his former general manager with the Texas Rangers, Doug Melvin, urged him to take it. They paid $4.075 million for two outfielders, Jim Eisenreich and John Cangelosi, who make a lovely pair of bench ornaments. They committed an average of $5 million annually until 2001 for the dynamic but brittle 30-year-old Moises Alou, who has never driven in 100 runs in a season."

Years later, though, baseball writer Rob Neyer noted in his 2003 book, *Rob Neyer's Big Book of Baseball Lineups*, that the criticisms weren't exactly warranted. "It's true that, prior to the 1997 season, the Marlins committed $89 million in long-term contracts to six free agents... But what's often lost, I think, is the fact that the Marlins' $48 million (or thereabouts) season-opening payroll was *lower* than that of five teams in the American League, and lower than that of the Braves in the National League. What's more, the Reds, Cardinals, Dodgers and Rockies weren't far behind." Neyer went on to note that the Cleveland Indians, who turned out to be Florida's opponent in the 1997 World Series, carried a payroll of $54 million, higher than that of the Marlins. "If the Indians had won the World Series—which, of course, they very nearly did—would anyone have accused them of 'buying' a championship? Probably not," Neyer opined, adding that the facts "are that the Marlins' payroll was *not* out of line with most of the other clubs with postseason aspirations…"

Cangelosi, of course, didn't mind the Marlins' spending spree. He still chuckles about it today. "You know," he says in jest, "I wish I could've signed for the other free agents' money… I was happy with my deal, obviously, and happy that I was gonna be playing for Jimmy Leyland again. Jimmy's a guy who never puts his players in a position to fail. He's a manager who utilizes each player on the ball club to his maximum performance. But, man, the contracts that Bonilla and Fernandez and Alou got… Man, it would've been nice if I'd signed for the money that those guys got!"

But the week that he signed with the Marlins, there wasn't a lot of laughing. He received horrible news during general manager Dave Dombrowski's teleconference with the media to announce the signing. After telling the media the name of the White Sox scout who over a decade earlier believed Cangelosi was a major league-caliber outfielder, Dombrowski shared something else about Walt Widmayer. "Walt's not doing so well these days," the general manager announced.

Cangelosi, who was listening, tracked down Widmayer's number and called the veteran scout from Dombrowski's office. He'd been meaning to call the scout for the longest time, but the years passed by before he finally made that phone call. "I got drafted by Walt Widmayer, and I had a relationship with him until the day he died," Cangelosi says now, confessing that he gets goose bumps thinking back to that day. "When [I signed with the Marlins], Dave Dombrowski [told me the bad news]. I went into the office [to make that phone call]. Walt Widmayer was on his death bed. He was dying of pancreatic cancer [but still] wanted to talk to me and congratulate me [for signing with the Marlins]… It was just a surreal moment for me how things all came full circle. I talked to him a little bit. He was in a lot of pain but he said, 'I'm proud of you. I'm proud of what you've done. Those son-of-a-bitches should've played you more. You had a lot to offer. But [you've] had a great career. I'm proud of you.' That was the last time I talked to him. A couple of days later, he passed away. So, I was able to close that chapter. But he was a big part of me getting to the big leagues."

Widmayer was in such pain that he had to end the phone conversation. Cangelosi badly wanted to talk to him again but never had another chance. Shortly after Widmayer's passing, Cangelosi received a called from Widmayer's wife. She said something that sent shivers down Cangelosi's arms. "She told me that I was Walt's pet project. After I'd called Walt, he told her that over the years, I was the player he really wanted to succeed because he took such an interest in me. It gave me chills hearing that. To think that, in his final week, he was thinking like that about me... Walt Widmayer was the one who made me become a switch-hitter. I owe him an awful lot. I'm glad I got to let him know."

And he was glad that Leyland wanted him on the Marlins, who now had a stacked roster and was ready to challenge Atlanta in the NL East. Prior to the arrivals of Leyland and the six free agents, the club already had some star players: pitchers Kevin Brown and Al Leiter, closer Robb Nen, catcher Charles Johnson, and outfielders Gary Sheffield and Devon White. (It should be noted, too, that the Marlins had gone on a free-agent spending spree the previous off-season, when they spent $36 million to sign free agents Brown, Leiter, White, and Cuban-born pitcher Livan Hernandez, who had defected to the United States in 1995. In addition to those 10 free agents over the two off-seasons, the club also gave Nen a four-year, $17.5 million contract to buy out his final two years of salary arbitration plus two years of free agency and gave Sheffield a six-year, $61 million extension that would kick in during the 1998 season.) Like Cangelosi, the other newcomers were excited about the 1997 Marlins' chances. Fernandez, who'd left Chicago and a potent White Sox lineup that included future Hall-of-Fame sluggers Frank Thomas and Harold Baines (along with hard-hitting veterans Robin Ventura, Danny Tartabull and Tony Phillips), knew his new ball club could contend. "I had a decent lineup in Chicago," the right-hander would tell Chicago sportswriter Bruce Miles in early April. "This lineup is a little beyond what I had in Chicago. When you have [Jeff] Conine hitting seventh, that's pretty tough. These guys want to win."

For Cangelosi, being with the Marlins also meant he no longer had to face Kevin Brown, who, in his opinion, was one of the toughest guys to hit in the National League. The previous July, Cangelosi had helped Houston beat the Marlins in back-to-back games, including one started by Brown, in the midst of the Astros' seven-game winning streak. On July 1, Brown struck him out in each of his first two at-bats, but in the fifth inning Cangelosi smacked a triple off the Marlins right-hander and wound up scoring the winning run as Houston won 6-2. The following night, Cangelosi led off the bottom of the 12th with a double off reliever Terry Mathews, went to third on a groundout, and came home to score the game-winner on Bill Spiers' single to center. While he had those two big hits in that particular series, Cangelosi actually batted just .167 against the Marlins in 1996, and that triple was his only hit ever off Brown. Still, being in the same dugout with Kevin Brown, as far as he's concerned, was better than having to step into the batter's box against the right-hander.

"There were a lot of guys that I didn't like to face," Cangelosi says now. "One that comes to mind was Kevin Brown, my teammate. I hated facing him. His ball was like a 10-pound weight. He worked both sides of the plate really well. He had a good two-seam sinker. He had a cutter. I mean, he dominated, man. He was good. But there were a lot of tough guys in the big leagues. But Kevin Brown comes to mind right away. I faced him when he was with the Marlins and I was with Houston, and I got a triple off of him. When we teammates in Florida and I reminded him about that triple a couple of times, he just said, 'You got lucky.' And actually, he was right. I did get lucky!"

Brown wasn't as lucky either on July 16, 1997, against the Dodgers. That night, he threw a one-hitter to beat Hideo Nomo and Los Angeles, 5-1. But, according to the *Los Angeles Times*' Steve Springer, it should have been a second no-hitter for Brown, who had already no-hit the San Francisco Giants one month earlier; the Dodgers' only hit—a fifth-inning line-drive single by Raul Mondesi—"might have been caught if left fielder John Cangelosi had chosen to dive for it." Today, however, Cangelosi refutes that report. "If I could've caught it, I would've tried to dive. But I probably didn't think I was gonna catch it. If I could've dived and should've dived, I'm sure Kevin Brown would've said something to me after the game. There was no conversation about it or even any ribbing. Nobody said anything like, 'Hey, Cangy, why didn't you dive for it? C'mon!' So, they probably agreed I wouldn't have caught the ball."

* * *

When the 1997 regular season began, it was a dream come true for Cangelosi. After all, he grew up in nearby Hialeah, attended Miami Springs High School, and played at Miami Dade-North Community College. "It was a wild dream just to play in the big leagues. But especially to play where I grew up, in front of my family… it was awesome."

The first two weeks of the season were also a dream come true for the Marlins, who were in first place in the NL East with an 8-1 record following a 10-0 victory in Cincinnati on April 11. Alas, they promptly lost eight of 10 to fall four games back of Atlanta, which won 14 of its first 19 games. Soon the Marlins were six games back—and having difficulty holding off low-budget Montreal for second place—but rookie left-hander Tony Saunders, Florida's fifth starter, stopped the Braves 5-1 on May 8 for his first major-league victory. Saunders, who worked six scoreless innings that day in his fifth big-league appearance, would post a pedestrian 4-6 record with a mediocre 4.61 ERA in 1997. But he would be a perfect 3-0 with a 1.65 ERA against Atlanta, outpitching future Hall of Famer Tom Glavine twice. (He was such an unknown that at least one newspaper columnist referred to him as "Tracy" Saunders.)

The aces on the team, though, struggled in the season's first three months as the Marlins remained in second place behind the Braves. Yes, there were moments of brilliance with Kevin Brown throwing a no-hitter against the Giants on June 10 and Alex Fernandez twirling a one-hitter against the Cubs on April 10. Unfortunately, through mid-June the trio of Brown, Fernandez and Al Leiter was just a combined 17-14, with Leiter owning a 5.20 ERA. As for Cangelosi, the switch-hitting outfielder also got off to a slow start. Through May 15, he was hitting only .171 in 22 games, six of them starts. A hot streak from May 17 to June 11—where he batted .375 in 32 at-bats—moved his season average to a more respectable .269.

Although Cangelosi would go on to collect only 192 at-bats in 1997—and didn't make headlines the way the other stars on the team did—it didn't mean he wasn't a valuable member of the ball club. Tommy Sandt, who first met Cangelosi when he was the Pirates' first-base coach in 1987, had joined Leyland's coaching staff in Florida in 1997. To Sandt, Cangelosi was an important piece of the Marlins' puzzle that year, even if he wasn't an everyday player. "He was a pretty good player," Sandt says now. "He fit a role with our team. When he came up with the White Sox, he played every day and stole a bunch of bases. He did pretty well. But with our team, he fit in as a fourth outfielder, pinch-hitter. He filled a role. Played good defense for us. Late in the game he would get on base via a walk or a hit, or whatever. He played an important role for us."

One such example came on June 15, in the second game of a doubleheader against the visiting Yankees—as interleague play began in Major League Baseball in 1997. Pinch-hitting for pitcher Livan Hernandez in the fifth inning, Cangelosi hit his only home run of the season in a game which the Marlins would win 6-5. It would turn out to be the second-to-last homer in his big-league career. It was also the first—and only—homer he hit as a left-handed batter in the major leagues. Cangelosi remembers that dinger for several other reasons. "I liked interleague play. You know, I didn't like playing in the American League at all because I'm not an American League player. But once in a while, playing against American League teams, you got to see old friends that you hadn't seen in a while. It added a little bit of a different twist and vibe to it. It was cool. I actually hit the [second] interleague home run for the Marlins and it was against Dwight Gooden, my teammate in New York. [Gary Sheffield had hit the first one in the first game of the doubleheader hours earlier, off Kenny Rogers.] It was on Father's Day. I'm like, 'Hey Doc! Thanks for the Father's Day gift!' That was my only home run hitting left-handed my whole career."

That home run wasn't the only "gift" he got from Gooden. Today, Cangelosi still has the present the former Mets ace gave him back in 1994. "Dwight Gooden was a great guy, and he was a class act. He belongs in the Hall of Fame," Cangelosi says. "I love that man. I talked to him several months ago. He was my locker mate in New York. Just a low-manner, low-key guy. Great teammate. Always approachable. Very talkative. You can talk to him about anything. One time, he had this briefcase. It was ostrich. It was really nice, really expensive. That's what we used back then, in the early '90s. It wasn't like you had a carry-on; we used briefcases back then. I was sitting next to him, and I said, 'That's a really nice bag. It's really cool, dude.' The next day, I had one on my seat. I mean, that's the kind of guy Doc is. I didn't want it; I didn't ask for one. I don't use it, but I have it because it's a special gift. He just went out and got it and put it on my seat. 'Here you go, Cangy. It's yours.' The briefcase was made out of ostrich; it was very expensive. He just gave it to me. Just a good guy, man.

"I think Dwight Gooden belongs in the Hall of Fame—but he doesn't have the numbers to be in the Hall of Fame. Unfortunately, he had demons and struggled with many things. I faced him in A-ball, rookie ball, my first year, when he first got signed. He was throwing 99 miles an hour back then. I think he was 18 years old at the time. Two months later he was in the big leagues. He was throwing 98, 99 miles an hour with a 12-to-6 breaking ball. It was phenomenal. He was untouchable. Just look at the years where he had 200 strikeouts. Unfortunately, things got in the way. He had everything. Unfortunately, things happened."

* * *

There were other moments for Cangelosi during the 1997 championship season. On June 25, he started in right field—in place of Gary Sheffield, who was given the day off—and had a season-high four hits in five at-bats with three RBIs in a 7-5 victory over Philadelphia, upping his batting average to a season-best .296. On a scorching day—a thermometer on the artificial field at Veterans Stadium registered 165 degrees an hour before the 1:05 pm starting time—manager Jim Leyland rested his regulars, and Cangelosi led the way. "You've got to give the Marlins' B-squad credit for the latest win," a scribe from *The Palm Beach Post* noted, referring to a starting lineup that featured Cangelosi and fellow backups John Wehner, Jim Eisenreich, Kurt Abbott, Todd Dunwoody and Gregg Zaun. "… Their leader was a 5-foot-8-inch reserve outfielder who had 76 at-bats all season." The win marked the first time in franchise history that Florida had been 15 games over .500. "It's fun to get the B-bombers in there," said Cangelosi that day. "We gave the starters a day off and still came up with the win. I'm not known for my RBIs in key situations. And I'm not blessed with all the ability in the world. But if I go out and play hard, that may rub off on the team."

Four days later, Cangelosi started in left field and batted leadoff against the Montreal Expos. In the first inning against left-hander Carlos Perez, he drew a walk and stole second, the 150th stolen base of his career. It led to a four-run inning off Perez, as Florida won 5-3. It had taken him just one season—his rookie year in 1986—to steal the first 50. But being a reserve player—and spending time in the minors along the way—meant taking longer to achieve these milestones. For example, while No. 50 had come in 1986, it took six years to reach the century mark; No. 100 came in 1992 with Texas at Yankee Stadium, when he came on as a pinch-runner for Kevin Reimer in the late innings in a blowout game and stole second base off pitcher Rich Monteleone and catcher Matt Nokes.

It had taken a while to go from 50 to 100 to 150 stolen bases—Cangelosi feels if he had been a starting center fielder in his first two big-league seasons, he would have surpassed 150 by his second year—but he is still proud of those milestones. Stealing bases when everybody in the ballpark knows you're going to try to steal, after all, isn't an easy job. But along the way, he did it against some of the best pitchers and, earlier in his career, frustrated guys such as Nolan Ryan, Jack Morris and Roger Clemens. "If I was standing on first base and the pitcher was slow to the plate, I was gonna steal two bases off of him," he says matter-of-factly. Left-handers, he adds, were the most difficult to steal against. Surprisingly, knuckleballer Phil Niekro, for Cangelosi, was also one of the toughest.

"He was really quick to the plate but he also threw a knuckleball," Cangelosi says of the Hall-of-Fame knuckleball specialist, whom he faced in 1986. "He just was really quick and he kinda had his back knee buckle a little. For a guy who threw a knuckleball, he didn't have that big of a leg kick. So, he was pretty much 1.1 [seconds getting the ball] to the plate. Even though he threw a knuckleball, he was very hard to steal off of. The longer it takes the pitcher to get to home plate, you have more time to get to second base. If a pitcher is 1.1 [seconds to home], like a slide step, it's very hard to get to second base. I was probably at 3.3 timing-wise, or 3.25."

A speedy base stealer may, from his normal lead, make it from first to second in roughly 3.2 or 3.25 seconds, according to sports magazine *Baseball America*. Of course, the other part of the equation is the catcher. A strong-armed catcher with good footwork can get the ball from his mitt to the second baseman's or shortstop's glove in 1.85 to 1.9 seconds. Hall-of-Fame catcher Ivan Rodriguez, in his prime, was at 1.75 to 1.8 in getting the ball to second base.

"If the catcher is 1.9 and the pitcher is 1.1, it's very hard [for the base stealer]," continues Cangelosi. "That's the time [it takes] the pitcher to get rid of the ball. The bigger the leg kick, the longer it takes for the ball to get to home plate. If the pitcher's 1.35 or 1.4, he's really, really slow. If a pitcher's 1.25 or 1.3, that's average. But if a pitcher's 1.1 or 1.2, then he's really quick to the plate. Lefties were a little bit harder. When I first came up in the American League, guys like [Scott] McGregor and [Mike] Flanagan, the two lefties with the Baltimore Orioles, were tough. They had the best left-handed moves because they would balance themselves really good. Let's say if I decided to steal and he was going home, he could re-direct his balance towards first base to pick you off. They were really, really good."

But for right-handed pitchers, it's a different story in terms of picking runners off. "The only way for right-handers to have a really good move to first base is if they have a 'close-to-a-balk' move, where their front knee buckles first and then they spin over. They're deceiving you."

There was no deception on Cangelosi's part on July 21—when he took the pitcher's mound and threw 70-mph fastballs to tough veteran hitters Steve Finley and Wally Joyner. No knuckleballs needed. No trick pitches necessary. No deception needed. "Here's my fastball; go ahead and hit it," was his message. That afternoon, with staff ace Kevin Brown having an unusually bad game—allowing seven runs on 11 hits and five walks in six-plus innings—and the Marlins getting blown out by the Padres, Jim Leyland needed a guy to mop up in the ninth to protect the other arms in the bullpen. In came Cangelosi, who pitched a hitless inning while giving up only a walk, finishing up the 10-2 loss to San Diego. He became the first ever Marlins position player to pitch for Florida.

Remarkably, he even kept Joyner—who had a single, double and triple earlier in the game—from hitting for the cycle. "He wasn't gonna hit one out of the park off a 72-mile-an-hour fastball," says Cangelosi, whose scoreless inning gave him four shutout frames in his career. He also retired Finley, who was looking for his third hit of the afternoon. "I just threw a natural cutter under the radar. I threw a little batting practice fastball, about 65 miles per hour, and they couldn't hit it. You can say I was the 'short guy' out of the bullpen. I just wanted to get guys out. I couldn't throw a knuckleball. I threw a breaking ball one time but it didn't break. I just threw my cutter and let them hit it. They got themselves out."

"It's like hitting against a groundhog," quipped Marlins coach Rich Donnelly, noting that Cangelosi clearly used his height to maximum advantage. "The ball comes right up out of the ground. If they allowed him to pitch from behind the mound, he'd be unbelievable—because you couldn't see him. You couldn't even see him winding up. You'd just see the top of his head."

And you could argue Cangelosi, despite starting only two of the games against San Diego, wound up having a better series than Rickey Henderson, who was then with the Padres. In the four-game series, Cangelosi was 5-for-8 (.625) and reached base seven times. He was successful in his only stolen-base attempt in the series, and even scored the 300th run of his major-league career. Henderson, meanwhile, started all four games but was 3-for-14 (.214). While baseball's all-time stolen-base king also reached base seven times, he was just 1-for-2 in stolen bases.

* * *

For the third consecutive season, Cangelosi was part of a second-half pennant race. While his 1995 and 1996 Astros fell short, his 1997 Marlins had a key piece that was missing in Houston: manager Jim Leyland, who, according to Cangelosi, simply knew how to inspire his players to play to their potential.

"There are certain coaches out there who, when they walk into a room, try too hard to get respect from their players," explains Cangelosi. "Or, think about a business owner with his employees. But Jim Leyland had a way about him where he walked into the room and he could be himself, and he just automatically got respect. People call him a player's coach. Guys loved playing for him. To be a great manager in the big leagues, I feel like you have to be a psychiatrist. Every major-league player makes a lot of money and is a grown-up. But everyone's got different personalities. Jim Leyland knew how to get the best out of everyone. One guy might need a little bit of cuddling. One guy might need a little bit of ribbing. One guy might need a little kick in the butt. One guy might need a little pampering. He just knew everyone's strengths and weaknesses, and he just made everyone feel like they belonged. Especially guys like me who weren't everyday players or weren't able to contribute on a daily basis, he really made us feel like we belonged and we were a big part of the team. He got 25 guys to play hard every day—and it came natural.

"We all wanted to win it for Jimmy Leyland because he deserved it. I played for many guys and he's the best manager. He's the best baseball mind that I ever played for, along with being the best psychiatrist. He knew how to read guys. He knew how to motivate guys. He knew how to motivate the best players."

Leyland certainly needed to do so in the second half of the season, when it seemed the club was slipping. On July 28 against Cincinnati, Al Leiter pitched eight innings of two-hit ball with 11 strikeouts, but Florida still lost 4-0 as Jay Powell gave up a three-run homer to Joe Oliver and a solo shot to Mike Kelly in the ninth. The Marlins had lost three in a row, six of their last eight, and had fallen a season-high seven-and-a-half games back of

Atlanta. To make matters worse, the Marlins had also fallen out of the wild-card lead, dropping a half-game behind the New York Mets. Leyland, who had steam coming out of his ears after the game, lashed out at the ball club in a closed-door meeting.

"He was just a great storyteller, great motivator, great coach," says Cangelosi. "Not every coach out there knows how to use reverse psychology or get guys to play hard. Here was a scenario with the Marlins. We had a four- or five-game losing streak. We got [veteran catcher] Darren Daulton in a trade [with Philadelphia on July 21]. I think we just fell out of the wild card. And we were supposed to win the whole thing. We were getting good pitching, but we weren't hitting. We'd just gotten Darren Daulton—and Jimmy had gotten Daulton for his leadership and because obviously he could still play. We had a closed-door meeting—and Daulton was on the team—and he basically ripped us in the whole meeting. It basically got us back on track a little bit. We played okay."

Fast forward to September. The Mets had faded, and the Marlins were now trying to hold off the Dodgers and Giants for the wild card (although one of the California teams would win the NL West title). After beginning the month by sweeping the American League East-leading Baltimore Orioles in a three-game set—heading into September, Baltimore had the best record in all of baseball at 85-48 (.639)—the Marlins lost three straight in Los Angeles, unable to solve Tom Candiotti's excruciatingly slow knuckleball in the third defeat. Florida salvaged the finale of that four-game set when Kevin Brown outpitched Hideo Nomo, but then dropped back-to-back games in San

Diego in walk-off fashion. Next up, a 1-0 loss on September 12th to the Giants' Kirk Rueter, a soft-tossing left-hander, back at home. (The defeat marked rookie Livan Hernandez's first major-league loss following nine straight wins.) The Marlins had lost six of their last seven games. But surprisingly, Leyland, as Cangelosi recalls, didn't rip into the team this time.

"After that [closed-door] meeting [in late July], we lost five or six games in a row. [Actually, it was six out of seven games.] Every day we were waiting for a closed-door meeting where Jimmy Leyland would rip into us again. One game, we lost. Nothing. Two games, we lost. Nothing. Three games, we lost. Nothing."

The Marlins bounced back to beat San Francisco 8-1 and 5-4 in the next two contests, winning that three-game set. That was when Leyland stepped in again. "And then, as soon as we won a couple of games in a row, he called a closed-door meeting," Cangelosi says. "Everyone was on a high. Then, he kinda motivated us instead of ripping us when we were down. When you're down and playing like shit, you don't wanna hear that you're playing like shit. I've been in many meetings, where a coach is addressing the team, 'You guys are playing like shit. Come on, you gotta do this, you gotta do that.' Everyone's tying their shoes or untying their shoes. Guys are taking their clothes off. They're not really even paying attention. But when Jimmy Leyland did that reverse psychology meeting, I looked around the room, everyone was looking at him intently, and everyone was on board. He had our full attention. He would go around the room, 'Cangy, you go run your sprints! You be ready! That's how we win!' Or, it would be, 'Gary Sheffield, we're struggling; let us frickin' get on your back! You do this! You do that!' Or, 'Bobby Bonilla, you come in here! You do that!' Now we're playing as a team. Everybody listened to that. Everybody gravitated to that. And after that meeting, we were a different team."

In reality, Florida struggled in terms of wins and losses in September, going 12-15 in the final month of the season. Unlike Cangelosi's 1995 and 1996 Houston Astros teams which collapsed down the stretch and missed the postseason, though, his 1997 Marlins didn't fold. While they weren't able to catch Atlanta for the NL East title, they still made the postseason in just their fifth year of existence. The Kevin Brown-Alex Fernandez-Al Leiter trio might have started out 17-14 through mid-June, but the three aces pitched well down the stretch, combining to go 27-15. Livan Hernandez came up from the minors to win his first nine decisions. And while Sheffield was having an off-year—he had batted .315 with 42 homers and 120 RBIs in 1996 before slumping to .250 with 21 dingers and 71 RBIs—but he contributed in other ways. In a season which saw him spend two weeks on the disabled list with a sprained left thumb, Sheffield drew 121 walks, scored 86 runs and posted a .424 on-base percentage. His 21 homers were second on the team behind only Moises Alou, who led the club with 115 RBIs. Bobby Bonilla, the everyday third baseman, hit .297 and drove in 96 runs. Even Charles Johnson, known more for his throwing arm from behind the plate, contributed 19 homers.

And, Cangelosi, of course, delivered when he was called upon. On September 16 at Pro Player Stadium, he went 3-for-3 against Colorado, but it was his ninth-inning walk that was one of the keys as Florida rallied past the Rockies. Down 6-5, the Marlins had a runner on first with Cangelosi at the plate. Cangelosi, up there in an obvious bunting situation, took a strike before bunting the ball foul. With the count 0-and-2, Rockies closer Jerry Dipoto inexplicably threw four straight balls, putting Cangelosi on base. Three batters later, Bonilla smacked a walk-off grand slam, the first homer coughed up by Dipoto in 65 innings, to give Florida the dramatic 9-6 victory. "The grand slam is not really what puts a stake in your heart," Rockies skipper Don Baylor lamented later, pointing to the walk to Cangelosi that was maddening—especially since Cangy was up there to bunt and he instead reached base. "I'm more disturbed about that one than the grand slam," added Baylor.

Seven days later on September 23, Florida clinched the NL wild card, beating the Expos 6-3 in Montreal. The Marlins were going to the playoffs, ready to dethrone the Braves as league champions. "On paper they stack up well," Atlanta third baseman Chipper Jones had been quoted as saying in the *Rocky Mountain News* earlier that year of the Marlins. "But nothing's won on paper... I think everybody realizes that if you want to be the National League representative in the World Series, you have to go through Atlanta."

Cangelosi only scoffs when thinking back to the cockiness of the Braves, who ended up finishing nine games ahead of Florida in the NL East standings. "We had a better team offensively," he insists now. "We weren't afraid of them. We were ready for them. We were quite confident that in a seven-game series, we could beat the Atlanta Braves."

Chapter Eleven
Forever a World Champion

John Cangelosi… He was known for his defense, base running and handling of the bat. John was known for fouling off pitches and taking a walk. …a great bunter…
—Tom Gamboa, Indios de Mayaguez
manager (2017)

In 1997, Cangelosi was in the playoffs for the second time in his major-league career. The first time around in 1990, he wasn't on the active roster as the Pirates lost to Cincinnati in the NL Championship Series in the pre-wild card era. This time, Jim Leyland, believing Cangelosi could be counted upon in key situations in the late innings for a pinch-hitting role, included him on the postseason rosters. Cangy, as far as the manager was concerned, was a valuable member of the Marlins. "Cangelosi is a lot, to me, like the bullpen," Leyland had told a reporter from *USA Today* back in spring training. "If you can use him like you want to, and not because you have to, that's a real big plus for the ball club."

"That was huge," Cangelosi reflects. "I mean, you think about the history of the game. Many great players never made it to the postseason, let alone win a World Series. Thank God for the wild card, which allowed us to make the playoffs. But I mean, here I was, a guy who was too short to make it to the big leagues, a guy who wasn't supposed to stay in the major leagues, a guy nobody wanted for a few years in the '90s, a guy who was an underdog, a guy who played hard and got a lot out of his ability, having a chance to play in the playoffs and win a World Series. How cool was that?"

The Marlins' first playoff opponent were the San Francisco Giants, who'd stunned the baseball world by holding off the talented Dodgers to win the National League West. But in the best-of-five NL Division Series, San Francisco was no match for the Marlins. While the Giants' trio of Barry Bonds, J. T. Snow and Jeff Kent had combined for 97 home runs and 326 RBIs during the regular season, those three players drove in a total of just four runs in the NLDS. The Marlins swept the Giants, taking the first two games in walk-off fashion at Pro Player Stadium before winning Game Three at San Francisco's 3Com Park on Devon White's sixth-inning grand slam off Wilson Alvarez. Cangelosi, who'd batted .500 (16-for-32) from 1995 to 1997 off Giants pitching, had only one at-bat in the series, grounding out to short in a pinch-hit at-bat against left-hander Rich Rodriguez in the eighth inning of the second game. (While with the Astros in 1995 and 1996, Cangelosi batted .588 (10-for-17 in 1995) and .417 (5-for-12 in 1996) off Giants pitching. In 1997, he went 1-for-3 against San Francisco during regular-season play.)

On a ball club that also included outfielders Jim Eisenreich, Cliff Floyd and Alex Arias on the bench—as well as other reserve players including infielder Kurt Abbott, catcher-turned-first baseman Darren Daulton, infielder-outfielder John Wehner and backup catcher Gregg Zaun—Cangelosi wasn't going to get a lot of playing time in the postseason. And he accepted that fact. "I knew my role on that team," Cangelosi, who batted .245 in 192 regular-season at-bats in 1997, says matter-of-factly, without any hint of bitterness. "We had Moises Alou, Devon White and Gary Sheffield in the outfield. I knew that I could be pinch-hitting in the late innings if the game was close, if the matchup was right. It was about being ready in that role when the time came, when Jimmy Leyland called upon me. We had a really good team with a lot of good hitters and a great bench, and that's what winning was about, being there to support each other, being ready when it's your turn to go up there to bat."

Following the Giants series, the Marlins finally had their shot against Atlanta, the two-time defending National League champions, in the NL Championship Series. The Braves, who led the majors with 101 victories during the 1997 season and had appeared in four of the previous five World Series (winning it all in 1995), were widely regarded as the team of the '90s. With a starting rotation that included Hall-of-Famers-to-be Greg Maddux, Tom Glavine and John Smoltz, as well as a solid lineup featuring speedster Kenny Lofton (who'd averaged 65 stolen bases from 1992 to 1996 with Cleveland before swiping 27 bags in 1997, his first season in Atlanta) and sluggers Fred McGriff and Chipper Jones. The Braves were so deep that fourth starter Denny Neagle went 20-5 and seven players reached double figures in home runs.

Yes, the Marlins lineup included the hard-hitting bats of Sheffield, Alou and Bonilla—and the playoff experience of veterans White and Daulton—but how was Florida supposed to score enough runs against an Atlanta starting staff which had captured the last six NL Cy Young Awards—Glavine (1991), Maddux (1992-1995) and Smoltz (1996) were named the league's top pitchers in those seasons—and produced the league's only 20-game winner in 1997? As good as the Marlins' rotation of Brown-Fernandez-Leiter was, the Braves' staff, on paper, was clearly superior. Even if Florida somehow got past Maddux in Game One, there was Glavine, the 1995 World Series MVP, waiting in Game Two. And those two might not even be the best the Marlins would be facing. Smoltz, the Game Three starter, was arguably Atlanta's best big-game pitcher; he'd already pitched in three Game Sevens in his career—allowing a total of two runs in those starts—and would be ready when the NLCS shifted to Miami.

But the Marlins, according to Cangelosi, didn't fear the Big Bad Braves when the NLCS began; Florida, after all, won eight of the 12 games against Atlanta during the season. "We played them that year pretty good. I don't know if we were .500 against them or what. But that year, we weren't afraid of them," says Cangelosi now. "We were a better team offensively. We had a great team. Then we had a couple of additions with pitching. We had a couple of injuries; we lost Alex Fernandez [during the series with Atlanta]. But offensively, we had a good mixture. I feel like they just had more experience playing in the playoffs and all that other stuff. But at the end of the day, we had a great manager in Jimmy Leyland. He motivated us every game, every inning. And when you have that kind of a manager that you love playing for, it just gives you that extra confidence that you're gonna get the job done for him. Either team could've won that series, but in a short series we knew that we could beat them. If we got to their first two—Greg Maddux and Tom Glavine—we knew that we could beat them."

The Marlins certainly got the job done when the series began, capitalizing on shoddy Atlanta fielding in the early innings of Game One. Sparked by Moises Alou's three-run double in the first inning, Florida struck for five unearned runs off Maddux—thanks in part to fielding errors by McGriff at first base and Lofton in center field—and won 5-3 behind the five-hit pitching of Kevin Brown (who went six innings) and three relievers.

But there was trouble ahead for the Marlins. Alex Fernandez, who started Game Two, had been pitching hurt and would be knocked out in the third inning, as Atlanta cruised to a 7-1 victory to even the series. Results of his shoulder examination two days later in Florida revealed the star right-hander had a complete tear of his right rotator cuff, meaning he would miss the remainder of the postseason. "[In the clinching game against the Giants] he actually pitched [seven innings] and we won that game," said Cangelosi, who didn't play in Game One in Atlanta but had a pinch-hit at-bat in the second contest. "He pitched great. He pitched a great game. He might've been complaining about his arm in 'Frisco. And then he got one more start [against Atlanta]. We really didn't know anything until we got back to Florida. They kept things hush hush, so we didn't know anything on the flight home [following the split in Atlanta]. I mean, we knew his arm was hurting, but they waited until we got home to give him an MRI or something. Then, when we got home—or when we got to the stadium the next day— he was in the trainers' room crying, and obviously devastated. We all didn't know the severity of his injury until we got to the ballpark the next morning.

"Obviously, the loss was devastating. I mean, he was Alex Fernandez. He was our second guy or third guy in the rotation behind Kevin Brown. I don't remember if he was our second or third guy, but it was either Kevin Brown, Alex Fernandez and Al Leiter, in that order, or Brown, Leiter and Fernandez. Either way, when you lose Alex Fernandez, you're losing our personality, along with a pretty damn good pitcher in a seven-game series. From a team standpoint, that was obviously a devastating loss. The other thing was, from a personal standpoint, he was the personality of our team. He was a great guy. Fun. Kept everybody loose. Then, to have that personality go away right away… obviously, he couldn't be fun anymore because he was worried about his career. So, that was definitely devastating.

"But instead of feeling sorry for ourselves, I guess any good team rallies behind their injured [player], you know what I mean? We obviously put his number on our hats. And, you know, Alex was there with us. So, he wasn't pitching, but, you know, the kind of guy Alex was, he put all his worries aside, and he was a cheerleader, man. I mean, he was at every game, in the dugout, with all our emotions, the ups and downs, and he was into the game—where he could've easily been in the clubhouse or not even at the ballpark. He could've been worried about himself, but he was actually there wanting us to win and being a part of it. I mean, Alex is a great guy, a standup guy."

The loss of Fernandez wasn't the Marlins' only concern. Moises Alou, their top run producer, was bothered by a sore left wrist. The injury had occurred in the opening game in Atlanta when the left fielder banged that wrist against the outfield fence while leaping for a Ryan Klesko home run. With Alou not at a hundred percent and with Atlanta sending John Smoltz to the mound in Game Three, Jim Leyland decided to insert Cangelosi, the Smoltz-killer, into the starting lineup when the series shifted to Florida. "He's fine and he's ready to play," Leyland said of Alou prior to Game Three. "But he's not starting tonight… You read the numbers just like I have." The numbers Leyland was referring to, of course, were the career batting averages of Alou (3-for-27, .111) and Cangelosi (10-for-19, .526) against Smoltz. "Rather than take a chance against a guy like Smoltz, who [Alou] hasn't had success against, it made sense to rest him one more day," added the Marlins skipper.

"Jimmy Leyland is a numbers guy," says Cangelosi now. "John Smoltz and I had a lot of history. I charged the mound in 1994 against John Smoltz when I was with the Mets. There was a grand slam hit. I was on deck, [but] I thought, 'Well, he'll hit Bobby Bonilla [our cleanup hitter that afternoon]. He's not gonna hit me. I mean, who am I?' He ended up drilling me, and I just charged the mound.

"Fast forward to 1995. Terry Collins played me against him when I was with the Astros for the first time, and I went 3-for-4 against him [on May 27]. It had nothing to do with the fight. But I just saw the ball really good off of him. I saw the ball really well. So, we go into

Atlanta. You're stupid not to play me if I'd gone 3-for-4 against John Smoltz." Smoltz got the start in the opening game of that June series—and so did Cangelosi, who made Collins look like a genius. Cangelosi went 1-for-2 off him with a pair of walks, one of them intentional. He would be a combined 9-for-17 off Smoltz in 1995 and 1996. "McGriff came up to me and goes, 'Cangy, man. That guy's afraid of you. Every time he sees you in the lineup, man, he starts going crazy.' I just really saw the ball well off him. It had nothing to do with the fight. And in [the playoffs in] 1997, Jimmy Leyland started me against him. I hit the ball well. I hit the ball hard three times [including the final at-bat against reliever Mike Cather] but I didn't get a hit. I think I went 0-for-2 [off Smoltz] with a walk."

Down 2-1 to the Braves in the sixth, Cangelosi led off and lined out to center, failing to ignite a rally. The rest of the Marlins, though, came through against Smoltz. Edgar Renteria, Darren Daulton and Charles Johnson all stroked doubles off the future Hall of Famer, with Johnson's coming with the bases loaded and two outs. The Marlins, behind the relief work of Livan Hernandez, Dennis Cook and Robb Nen, shut out the Braves on just one hit over the final three innings in the 5-2 victory. (Tony Saunders, a rookie who went 4-6 on the season, started that game. Though he finished the year with a losing record, he went 3-0 with a 1.65 ERA against Atlanta and got the start over Al Leiter.)

Florida had taken a two-games-to-one series lead, but once again, there was more concern for Leyland. With Alex Fernandez done for the rest of the postseason, the Marlins needed Kevin Brown to step up in his scheduled Game Four start. Alas, their ace, bothered by a severe flu virus, would miss the contest, a 4-0 loss by Al Leiter, who took Brown's spot, to Denny Neagle, the Braves' fourth starter. With the series now 2-2, Leyland needed Brown even more, as Atlanta had Maddux, Glavine and Smoltz—three Hall-of-Famers-to-be and recipients of the past six NL Cy Young Awards—lined up for Games Five through Seven.

But once again, Brown could not pitch Game Five because of that flu, meaning the Marlins had to rely on Livan Hernandez, a rookie, against the four-time Cy Young winner Maddux. Hernandez had gotten the win in relief in Game Three—but had also gone 0-3 down the stretch after beginning his major-league career by winning nine consecutive decisions. How were the Marlins, without Brown and Fernandez, going to beat Maddux, Glavine and Smoltz? With Hernandez and fellow rookie Tony Saunders?

As it turned out, Livan Hernandez pitched the game of his life in Game Five, and Florida went ahead three games to two with a 2-1 victory. "He [had] pitched a few times [already]," recalls Cangelosi now, referring to the fact that Hernandez, having been part of the starting rotation during the regular season, was ready to go when called upon in the playoffs. "So, they knew what he could do. He was gonna be on our [playoff] roster anyway [and pitching out of the bullpen], and then when Alex got hurt [and Brown had the flu], he just went into the rotation. Obviously, the rest is history. But I'm telling you, man, the kid was awesome. Livan came in and, you know, we were just hoping to get innings out of him. We were just hoping that he would keep us in the game, and then turn it over to the bullpen in the sixth inning. We didn't really expect that he would be MVP of both series [the NLCS and World Series]. I mean, sometimes in those short series, you don't count on somebody, but at the end of the day, he becomes a hero like that. On a personal side, it was great for him. But it made us stronger. In a seven-game set, now we've got three quality starters. You know, and when you're going against guys like Maddux, Glavine and Smoltz, you gotta have guys on your side who can match up against them in a short series. But Livan stepped up, and I'm greatly appreciative of that.

"And we actually beat Maddux in Game Five. We kinda got into his head a little bit. And this came from Jim Leyland too. Greg Maddux worked quick all the time, and he threw strikes all the time. We had to get him out of his game plan. Our game plan was once in a while, everybody [would] step out, get him out of his rhythm, just kinda like piss him off a little bit. Don't let him continue with that groove where he gets the ball, throws it, gets the ball, throws it… Let's not be too aggressive too early in the count. He knows that you're gonna be swinging a lot, so he throws a lot of first-pitch change-ups. Very smart pitcher. Phenomenal off-speed pitcher. Changes speed. Our game plan was to get into his head a little bit. Step out, slow the game a little bit. Get into his head. Every time we got two strikes, we asked to check the ball. You know what I mean? That was basically just to ruffle his feathers, and it worked."

It only worked because Hernandez, starting only because of Fernandez's injury and Brown's flu, gave up just one run on three hits in a complete-game effort, striking out an NLCS-record 15 batters. That game is also remembered for the controversy surrounding an unusually wide strike zone given to Hernandez by home-plate umpire Eric Gregg. When reminded about Gregg's generous strike zone, Cangelosi says it was that way for both teams. He didn't feel sorry for the Braves, whose pitchers—particularly Maddux and Glavine—routinely benefited from wide strike zones during regular-season play.

"I mean, it is what it is. He called that game like that for both sides. It wasn't like it was uneven. It wasn't like we got all the calls and they didn't. He had a wide zone, and basically it was for both sides. If you looked back at the game, there were pitches that were three or four inches off the plate for both sides. And quite honestly, kudos to the Atlanta Braves—Greg Maddux, Glavine—had pinpoint control and they had their catcher set up on the outside part of the plate. For years, those guys had that perfected, and I have no argument that they deserved it. But their location was so good that they got pitches off the plate all the time. That's a craft. That's an art. They worked at it. They worked from the outer third off the plate. From a visual standpoint, it looked like a strike all the time. But from hitting, you know, it was three inches off the plate! For Bobby Cox to argue and all that stuff, I mean, they always got those calls. But in that particular game, both sides had the same big plate. And, you know, umpires are human. Eric Gregg was a great umpire for his whole career. That game, he was very consistent with three or four inches off the plate. Everybody got it. The Braves got it, and Livan Hernandez got it."

The Marlins had beaten Maddux but still needed to face Glavine and, if necessary, Smoltz. They received good news when Brown, who'd originally been scheduled to start Game Four (and then Game Five), finally returned to the mound with Florida just one win away from capturing the NL pennant. Perhaps inspired by their ace's return, the Marlins beat up an ineffective Glavine for four runs in the first inning. Atlanta got three runs off Brown in the first two frames to cut the deficit to 4-3, but the Marlins scored three more off Glavine in the sixth to put the game out of reach. The Braves plated one more run off Brown in the bottom of the ninth, but the Marlins ace, on his 140th pitch of the evening, got Chipper Jones to ground into a force play for a complete-game victory and the pennant for Florida.

It was also the first pennant for Leyland, who'd lost to the Braves in back-to-back NL Championship Series in 1991 and 1992 while with Pittsburgh. "Everybody wanted to win it so badly for Jimmy Leyland," says Cangelosi now. "He's the greatest manager I ever played for." And the Marlins had to beat, in his mind, the game's best left fielder, the Giants' Barry Bonds, to have a shot against Atlanta. "We were fortunate to be able to keep Barry in the ballpark and beat the Giants in the first round, but that wasn't easy because Barry was a great player," Cangelosi says. "Barry could beat you with his bat, with his glove, and with his speed. He could hit it out of the ballpark. He won seven MVP awards and eight Gold Gloves in his career, and he hit 762 homers in the big leagues. I know we swept the Giants in the first round in '97 but all those games were close. But it's a great feeling to beat the best to move on in the playoffs." What about the best pitchers too, on the Braves' staff, to get to the World Series?

Cangelosi doesn't think so. While he has Leyland and Bonds on his all-time team, that roster does not include Smoltz, Maddux, or Glavine. "Nolan Ryan would be my right-handed pitcher," begins Cangelosi. "What a class act. Just a tremendous pitcher with an intimidating presence on the mound. He won 324 games, threw a record seven no-hitters, and is the major-league leader in strikeouts, with 5,714. He threw hard in his 40s too, with a no-hitter at the age of 44 in 1991. The greatest right-hander in baseball history.

"Sandy Koufax would be my left-handed pitcher. I never saw him pitch, but Koufax was the greatest left-handed pitcher in baseball history. Four no-hitters and 40 career shutouts. Won 25 games three times with three Cy Young Awards. Injuries ended his career prematurely—but you can't leave the best left-hander in history off your all-time team!

"Mariano Rivera, the first player ever to be elected unanimously to the Hall of Fame, would be the closer. He goes into the Hall of Fame in 2019 with Harold Baines, my ex-White Sox teammate. With Mariano, what a dominant reliever. I mean, he was consistent and pitched with longevity in a role that usually sees very high turnover. He pitched for 19 seasons in the big leagues, and he was a closer for 17 of those years. And, obviously, Mariano's the career major-league leader with 652 saves. He had an incredible cut fastball that was almost like a slider. It was unhittable. And he threw it every day. Hitters knew it was coming and they still couldn't hit it. When he came out of the Yankees bullpen and stepped onto the mound, the game was over. He was incredible, the way he went through big-league hitters and dominated for all those years.

"At designated hitter, I've got to go with my ex-teammate, Harold Baines. He was a great hitter who was overlooked for many years for the Hall of Fame [before finally being voted in by the Today's Game Era Committee, a veterans committee]. He almost had 3,000 career hits, finishing with 2,866 in his career. Eight times he drove in 90 or more runs in a season, and he finished with 384 career home runs. He was an All-Star six times. A great hitter. Definitely belongs in the Hall of Fame. I think maybe a lot of people don't understand how good you have to be to do what Harold did. Pinch-hitting is a tough job, but DHing is essentially like pinch-hitting four times a night. And Harold did it for many, many years... He was great in that role, and I'm glad the veterans committee selected him for the Hall of Fame.

"Barry Bonds, Willie Mays and Mickey Mantle would be in the outfield. Willie was a five-tool player and defensively he was graceful in the outfield. He was great at charging the ball and throwing runners out. He could hit for power and he had speed on the base paths.

"Mickey could crush the ball. If he'd been healthy during his career, he would've hit a lot more home runs. He still hit 536 homers in the big leagues. Triple Crown winner [in 1956]. The greatest switch-hitter in the history of the game."

Then, things get interesting when first base is mentioned. Throughout the history of the game, many great players have played at "the other hot corner," but... "Did Babe Ruth play first base?" Cangelosi asks rhetorically. When told that Ruth did indeed play at least one game at first base in 10 different major-league seasons—and a total of 32 times in his career, including 23 starts—Cangelosi only smiles. "You gotta have Babe Ruth in there. He hit 714 homers, 60 in one year, and was part of those Yankees dynasty teams. You can't leave him out [of the all-time lineup].

"Pete Rose would be at second base. All-time hits leader, with 4,256. I gotta have Pete Rose in there. He played in a lot of positions—all three outfield positions, first base, third base—but he started his career at second base.

"Mike Schmidt would be the third baseman. Hit 548 homers in the big leagues. Three-time National League MVP. World Series MVP for the Phillies [in 1980]. Even though he was a power hitter, he was also known for his defense at third base. He's often considered the best third baseman in baseball history.

"[Derek] Jeter would be at shortstop. Had so many clutch hits for the Yankees in the playoffs. Had 3,465 hits in his career. Five-time World Series champion. Great player.

"Ivan Rodriguez would be at catcher. That's a tough one. It's a toss-up between Rodriguez and Johnny Bench. But I'll go with Ivan Rodriguez. He had the best arm in the game during the 1990s and won 13 Gold Gloves. Could hit for power and for average. Helped Texas get to the playoffs. Won a World Series with the Marlins in 2003. Helped the Tigers get to the World Series in 2006 under Jimmy Leyland..."

Cangelosi might get some arguments for some of the choices on his all-time team, but few Marlins would argue about Leyland's spot on that list. A big-league manager since 1986 with the Pirates, Leyland was long considered one of the best skippers in baseball—but a league pennant had eluded him during his managerial career until Florida broke through against Atlanta in 1997. "And after beating Atlanta," says Cangelosi, "we had one more step after that, winning the World Series."

While critics scoffed at the notion of the World Series being played in Florida—the first time ever the Fall Classic had arrived in the Sunshine State— Cangelosi couldn't care less. The afternoon before the World Series opener, Cangelosi and several Marlins players were seen tossing baseballs in right field at Pro Player Stadium while wearing T-shirts and shorts. Those were "the kind of shorts that kids wear in gym class and intramural basketball," one Boston scribe covering the 1997 World Series noted in *The Boston Herald*, adding that the hot, humid conditions in Miami weren't exactly the type of climate the Series should be played under. "Florida? This is not the way the game was designed," continued the scribe. "Baseball is supposed to begin in Florida, or Arizona, with wind sprints and split-squad doubleheaders and overnight stays in Punta Gorda. And baseball is supposed to end in some cold, autumnal northern city… in New York or Cincinnati or St. Louis or Pittsburgh…"

"Everybody was talking about the Florida weather," recalls Cangelosi. "But I didn't care about the weather. None of the players did. I mean, we would play in a blizzard if it meant we could be in a World Series. No problem. It just happened that we were playing for the Marlins and we had nice weather in Miami. It is what it is. But it was fun to get to the World Series. That's the ultimate goal of every Major League Baseball player, to get to the playoffs and play in the World Series."

* * *

The Marlins' World Series opponent was Cleveland, a team that hadn't won a world championship since 1948. It was the Indians' second appearance in the Series in three years, but it was also just their second appearance since 1954. Florida, meanwhile, was in the Fall Classic in only its fifth year of existence.

And while the Indians had a potent lineup two years earlier when they went 100-44 in the strike-shortened season, the 1997 team wasn't the same. Gone were sluggers Albert Belle and Eddie Murray, as well as fan favorite Carlos Baerga, the hard-hitting switch-hitting second baseman. Kenny Lofton, the speedy leadoff hitter and center fielder, had been traded to Atlanta in a controversial deal prior to the start of the regular season (with outfielders Marquis Grissom and David Justice heading to Cleveland). Veteran starter Dennis Martinez was also gone, while right-hander Jack McDowell's season ended in mid-May because of an arm injury. (McDowell wasn't around in 1995; he was signed as a free agent prior to the 1996 season. Over the previous seven seasons from 1990 to 1996, McDowell had been a workhorse, averaging 224 innings and 16 victories a year. He was also the AL Cy Young Award winner with Chicago in 1993, a year after being runner-up to Dennis Eckersley for the award.)

There was also the saga with closer Jose Mesa, who had an off-year with only 16 saves after recording 46 of them two years earlier. Mesa, who logged a 6.94 ERA during spring training in 1997, had lost his closer job to Mike Jackson early in the season. Through his first 19 regular-season appearances, Mesa had a 7.45 ERA and a record of 0-3 with three saves in five opportunities, prompting manager Mike Hargrove to hand the closer job to Jackson. Mesa regained the closer role in August, and pitched to a 0.52 ERA in his final 31 appearances. But the on-field struggles weren't the only crisis that he had to deal with in 1997. Prior to the start of the season, Mesa had to stand trial on charges of rape, felonious assault, theft and gross sexual imposition, with the charges relating to a complaint by two women who alleged the Cleveland reliever and a friend groped them after meeting in a nightclub in December. On April 9, 1997, the jury found Mesa not guilty of all charges.

And although they had won the AL Central for the third consecutive year, the Indians had gone just 86-75 during the season—only the fourth-best won-loss record in the American League (behind Baltimore, New York and Seattle)—and were underdogs in both the Division Series and AL Championship Series. The Indians did manage to upset the Yankees and Orioles to claim the AL pennant, but the Marlins, after dispatching both the Giants and Braves, were ready for them.

Regardless, Cleveland probably should have won the World Series, beating Kevin Brown twice and battering Al Leiter and Tony Saunders in two other contests. But the Marlins managed to defeat Orel Hershiser twice, beating the Cleveland ace 7-4 and 8-7 in Games One and Five behind Livan Hernandez (and their big bats). (In a postseason which featured many surprises, several aces went 0-2 during their playoff series. While Brown and Hershiser were each 0-2 in the 1997 World Series, they were not the only ones in that year's postseason. Seattle's Randy Johnson went 0-2 in the Division Series, Greg Maddux was 0-2 for Atlanta in the NLCS, and Andy Pettitte was 0-2 for the Yankees in the Division Series.) The Marlins also managed to rally for a wild, 14-11 victory in Game Three—bailing out Leiter, who was roughed up for seven runs in 4.2 innings—by striking for 11 runs over the final four innings to overcome a 7-3 deficit. Yes, it was a contest that saw 25 runs being scored, but because that game was played in Cleveland, in an American League ballpark, the designated hitter was used—and Cangelosi didn't come off the bench to make an appearance. That rally in Game Three, though, was surpassed in Game Five, when the Marlins trailed Hershiser 4-2 going into the sixth. But in that inning, Moises Alou delivered his second three-run home run off Hershiser in the Series, putting Florida ahead to stay.

"Moises had an awesome Series," Cangelosi recalls fondly. "With the Marlins, I hung out with Moises Alou. It's funny because his locker was just down the way from mine in the Marlins' clubhouse. It was funny because the year before, in 1996, there was that brawl between the Astros and the Montreal Expos. I played for the Astros and Moises was with Montreal." Cangelosi and Alou didn't fight each other that night, but they were both ejected from that contest for their roles in the brawl. "But we laughed about it. We joked about it all the time. It was kinda funny we were in that thing the year before, and now we were on the same team trying to win a World Series."

Cangelosi did get into Game One as a pinch-hitter, batting for reliever Jay Powell with Florida already ahead by three runs in the eighth inning. Facing southpaw Paul Assenmacher, Cangelosi struck out swinging on the fourth pitch, a big curveball low in the dirt where Cangy couldn't check his swing. That came one pitch after he had hammered a high fastball from Assenmacher to deep left field that went foul. That eighth-inning at-bat was his lone plate appearance of the evening, but he did see some unexpected action in the dugout two innings earlier, when Livan Hernandez came out of the ballgame. After Hernandez had given up a one-out home run to Jim Thome and back-to-back singles, he struck out Jeff Branson for the second out in the sixth. But he'd already thrown 101 pitches, and in the era of teams monitoring pitchers' pitch counts and starters being removed after having reached 100 pitches for the evening, the rookie pitching sensation was pulled in favor of left-hander Dennis Cook. The fiery Hernandez walked to the dugout, accepted a few high-fives from teammates, and then threw a violent tantrum. NBC television cameras, in fact, caught him throwing his hat and glove away violently and kicking something in his path in the corner of the dugout. When he stormed up the tunnel toward the clubhouse, Cangelosi tried to restrain him. "There wasn't any conflict between me and Livan Hernandez," Cangelosi explains. "He wasn't mad about being taken out of the game. He was mad about his pitching, and I just wanted to make sure he didn't hurt himself."

Cangelosi wouldn't see any action in the next four games. He wouldn't have minded playing in the cold weather in the three games in Cleveland—Games Three through Five—as the Series went from the warm climate in Miami to the frigid temperatures in Northeast Ohio, but there was no role for him as the designated hitter was used in the AL ballpark. There was no pinch-hitting for pitchers or double switches. "I hated playing in the cold," he says now. "But I mean, throughout my career, at the beginning of the season, you played in 40-degree weather. It really wasn't foreign to use because you played in cold weather at the beginning of the year. In Game Five, I believe, in Cleveland, it was snowing in batting practice. It was cold. But we were used to it. Both sides had to play in it. Don't get me wrong; I'd rather play in the heat. It is what it is. You just had to deal with it. It is cold but you had to get through it. At the time, a couple of the games, it was extremely cold. It got close to where they were gonna reschedule the games because of the coldness. I don't wanna downplay it, but we'd played in cold weather before [so the Marlins didn't mind going out there to compete]. In Game Five, they were close to rescheduling that game. It was close."

The Marlins went home with a three-games-to-two lead and had Kevin Brown on the mound in Game Six, ready to close out the Series. But Cleveland handed him a 4-1 loss—Brown's second defeat of the Series—thanks to the bat and arm of unheralded pitcher Chad Ogea, who drove in two runs on a bases-loaded single while allowing just four hits over five-plus innings. Ogea, who'd lost both of his starts in the AL Championship Series, even doubled and scored on a sacrifice fly for the Indians' final run of the night. With the score 4-1 in the seventh, Cangelosi finally got into the contest. With a runner on first and none out, Cangelosi pinch-hit for reliever Felix Heredia and singled to center off Indians set-up man Mike Jackson, bringing the tying run to the plate. (That single turned out to be the only hit of Cangelosi's career in World Series play.)

Shelly Dunkel, Cangelosi's old high school baseball coach, was in the stands at Pro Player Stadium in Game Six with his family—and was proud of his former player. Cangelosi, Dunkel says, worked hard throughout his baseball life and deserved his moment in the spotlight. "It was a thrill to see Johnny play in the World Series, and we were all so happy to see him not only play in the Series but also get a hit," the coach says now. "If you look back at the history of the game, not too many guys can say they got a hit in the World Series. But Johnny did it that night."

Tommy Sandt, the Marlins' first-base coach, wasn't surprised that Cangelosi came through against a tough set-up man like Mike Jackson, who'd served as the Tribe's stopper earlier in the season when regular closer Jose Mesa struggled. "You know, Cangy had a lot of guts. He was a gutsy player," says Sandt. "He was determined; he wasn't gonna let anything stop him. That's one thing about him—being the height he was. Most guys wouldn't even try to play in the big leagues. He had a 10-year career out of it. He was a competitor. A true competitor. I think John knew his role. He was trying to get on base. It was to get a rally started. It wasn't easy to throw strikes to him because he was a small target and he had a good eye. He would make the guy work, which benefited everybody, but his main job was to get on base, not to let everyone see what [the closer] was throwing. With closers, [the players already] know what he's throwing. [Cangelosi] would work guys for a walk as much as anything. It wasn't just to see what the guy was throwing. That did happen, but his job was to get on base."

He did that in the seventh inning of Game Six. The tying run was now at the plate with nobody out, with the top of the Marlins' batting order coming up. But alas, Jackson, who remained in the game, fanned both Devon White (who would hit a triple in the ninth with nobody on base) and Edgar Renteria for the first two outs, walked Gary Sheffield to load the bases, and then got Bobby Bonilla to pop out to center. That was as close as Florida got to tying the game—as Paul Assenmacher and Mesa then came on and pitched effectively to get the final six outs—and the Series was extended to a seventh game.

The Series came down to extra innings in the seventh game at Pro Player Stadium on Sunday, October 26, 1997. Cleveland went ahead 2-0 on a two-run single by Tony Fernandez off Al Leiter in the third inning before Bonilla homered off Indians rookie starter Jaret Wright leading off the seventh to put the Marlins on the scoreboard. (Wright was looking to be the first rookie since Pittsburgh Pirates right-hander Babe Adams in 1909 to start and win the seventh game of a World Series. The Cleveland pitcher would fail to do so, and it wasn't until 2002 when the feat was accomplished again as Anaheim Angels rookie John Lackey joined Adams in the record books by starting and defeating the San Francisco Giants in the seventh game of that year's World Series.) In the ninth, Florida tied it against Jose Mesa—with Craig Counsell delivering a sacrifice fly to cash in Moises Alou from third base—sending the game into extras. Cangelosi, who hadn't gotten into the game through nine innings, would get his opportunity in the 10th.

"In Game Six, I got a pinch hit, a base hit," Cangelosi recalls. "In Game Seven, I struck out. I came up in a situation where a hit would've won the game. That kinda still haunts me. I'm over it. But sometimes, I'll dwell on it. That moment was so severe. People really don't realize that, you know, in past history, a lot of players could not get by that. Some have committed suicide over it."

Indeed. There was the sad story of Donnie Moore, the California Angels closer best known for giving up a home run to Boston outfielder Dave Henderson in the 1986 AL Championship Series with the Angels one strike away from advancing to the World Series for the first time in franchise history. California never won another game that October, blowing a 3-1 series lead. Moore, meanwhile, never recovered from that home run. He committed suicide less than three years later, shooting his estranged wife three times before putting the gun to his own head.

Fast forward to 1997, and Cangelosi's big moment came in the bottom of the 10th inning in Game Seven of the World Series, with the Indians and Marlins tied 2-2 and two men on. Mesa, still in the game despite blowing the lead in the ninth, had given up back-to-back one-out singles to Edgar Renteria and Gary Sheffield. With reliever Robb Nen due up to bat, Leyland sent in Cangelosi to pinch-hit against the tiring Mesa.

Here was John Cangelosi, batting in extra innings in the seventh game. A guy too short to play in the big leagues. A guy not good enough to be a regular on the White Sox or the Mets. Or the Rangers. A guy not good enough to make it onto the big-league rosters in Detroit or Milwaukee. Yet, the undersized "Kid from Nowhere," improbably, had a chance to be the hero in the 1997 World Series.

First pitch from Mesa, low and in. Ball one.

The second pitch, swing and a miss at a low offering, 1-and-1.

Cangelosi took the next pitch, which was right down the middle for a called strike, and the count was now 1-and-2.

The next offering was high. Ball two, 2-and-2. Cangelosi breathed a sigh of relief and stepped out of the box to gather his thoughts.

The 2-and-2 pitch was low and in. Ball three. Cangelosi again called time and stepped out of the box. The count was full. One more pitch outside of the strike zone, and the bases would be loaded with just one out. "I didn't wanna let Jimmy Leyland down in that situation. I wasn't nervous to be up there with the World Series on the line. I mean, a hit would've won it right there…"

The 3-and-2 pitch from Mesa was a breaking ball that seemed low—and Cangelosi took the pitch thinking it was ball four—but home-plate umpire Ed Montague instead rung Cangy up. Strike three called.

Cangelosi headed back to the bench, and the game continued on. At that juncture, Charles Nagy came on in relief and retired Moises Alou on a pop-up and the Indians escaped the jam.

Marlins first-base coach Tommy Sandt remembers that night vividly. He, like all of the Marlins and the 67,204 fans in attendance, was hoping for a Series-winning hit in that inning. For Sandt, it would have been fitting had Cangelosi been the World Series hero. But it wasn't meant to be. "He played an important role for us," says Sandt now about Cangelosi's value on that 1997 ball club. "In fact, he pinch-hit in the seventh game of the World Series. I was hoping somebody would get a hit! I was hoping he would be the guy to get the hit. He's a guy who worked hard every day at his craft—and you'd love to see a guy like Cangy be the one who got that hit for us. Unfortunately, he didn't, but it would've been nice to see him do that."

Cangelosi remembers that at-bat well, too. He could have gone down in World Series lore, joining Joe Carter (1993 Toronto Blue Jays), Gene Larkin (1991 Minnesota Twins), Bill Mazeroski (1960 Pittsburgh Pirates), Billy Martin (1953 New York Yankees), Goose Goslin (1935 Detroit Tigers), Bing Miller (1929 Philadelphia Athletics) and Earl McNeely (1924 Washington Senators) as the only players who delivered walk-off hits in the final game of the World Series. (The 1912 Series also ended on a walk-off, on Red Sox infielder Larry Gardner's game-ending sacrifice fly against the New York Giants.) To this day, striking out against Mesa still haunts Cangelosi. "I mean, it was the most elevated experience I was ever in. I wasn't nervous. I was excited to be in that situation. If you fail in that situation, you feel like you let your team and your [coaching] staff down. I'm still struggling with the fact I feel like I let Jimmy Leyland down in that position. And it just stays with you. That's one chapter when you get older, you circle back and you talk to your friends. And you thank people for [giving you that opportunity]. You look back at your story and you wanna thank people for opening a certain door. You wanna thank people, like, 'Hey, if you weren't there at this particular time, maybe I wouldn't have been here.' That's one story that I wanna close. It sounds stupid, but I'd like to call Jimmy Leyland myself and say, 'Hey man, I'm sorry that I didn't come through for you in that position.'"

While that at-bat was the most elevated experience for Cangelosi as a major-leaguer, it didn't mean he hadn't been involved in late-game dramatics in big games prior to that moment. There was the time in 1990 when he was a pinch-runner and scored from third base on a sacrifice fly to plate the go-ahead run as the Pittsburgh Pirates clinched the NL East title. There was the final weekend of the 1995 season at Wrigley Field, when his Houston Astros were battling for a wild-card spot and Cangelosi collected four hits over the final two games—including a game-winning, seventh-inning RBI single in the penultimate game.

But Game Seven of the World Series was obviously the bigger stage and, to this day, he still feels he let Jim Leyland down. He still feels the need to, someday, find closure. "I know it sounds stupid, but I would like to call up Jimmy Leyland and say sorry," Cangelosi continues. "I'd been a utility player for a few years in the big leagues. When I'm up there, I try to contribute with each at-bat. My position was to be in pressure situations all the time, be prepared in those late-inning situations. There are no excuses. I shouldn't have let Jimmy Leyland down in that situation."

Cangelosi's thoughts then go to former Boston Red Sox first baseman Bill Buckner, who infamously allowed a Mookie Wilson ground ball go through his legs as the New York Mets won Game Six of the 1986 Series. The Red Sox then lost Game Seven, and Buckner, for years, was crucified by the Boston fans and media. Despite collecting 2,715 hits in his major-league career—and being the 1980 NL batting champion—he is remembered today for that one error. "Look what it'd done to Buckner for missing the ground ball," laments Cangelosi. "He had to move his family. The man should be in the Hall of

Fame, and [yet] everyone remembers him for missing the ground ball."

In the 1997 Series, it was another infielder who would wear the goat horns: Indians second baseman Tony Fernandez, whose two-run single would have been the Series-winning hit had the Marlins not come back in the ninth. Bonilla led off the 11th inning with a single, and with one out Craig Counsell squibbed a roller between first and second that could have been turned into an inning-ending double play. But Fernandez, who had hit the ALCS-clinching homer to send the Tribe to the Series, muffed the squibbing grounder instead, putting two Marlins on. An intentional walk loaded the bases, and with two outs, Edgar Renteria lined a slider up the middle off Charles Nagy, and the Marlins were the World Champions.

It was an improbable championship. The Indians' defeat, according to *Sports Illustrated*, marked the first time in the history of the World Series that a team began the ninth inning of Game Seven with the lead and lost. It had never happened before in 92 previous World Series played. But for Cangelosi and the rest of the Marlins, it didn't matter. They were champions. And when the ball went off Nagy's glove and into center field, bringing home the Series-winning run, one of the first people Cangelosi thought about was Walt Widmayer, the old White Sox scout who'd passed away less than a year earlier. "Walt was the one who drafted me, and I get goose bumps thinking about that night when we won the World Series," Cangelosi explains. "For me, it all came full circle. That night, during the celebration, I remembered my last conversation with Walt. He told me he was so proud of me and told me I had a great career."

Back in the clubhouse after Game Seven, Cangelosi's thoughts then went to all the baseball coaches he'd had in his life. "Shelly Dunkel was my baseball coach in high school and Carlos Perez was the assistant coach. You just remember the things they taught you and the impact they had in your life. Everything really came full circle." Of course, Cangelosi's thoughts also went to Demie Mainieri, his college baseball coach, and Demie's son Paul. "[Back in high school] I just played really, really well against [Paul Mainieri's team]. There was one specific game where we went extra innings, and they intentionally walked me with the bases loaded. Those were some great games. And that's how the ball started rolling. Paul Mainieri went to his dad and said, 'Hey man, you gotta go see this little kid play at Miami Springs.' That's how I got recruited. Paul Mainieri recruited for his dad, and his dad basically came to my house to sign me. And if it wasn't for Demie, talking to the scout Walt Widmayer, I would never have known that I had to switch-hit to get to the big leagues, and Demie helped me through that.

"And there's another story with me and Demie, which is kinda touching. The scout, Walt Widmayer, came to my house. I was a fourth-round pick. Walt goes, 'Hey, look. There's no negotiation. I believe that your son can play in the big leagues. I'm gonna offer your son $20,000. It's not negotiable. Let me know if you wanna take it.' I excused myself and went into my mom's bedroom and I called Demie. 'Doc, what do I do? He just offered me $20,000. I mean, I don't wanna leave you. I wanna play baseball for you.' I felt like I was leaving Doc after all the good things he'd done for me; it was like I had a sense of loyalty to him. It happens all the time in junior college. I guess that's why you go there—to get drafted. He said, 'John, as much as I want you on my team, that's a very fair offer. You need to take it, and you need to start your career. I wish you nothing but the best.' Doc gave me his blessing. He could've easily been selfish and said, 'Hey, no, no, no. Stay with me.' But in that conversation, he was more concerned about my welfare."

Paul Mainieri isn't surprised that Cangelosi made it to the big leagues and played long enough to win a World Series ring. "I wasn't surprised," says the younger Mainieri, "because I thought Johnny Cangelosi was one of the best ballplayers I ever saw, as a player and then in my short time as a coach at that point. I'm 60 years old now, and I was only 23 back then—22 or 23, I can't remember exactly—but I thought Johnny was one of the best players, the most electric players, and dominating players, that I'd ever seen. I mean, I fell in love with him as a ballplayer and that's why I made such a strong recommendation [to my father]. I wasn't surprised at all that he got to the major leagues or that he had a long career in the major leagues. The only thing, I guess, that would've made me surprised was administrators and executives in Major League Baseball seem to think that a little guy doesn't have the ability to play in the major leagues. And Johnny was considered 'a little guy.' But he had to prove himself all the way up, and he did. When he got his opportunity, he took advantage of it."

In Paul Mainieri's mind, the fact that Cangelosi had a chance to play in the World Series was something he and his father were proud of. It was a big deal because Cangelosi was doing it for all the smaller players out there, to give them hope and inspiration. In the seventh game of the Series, there was the undersized Cangelosi, batting in extra innings with a chance to drive in the winning run. And while he didn't deliver the winning base hit, his team still went on to win the World Series. "I didn't stay in close touch with Johnny through the years but every time we saw each other, we would reminisce about those days when he was playing in high school and I was coaching in high school," Mainieri continues.

"He stayed very close with my father, and my father was always very proud of Johnny. Speaking for my father, he's very proud of Johnny's career, probably as proud of him as any player he ever had—because my dad's a little guy and I'm a little guy. My dad used to tell me all the time that little guys had to go to the ballpark and prove they could play, whereas big guys had to prove they couldn't play. It's just a natural human perception that when people are big and physical, they must be good athletes, and little guys are insufficient. But when a little guy like Johnny made it to the big leagues and did well, I think it gave my father a little bit of an extra sense of pride, to see one of the players who played for him be able to make it to the major leagues."

Shelly Dunkel, Cangelosi's old high school baseball coach, was one of the 67,204 in attendance at Pro Player Stadium that night. A baseball coach for 37 years, he considers Cangelosi one of his favorite players. Naturally, he was proud that his former player was a World Champion. "I was ecstatic," Dunkel says now. "I was at the ballgames, including the seventh game, with one of my grandsons. We were just ecstatic. I remember everything about Johnny. He was one of my favorite dudes. I can remember the first day I met him. He was a

10th grader. His mother brought him out to practice and said, 'He's a little bit afraid of you for your reputation... His friends played for you and they said you're a tough guy!' But we ended up being friends. Johnny was a gamer. That's what he was for me for three years. He had a stolen-base record for three years with my ball club. And he was just a great kid to have.

"It was a long-time Chicago White Sox scout, Walt Widmayer, who signed him. Walt came over to me and said, 'Shelly, you think this kid can play pro ball?' I told him, 'Absolutely, I think he can play.' He'd signed two of my kids prior to Johnny, and he wound up signing Johnny as well. So, I always thought Johnny could play pro ball. But getting to the big leagues is another story. Not too many guys go to the big leagues. But he played 10 years. Not too many guys can say that. And he won a World Series, in front of his family in Miami. I was just ecstatic, just so proud of Johnny."

"It's a great story," Cangelosi acknowledges today about being a member of a World Series champion. "You know, if my story was a movie script shown to a Hollywood producer, he would say, 'Nah, it couldn't happen in real life.' But it did in real life. An underdog like me, an undersized player—a guy who's 5-8—making it to the big leagues against all odds, getting sent down a few times and being out of a big-league job, and now his team wins the World Series? It's a great inspirational story for anybody who's ever had any doubts about what they're doing. You know, it could happen in real life. It did for me. You know, there are others out there not blessed with a lot of size. They can make it just like I did."

Of course, he is thankful to the two managers he had in his final seasons in the big leagues. "I wouldn't have been in a situation to win a World Series if not for Terry Collins, who played me and gave me my at-bats the two years I was in Houston. Then Jimmy Leyland called me to say he wanted me on the Marlins. He said, 'Hey man, I've got something brewing. Just keep watching the news. It ain't over yet.' Obviously, it wasn't because he thought I was a nice guy. Jimmy was trying to build a winning ball club—he signed Moises Alou, Alex Fernandez, Bobby Bonilla, [and] Jim Eisenreich—and he appreciated what I'd done for him in Pittsburgh and knew I could still contribute in the big leagues. He knew I could play any outfield position if one of the guys needed a day off. He knew I could still run and steal bases. He knew I was still an effective pinch-hitter from either side of the plate, that I would be prepared whenever he called upon me to come up in a pressure situation.

"I mean, that Marlins team was a great team, and for Jimmy to stick his neck out for me and have me on that ball club was flattering. And then when Edgar Renteria got that base hit to win Game Seven... there's just no way to express my feelings about winning a World Series. Just no words for it. Everything that I'd gone through as a player, the successes and the failures, I wouldn't change for the world."

Chapter Twelve
The Final Seasons

He was the perfect player for us. He could fill in on the Sundays after a Saturday night game. He could give us a spark and he was great to have on the club. He never complained about his playing time and was just the perfect fit.

> —Jim Leyland, Florida Marlins manager,
> as told to *USA Today* (1998)

The Florida Marlins won the World Series in 1997, but Cangelosi, like the other players on the team, knew there would be no chance for the club to repeat. Frustrated by poor attendance—the club drew 2.36 million fans, a figure good only for 11th out of the 28 major-league clubs, or just over 29,000 per game—and his failure to swing a deal for a new ballpark built with taxpayer money, club owner H. Wayne Huizenga ordered the Marlins' roster dismantled following the World Series. Huizenga, who had, in fact, announced his intention to sell the team during the summer of 1997, claimed in the off-season he suffered a financial loss of $34 million running the club that year and was unwilling to continue losing even more money. And so, just weeks after winning the Fall Classic, the billionaire owner elected to purge the payroll rather than give the ball club another shot at competing for the postseason in 1998.

Cangelosi acknowledges that the players knew during the championship year that things would be different the following season. "In 1997, we won the World Series. We had a perfect team, perfect chemistry. We had the perfect staff. The perfect bench. Everybody had their roles. Everything was good. Even that year, Wayne Huizenga came in and said, 'Hey, from a financial standpoint, from a business standpoint, next year we might not have this. But I'm gonna let you guys know, I'll do anything this year. Buy a player, do whatever, so that we can win this World Series.' And he honored that. And he actually came out years later after he dismantled his team, and he said he made a bad business decision; he listened to the wrong people. After all of the veteran players were traded, we had one pitcher on that staff, Livan Hernandez. Everyone else was gone. We had no outfield. Edgar Renteria was the only one left."

By May 1998—just seven months after World Series glory—the Marlins had become a completely different ball club, with outfielders Moises Alou (Houston), Devon White (Arizona) and Gary Sheffield (Los Angeles) each traded to another National League team. Also gone were closer Robb Nen (San Francisco), first baseman Jeff Conine (Kansas City), third baseman Bobby Bonilla (Los Angeles), catcher Charles Johnson (Los Angeles), along with pitchers Kevin Brown (San Diego), Al Leiter (Mets) and Dennis Cook (Mets). All of the moves were made to dump payroll, with the Marlins receiving prospects in return. Right-hander Alex Fernandez, in the second year of his $35 million contract, was not traded; however, the torn rotator cuff he suffered during the NL Championship Series kept him sidelined for the entire 1998 season.

For a while, it seemed even Cangelosi was on his way out. Rumors during the spring had him going to Atlanta—with Boston, San Francisco, Kansas City, the Mets and the Dodgers also reportedly interested in the services of the switch-hitting outfielder—leaving him to answer all sorts of questions about his status on a daily basis. "It's tough to take, but I have no control over it," Cangelosi, who had been told for months that he'd likely be traded as the Marlins continued to cut salary, told *USA Today* then. "Everybody talks about it, so I can't really get away from it. They want to know, 'Are you here? Are you there?'… I can say I want to stay here over and over, but it's not going to matter. It's up to [management] and I really have no say in the matter. I just want to be with a team that wants me." But the Braves, along with the other teams, pulled back in the final week of spring training, and Cangelosi remained a Marlin when the 1998 season began.

When the Marlins traded Sheffield, along with Bonilla, Johnson, outfielder Jim Eisenreich and rookie pitcher Manuel Barrios to the Dodgers in a blockbuster move in May, future Hall-of-Fame catcher Mike Piazza and third baseman Todd Zeile were the players who came to Miami. Piazza, however, didn't stay with the Marlins long; he was dealt to the Mets eight days following the trade. The rebuilding Marlins also traded Zeile to Texas on July 31. That meant, out of all the free agents the Marlins signed in the 1996 off-season (including the manager), only Leyland and Cangelosi were left while Fernandez was injured.

"Eisenreich got traded when we traded Sheffield," Cangelosi says now. In return, the Marlins received a future Hall-of-Fame catcher, but Cangelosi, who had previously been teammates with other Hall-of-Fame catchers in Ivan Rodriguez and Carlton Fisk, didn't get a chance to know his new Florida teammate much. "Piazza was a nice guy, but very quiet. He was just quiet, to himself. Nice guy. If you talked to him, he talked to you. But he was there with us for only a week; it was a very short-lived thing. He wasn't there for very long. Really nice guy but really quiet. He was really private."

Although Cangelosi wound up staying in Florida for the entire 1998 season, he says now that there was at least one contender interested in his services that summer. With the Chicago Cubs dealing with injuries to outfielders Lance Johnson and Brant Brown in June, it was reported in multiple newspapers that the club inquired about Cangelosi. But during the All-Star break in early July, the Cubs opted instead to claim veteran outfielder Glenallen Hill, a right-handed power hitter, off waivers from the Seattle Mariners. Two weeks later, they picked up minor-league outfielder Derrick White off the waiver wire from the Colorado Rockies. Cangelosi, meanwhile, ended up staying with the Marlins, and watched as the Cubs signed third baseman Gary Gaetti (released by St. Louis) in August and outfielder Orlando Merced (released by Boston) in early September.

According to his recollection, Cangelosi could have—and should have—gone to Chicago too. He was, as he remembers now, nearly a late-season acquisition but the deal fell through at the last minute. "The Cubs were gonna pick me up off the waiver wire [right after the August 31] deadline in '98," Cangelosi recalls today. In baseball, following the July 31 trade deadline, teams can still make trades. In August and September, a major-league player must first pass through revocable waivers before his team can trade him without restriction, with August 31 being the deadline for teams to acquire players and have them be eligible for the postseason roster. After July 31, it's common for teams to place players on revocable waivers—in fact, sometimes clubs place their entire rosters on waivers—and Cangelosi was one player the Marlins placed on the wire in 1998.

"Jimmy Leyland called me into his office," continues Cangelosi. "He goes, 'Cangy, I got you traded. It's awesome, man! You're gonna go to the Cubs. Pack your bags. It looks like the Cubs are gonna take you. Just come into my office tomorrow, and we'll see what happens.'" The Cubs, in a three-way battle with the Mets and Giants for the NL wild card, were interested in acquiring him, according to what the Marlins skipper was telling him. "There was gonna be a deal that was made where I was going to the Cubs. But then, when I got to the office the next day, I found out that the deal fell through because Orlando Merced went on the waiver wire as well, and then they frickin' took him for their pinch-hitting role instead of me—because they wanted a guy off the bench with more pop instead of a base stealer."

It is understandable that Cangelosi feels like he missed out. He'd been bypassed earlier that summer when the Cubs decided not to trade for him, opting instead to sign Glenallen Hill once the power-hitting outfielder became available. It became agonizing as he read the Cubs' transactions in the papers throughout that summer. But he especially remembers being upset about the Merced situation. With Hill already on the Chicago bench, the Cubs were adding a similar type player—a guy with some pop—when the more logical move might have been to pick up a guy with some speed? "That kinda screwed me out of coming home to Chicago," Cangelosi adds. "It would've been perfect because I had family in the Chicago area. I was well liked in Chicago because I was a blue-collar type player, and I could've been a guy who came off the bench to pinch-run for somebody [and] steal a base late in the game, or pinch-hit late in the game... It was a done deal; the Cubs were gonna get me. But then, when Orlando went on the wire, they decided to go with a different type of player off the bench, which was him."

Merced, who arrived too late in Chicago to make the postseason roster, went 3-for-10 for the Cubs and hit a dramatic game-ending, three-run homer on September 12 against Milwaukee. That victory, one of eight walk-off wins on the year for the Cubs, gave Chicago sole possession of the NL's lone wild-card spot with two weeks remaining. Chicago, led by Sammy Sosa and his 66 home runs, went on to defeat San Francisco in a one-game playoff before being swept by Atlanta in the division series.

Cangelosi missed out on being part of that wild-card race. And although he wouldn't have been eligible for the postseason had he been picked up by the Cubs in September, he feels he lost out just the same. "The reason why that was kinda a really big thing for me is that if I could've got traded to the Cubs—or to any team, for that matter, that really needed a good role player—I probably could've played in the big leagues for another year or two. But I was with the Marlins [on a bad team] in '98 on the last year of my contract—at the age of 33, I think I was—it was hard for me to get a big-league job the following year.

"But if I'd gone to a team that was winning and it was a solidified utility role—and I was really good at what I did—and if I played well for the Cubs if I got traded there, then I would've had a job the following year. So, that kinda pushed me out, so to speak. If we don't dismantle the Marlins [after] '97, I could probably have had another two-year deal with Leyland there, in my role. But paying me what they were paying me, on a team that was gonna lose over 100 games... they cleaned house."

His comment about possibly staying with the Marlins—had they not been dismantled—appears to be a valid one. The ball club "*was* well-positioned for the future," baseball writer Rob Neyer opined years later in his 2003 book, *Rob Neyer's Big Book of Baseball Lineups*. "If owner Wayne Huizenga hadn't taken the money and run, there's no reason why the Marlins couldn't have challenged the Braves for National League East primacy for the next two or three seasons, at least." Even Leyland admitted in 1999 that he thought, when he signed on to be the manager in October 1996, the team was going to be battling for a pennant every year until at least 2001. While he didn't think the Marlins were ready to win it all in 1997, he believed the core players would at least stay together and the ball club would contend for several seasons. "My plan in Florida was totally different than it turned out... I had a five-year deal. We thought we were going to be competitive for five years," the Marlins skipper reflected when speaking to a reporter with the *Rocky Mountain News* in 1999, after he, too, had left the club. "There were no ifs, ands, or buts about it. I thought we'd have a chance to be in the World Series in 1998. I didn't think we'd get there in '97. But after the All-Star Game, it came together like hellbent for election. You could smell it."

Cangelosi did reach two milestones before the 1998 season ended. On August 12 in Los Angeles, he started in center field and went 1-for-4 as the Marlins beat the Dodgers 3-2. It was the 1,000th game of his major-league career. In the first game of a doubleheader against Philadelphia on September 27— the Marlins' penultimate game of the season— Cangelosi started in left field and went 3-for-3 with two walks. The third hit, an infield single off Phillies reliever Mike Welch in the sixth inning, gave him 500 base hits for his career. His second hit, meanwhile, drove in the first run of a six-run fifth inning against Tyler Green as the Marlins won 6-5. "I mean, when I was growing up, obviously I dreamed of playing in the big leagues... but for me to have a chance to get to 1,000 games in the big leagues and to have 500 hits... that just goes to show that if you're determined and you stick with it, no matter what field you're in, hey, things can work out for you."

After the season, Cangelosi was granted free agency, ending his two-year stint with the Marlins. The organization appreciated his two seasons as a utility outfielder, but it was time to part ways. "You can't play no more!" Leyland had told him. Cangelosi, who would be 36 in 1999, disagreed. Wanting to return to Chicago—and remain in the game—he agreed to a non-roster contract with the White Sox in January 1999 with an invitation to spring training. "All I want is a chance to prove I can still play," he would tell Chicago reporters in March. "…If it doesn't work out here, I think I can play somewhere else. I know what my role is and I think I can help another team. I'm not even thinking about retiring."

* * *

Baseball, as John Cangelosi found out throughout his playing career, can be a cruel sport. You might, for instance, have the numbers but still get cut due to circumstances outside of your control. Cangelosi saw it happen with the White Sox in 1991. He saw it again eight years later, again with the same organization.

During spring training in 1999, Cangelosi batted .308 and felt he'd done enough to make it to the big-league roster. But battling with him for a reserve outfield spot was veteran Darrin Jackson, who hit .462 in the spring. All throughout the spring, the White Sox maintained they were keeping only one veteran outfielder—either Cangelosi or Jackson—not both, because they wanted to give their younger outfielders more playing time during the season. "I made it very clear to each when we signed them that one might be kept to play a little and help the kids, but probably not both," general manager Ron Schueler told Joe Goddard of the *Chicago Sun-Times* then. "We're giving them an opportunity, but they know the situation."

By the end of the spring, it was clear Jackson was a better fit for what the organization was looking for, despite Cangelosi's strong spring numbers. Having made the decision to keep Jackson, the White Sox tried to traded Cangelosi in the final days of spring training. But when they couldn't work out a deal with another major-league team just before Opening Day, they wound up releasing him.

For Cangelosi, the release still hurts him to this day; he feels he never had a shot from the very beginning because the club had already made up its mind. "When I didn't make the White Sox in 1999—I should've made that team too, but they had plans for Darrin Jackson—I had a really good spring," he reflects matter-of-factly. "Darrin and I were neck and neck. I thought I brought more to the table. The role was more for me. I didn't know it at the time, but I had no chance going in. They had plans for Darrin Jackson. Kenny Williams [the White Sox's vice-president of player development who then became the team's general manager in October 2000] wanted Darrin to begin with…" Jackson would spend the 1999 season on the big-league roster before joining the team's broadcast booth the following year.

When he was released by the White Sox, Cangelosi realized his major-league career was probably over. He contacted other teams, but there weren't even any Triple-A jobs available, as all of the rosters, with the season around the corner, were pretty much set. "That was the first time I didn't have a Triple-A job. I tried to stay in shape. It was weird being home when the season was going on. It was the first time in 20 years I wasn't playing baseball. It was weird." Two months passed, and nobody was calling. "So, I just told my family, 'I think I'm done. Let's go to Pittsburgh for vacation—because I had a house in Pittsburgh.' I was driving the family to Pittsburgh, and then…" The phone suddenly rang. It was Jim Leyland, who had stepped down as Marlins skipper just days after the 1998 regular season ended and was hired the following week to manage the Colorado Rockies.

Cangelosi, thinking Leyland wanted him as a reserve outfielder in Colorado, quickly became excited. "I go, 'Damn. You're gonna give me a job!' So, I started talking to him," recalls Cangelosi today. "I go, 'Skip, man!' But he starts laughing. Jimmy says, 'Forget it, man, Cangy! You can't play no more!' We both laugh and chuckle." (Leyland made that point clear to Cangelosi, and even told the *Rocky Mountain News* the same thing later that season. "He's done [as a player]. You can quote me on that," he told the Denver newspaper. "He's well-done… [But] he's had a good career. That guy has gotten a lot out of his ability, and he plays hard.")

Leyland had a job in mind for Cangelosi, but not as a player. And not on the big-league club, either. "So, Jimmy Leyland goes, 'Hey, Cangy, I need an outfield base running guy in Colorado in the minor leagues. Would you be interested in being our outfield roving instructor?' I said, 'You know, let me think about it.' I thought about it and then I called him back and accepted the job. That's how I started coaching. I was an outfield roving instructor with the Rockies."

* * *

With Cangelosi's playing career seemingly coming to an end, he had no regrets. Even today, he feels the same. Obviously, baseball fans now know the height of the sport's so-called "Steroid Era" can be traced to the late 1990s, when numerous players were putting up monster power numbers in both leagues. Roger Maris' single-season home run record of 61, for instance, was broken in 1998—by both Mark McGwire and Sammy Sosa—after surviving for 37 years. Cangelosi, when asked to discuss the impact of steroids on the sport, shrugs. As far as he was concerned, he never needed the extra help; his ability was enough.

"I knew that steroids were around," Cangelosi says when asked to comment on his view on performance-enhancing drugs. "I really never personally saw it. But I knew guys that were taking it. I never really saw it. It really didn't bother me. But for years, pitchers have been cheating. So, it was their choice. If taking steroids might've helped me prolong my career a little bit, I don't know. I just refused to take it. I thought of my health first. I'm assuming if I took steroids, I could've been faster or wouldn't have lost a step here or there. I mean, it could've been maybe my legs wouldn't have lost a step or two for a couple of more years. Obviously, it's an advantage, but I elected not to take it.

"Honestly, I didn't feel cheated. I mean, in my opinion, you still have to hit the baseball. I don't care how strong you are or what it does for you; you still have to have baseball skill. And I'm not a doctor, but I think the advantage of taking steroids, your body doesn't break down. So, maybe your strength is there more often whereas I'm a little sluggish, a little slower. My bat speed isn't the same, their confidence is always up. Their energy is always there. So, maybe from that standpoint, they had an advantage. But you still have to hit the baseball."

Sure, he was disappointed that no teams wanted his services as a player, but he didn't have any regrets. Instead, he is proud that he managed to extend his career up till the late 1990s when it seemed he was pushed out after his rookie year in 1986. "The way I view things or the reason why I was successful at a high level, is one, I was mentally tough. But two, you can control what you can control. You're gonna be in great situations which are very easy. You're gonna be in bad situations that are gonna be difficult. It's just a matter of how you choose to react to that. So, I look it as making a negative into a positive or a bad situation into a better situation.

"At the end of the day, if you let someone else's actions affect your future or your moving forward, the only person that gets hurt is you. In that situation [in my rookie year], dealing with getting benched and Jim Fregosi not allowing me to play, I mean, he's my coach, he's my manager. Even though I don't agree with it, I have to accept it. And I just moved forward from that.

"Then when I got traded to Pittsburgh, I became a utility player, and again I could've complained or I could've just said, 'Hey man, you know, I'm an everyday player. I can steal bases. I'm more valuable as an everyday player.' But I opted to take the route of, 'Okay, if these are the cards that I'm dealt, then I'm gonna try to be the best utility player I can be and be the best role player I can be.' I'm not necessarily saying that's the right or wrong answer, but that's how I chose to apply my job, my future.

"Looking back, yeah, I wanted to play every day, I felt like I could play every day in the big leagues, and I'm more valuable as an everyday player. But, you know, I built a great relationship with Jimmy Leyland. I was blessed with a great career. I had longevity. Again, no one has a crystal ball. You don't know how things are gonna turn out. But I look at it as, 'I was blessed to play as long as I did.'"

Indeed. Cangelosi was part of the 1986 rookie class that featured, among others, Jose Canseco, Wally Joyner, Pete Incaviglia, Danny Tartabull, Ruben Sierra and Cory Snyder in the American League. Over in the National League, the list of rookies included Will Clark, Andres Galarraga, Robby Thompson, Kevin Mitchell, Barry Larkin, Darren Daulton, John Kruk and Barry Bonds.

Cangelosi, despite being told along the way that he wasn't big enough to be a Major League Baseball player, ended up staying in the big leagues longer than guys such as Incaviglia, Snyder, Daulton, Tartabull, Thompson and Kruk. (Among pitchers, Jamie Moyer ended up having the longest career out of the '86 rookie class, pitching in the majors until the 2012 season. Among position players, Bonds had the longest career, playing 22 seasons until his final year in 2007.)

"I mean, I was blessed to have played as long as I did in the big leagues," adds Cangelosi. "I wasn't supposed to make it. I played against guys like Rafael Palmeiro, Danny Tartabull and Jose Canseco, and I wasn't drafted out of high school. Nobody wanted to take me because I threw left-handed and hit right-handed. I had to learn how to hit left-handed and become a switch-hitter. But in Chicago, the White Sox gave up on me. I never played for the Tigers in the big leagues even though I should've made that team. Things didn't work out with the Rangers and the Mets.

"But I never gave up. I got the most out of my ability. Sure, I wanted to play every day, but I was blessed to have had a manager like Jimmy Leyland in my corner. John Boles was there for me. Same with Terry Collins. They knew I played hard and I played the game the right way. So, I have no regrets about my career. A guy my size, after all, shouldn't have been in the big leagues. That's what a lot of people said. But I was an overachiever and I had longevity. I had a great career."

Although he wasn't an everyday player during his career, he did hit well against some of the toughest pitchers in baseball. Of course, he had that .455 batting average off John Smoltz, the Hall-of-Famer-to-be, in 22 at-bats, and the following pitchers probably also hated seeing him come to the plate:

- He hit .467 in 15 at-bats against Hideo Nomo, the 1995 National League Rookie of the Year who was dominant in the NL in the early part of his career.
- He was 4-for-10 off Bert Blyleven (.400) and 4-for-12 versus Jack Morris (.333)—a pair of future Hall of Famers—and 3-for-10 against Roger Clemens (.300), a 354-game winner and seven-time Cy Young Award winner.
- There's also a .353 average in 17 at-bats off John Tudor, the tough left-hander with the

Cardinals in the mid-1980s who won 21 games in 1985.

- Houston ace Mike Scott, a one-time Cy Young Award winner who had a dominant run in the NL in that same era? Five hits in nine at-bats for a .556 lifetime average.
- Off Dennis Martinez, who won 245 games in the majors, Cangelosi batted .333 in 18 at-bats.
- Against Dodgers ace Ramon Martinez, it was .375 in eight at-bats. In the same number of at-bats, he hit .375 against Royals ace Kevin Appier.

"That wasn't a lot of at-bats," Cangelosi says when asked to explain his success against those top pitchers. "I went 4-for-4 off John Tudor in one game. I saw the ball well off him. Dennis Martinez, I saw the ball well. Jack Morris, I think I got a couple of hits off of him. Clemens... I don't know if I had a lot of at-bats against those guys in the American League. But I did do well when I faced them. I walked a lot against those guys. For me, I was up there to take pitches and try to get on base anyway I could. I guess I just hit the ball well against those guys and got on base a lot."

* * *

Cangelosi officially began working as the Rockies' roving outfield-base running coach in July 1999, and the organization was happy enough with his work with the young minor-leaguers that it seemed it would be a long-term fit. Paul Egins, the Rockies' player development director, was certainly impressed, telling Jack Etkin of the *Rocky Mountain News* as much in a story that ran on September 13. "I've seen all of the instructors and coaches we've had in this organization," said Egins, who had been with the Rockies since September 1991, before the franchise began play in the National League some 19 months later. "The effect that he has on kids... the only other person I've seen that with is Clint Hurdle. It's overwhelming how they respond to him and how he communicates to them."

Cangelosi, the Rockies' first full-time roving outfield-base running instructor, stressed the importance of on-base percentage, a statistical category with which he was familiar but was a revelation to many young minor-leaguers. Egins was amazed when he toured the Rockies affiliates and had minor-leaguers tell him how much they enjoyed working with Cangelosi. Some players even wanted Egins to let Cangelosi know they were working on nuances he taught them relating to base running and taking pitches.

With injuries mounting with the Triple-A Colorado Springs Sky Sox, though, there was a change in plans just one month into Cangelosi's new position. Egins and Cangelosi were together at Double-A Carolina in late July when Egins received word of a rash of injuries to outfielders at Colorado Springs. Chris Hatcher, who was leading the Pacific Coast League with a .360 batting average, was sidelined thanks to a dislocated thumb, and Edgard Clemente, who was hitting .299, was suffering from a sprained ankle. Finding a minor-league free agent then would have been difficult, so Egins asked Cangelosi to join the Sky Sox, initially expecting he would have to play for about a week.

And so, on August 1, Cangelosi was back in uniform, activated by the Sky Sox. Except he was needed for a month, not a week. "They [just] had a lot of injuries at the time," he says now. "The organization made me a player-coach in Triple-A. So, I started playing in Colorado Springs. Again, I got my legs back in shape. I still loved playing the game. I was hitting over .300." In 29 games, in fact, he batted .330 in 109 at-bats while posting a gaudy .452 on-base percentage.

Thinking he could still play in the big leagues the following season, Cangelosi decided he would work out in the off-season to be ready for 2000. The Rockies organization, meanwhile, realized what his plans were, and pushed hard to persuade him to stay on as a coach. "They heard wind that I was gonna go to winter ball and try to get a big-league job the next spring," recalls Cangelosi. "Leyland called me and said, 'Hey, you know, they really love what you're doing. They love you as a coach. If I were to call you up and give you your two weeks so that you'll have your [major-league] service time—and you'll be maxed out on your pension—will you agree? The only way they're gonna let me call you up is if you agree to retire and continue coaching.' And that was probably the only time that I really second-guessed myself because I still loved playing. I could've kept playing. I could've gone to Europe and Italy and played one day a week... I could've traveled the world and just kinda kept playing... even if I didn't get back to the big leagues."

In the end, Cangelosi accepted the Rockies' offer. The outfielder-turned-roving-instructor-turned-player/coach, who needed 12 days in the majors to give him enough service time to qualify for the 10-year major-league pension benefit, agreed to retire and return to the Rockies as a roving instructor for the 2000 season. In exchange, the Rockies would arrange for him to get those 12 days with the big-league club in September. "So, I decided to retire," Cangelosi says. "Jimmy Leyland called me up. I played for two weeks, got my time in, and then I went right to instructional league with the Rockies."

As Egins noted then, Sky Sox manager Bill Hayes and hitting coach Tony Torchia both assured him Cangelosi could still play center field. Had they said otherwise, Egins added, Cangelosi wouldn't have gotten the opportunity to be called up. As promised, the Rockies called him up in September, and he appeared in seven games in a Rockies uniform. On September 17, Cangelosi collected his final major-league hit, a double off the Dodgers' Robinson Checo while pinch-hitting for Rockies pitcher Darryl Kile. Five days later, he appeared in his final major-league game, pinch-hitting for Luther Hackman and grounding out against Arizona Diamondbacks right-hander Andy Benes. He was replaced in the next half inning and never appeared in another big-league contest.

His improbable playing career—one that saw him appear in 1,038 major-league games, collect 501 hits in 2,004 at-bats, record a respectable on-base percentage of .370, and steal 154 bases—was indeed over this time. "No, not at all," John Boles says when asked if he was surprised that Cangelosi wound up lasting that long in the big leagues. "People will say, 'He was a gamer. He was an overachiever.' I don't think the 'overachieving' thing was correct. He had plus-range in center field. He could cover the ground in center field. He was a plus-base stealer and a plus-base runner. Plus, he was a switch-hitter. So, he was a valuable asset on a major-league team. When I was with the Florida Marlins when we won the World Series in 1997, he was an integral utility player on that team."

Former White Sox teammate Harold Baines isn't surprised either at Cangelosi's longevity in the majors. "John," adds Baines, "wasn't blessed with all the tools but he played hard. He didn't have home-run ability, but he always got on base for you. John's a good guy, a scrappy guy. You surround yourself with good people like him."

Leyland had kept his promise and called Cangelosi up. What the Rockies wanted, in return, was for Cangelosi to remain in the organization as a coach. At the time, he gave every indication he would honor his agreement with the club. Things changed, though, after the season, when Leyland retired, and some of the personnel was no longer the same. In the off-season, Cangelosi himself left the Rockies organization and accepted the roving base running and outfield instructor position with the Chicago Cubs.

"That year, Leyland retired," Cangelosi, who wound up spending four seasons in the Cubs' farm system as a coach before leaving to run his own baseball school in the Chicago area, explains. "He didn't like what was going on. He was kinda burned out. Didn't like the way the players were just kinda, like, not the same kinda blue-collar players. He walked away from the game for four, five years, and did whatever he did. The personnel changed. And then that's when I called Jim Hendry and asked to be the roving coach for the Cubs."

Chapter Thirteen
Life After the Majors

There is a lot of Americana in this little guy's story.
—Ken "Hawk" Harrelson, Chicago White Sox
vice-president, as told to *Sports Illustrated*'s
Roger Jackson (1986)

Today, John Cangelosi still lives in the Chicago area, and does go out to a few White Sox games every season. "Cangy comes out to the ballpark about five times a year," confirms former teammate Harold Baines, who now works in the White Sox front office after spending 13 seasons as a coach on the big-league club. "We still stay in touch. We play golf maybe once or twice a year."

Cangelosi stays in touch with former teammates such as Baines, Dwight Gooden, Bobby Bonilla and Barry Bonds. It's always good to reminisce the old days. But he wouldn't call himself a baseball fan these days. "I really, to be honest with you, don't watch all that much baseball," he confesses. "I might channel surf." Naturally, when Houston, one of his former teams, made it to the World Series in 2017 against the L.A. Dodgers, he just had to tune in. "I actually watched that World Series, which was very exciting. I normally don't watch it, but, I mean, all the hitting that went on in that Series was just crazy. I really don't watch baseball because I'm in the baseball business to begin with. So, the last thing I wanna do is turn baseball on."

Which sports does he watch? "I watch the Golf Channel a lot," he laughs. He's also happy when the local Chicago Bears do well. "They're playing really good," he marveled during the Thanksgiving holiday in 2018, with the Bears in first place in the NFC North Division.

Obviously, he does realize the game of baseball has changed quite a bit since the last time he put on a major-league uniform. "I think the game's different today. I think it's just our generation now. Everybody works out. Everyone's in shape. Everyone's got specific training for their sport. So, when these guys get to the big leagues, I feel like, all of them are just in better shape.

"Back when I played, some guys kinda worked out. Some guys didn't. For me, I didn't really work out all that much—until the later part of my career. But I went to winter baseball to stay in shape. I played baseball year-round to make money and stay in shape."

Indeed. He recalls the days with the Pirates in the 1980s, when he played winter ball in Puerto Rico to get the at-bats he needed to stay sharp. He wasn't getting 400 at-bats during the major-league season, so playing winter ball gave him the opportunity to get the extra swings that he needed. For those who aren't aware, the major-league seasons in Latin America— Mexico, Puerto Rico, Venezuela and the Dominican Republic—occur during the winter months. At the end of those respective seasons, a Caribbean World Series which pits those four league champions is played in the first week of February. In order to get to the Caribbean Series during the era Cangelosi played in, there was first a 60-game winter schedule and the top four teams in the league played an 18-game round-robin followed by a best-of-seven league final.

For Cangelosi, playing in winter ball gave him the much-needed at-bats to stay in shape for the big-league season every year.

"Today, guys make so much money [that] they can afford to stay home, hire a strength and conditioning guy, and work out all winter. It's just the space now. Now, they have so much more time and money, and finances, to take care of themselves. I think today the guys are in way better shape. They have the ability to be in better shape."

Then, there's also the pitching aspect of things, with all the power arms in the game today. "From a pitching standpoint, I don't understand why there's multiple guys in the big leagues throwing three digits. I don't know if it's the radar gun. I don't know if it's legit. But back in the day when I played, you'd have guys that would, maybe, throw in the low 90s, high 80s, for an average. Then you'd have, maybe, three to five guys on your rotation that might throw 94 to 97, or 95 to 98, in that range. And then, in the big leagues, you might've had, maybe, five guys that threw a couple of pitches over 100.

"Now, it seems like you have two or three guys on *every staff* that are throwing over 100. So, I don't understand the scientific part of that. But it's just crazy how these guys are throwing over 100. It seems like everybody and their mother's throwing 97, 98, like it's nothing. I don't know, is it because they're trained all the way up to the big leagues?

"I just don't understand that concept. But what I see as far as changes in the game? I just see guys that are in better shape. I see guys hitting more home runs. I see pitchers throwing harder. It's the same game. Why are they able to do all these things? I think it's just from the training aspect of it."

One thing that hasn't changed since his retirement, of course, is that fact that the American League still uses the designated hitter while the National League still hasn't adopted the DH rule. It's obvious, because of his role on NL teams, what Cangelosi's stance is on the DH debate. "I mean, in hindsight, anyone will answer differently," he says now. "If you were talking to an older guy that is a DH, if he could prolong his career, he would want the DH. As far as my role in the big leagues, if you're a utility player, you don't want the DH. When I was in the American League, I very rarely played because there really weren't any double switches. There weren't really any moving components. The American League game, you just play. There really isn't much double-switching or pinch-hitting. It is what it is. You might have a defensive replacement at the end of the game. That's what I did with the Rangers. What I would do is go in for Kevin Reimer at the end of the game. After his last at-bat, I would go in and play two innings. But I wouldn't get an at-bat.

"For me, I was more valuable in the National League because I could pinch-hit, I could double switch, I could pinch-run... There's more moving components. Plus, in my opinion—because I know there are different opinions out there—I think the National League is a more exciting game to watch. As a manager, there are more things to do. 'Hey, do I take my pitcher out? I know he's pitching well… but it's the sixth inning and we're down a run...' There are more decisions to be made, more managing to be [done], more strategical moves to be made. So, I'm a fan of the National League, and I'm a fan of no DH. It's just a much more exciting game to watch, too. The American League is just... you've got one through nine; they all hit. When you have a pitcher hitting, there's just a lot more that could happen."

* * *

Cangelosi can look back now and wonder what could have been. What if he hadn't been benched in his rookie year? Would he have stolen 80 bases? Would he have been the White Sox's starting center fielder after 1986? What if Tony La Russa had stayed on as manager? Or, toward the end of his career, what if the Marlins hadn't dismantled the 1997 championship team? By how many years would his career have been extended?

But there's another what-if scenario. Remember Cangelosi's brother Vince? He had quit baseball after getting into an argument with Cangy on the field. There's more to that story, however. "My brother quit and started doing other things," says Cangelosi, continuing the story about Vince.

"So, he didn't play sports in high school. He got into bodybuilding for a little bit. He flourished. He was third-place Mr. Florida. Obviously, there was no money involved in bodybuilding at the time. He didn't play football in high school. Some of our friends went on to play college football. My brother wanted to be with them. He walked on and made the team, and became the starting cornerback. He made the team and then something happened, but he ended up quitting after two games and then just going to school."

In Cangelosi's first year in the major leagues, Vince called him. "He was on the phone. He said, 'Hey, call Demie. I wanna play baseball. I don't have any money to go to school. I wanna play baseball and get a scholarship and get the school to pay for it.'"

Cangy thought Vince was nuts. "I tell him, 'Vince, I can't. You're crazy. That's a top junior college program in Florida. The last time you played was 13 years old. I'm not gonna do that.'

"But Vince pleaded with me. He goes, 'Just call him.'

"I called Demie and I said, 'Hey, my brother wants a tryout. Can you just give him a quick look? Just give him a quick look, and don't embarrass him.' Not only does he make the team, but he starts too. I think he has, like, 70 stolen bases, which I think was fourth in junior college. To me, if he wasn't older—I think he was 23 years old at the time—he might've got drafted. He played two years in junior college at Miami Dade-North. Then he got a scholarship to the University of Central Florida, and he finishes playing Division I baseball. And then he was done. I mean, think about it. The last time he played baseball was 13 years old. He goes to a top junior college. Then he goes into Division I—and has it paid for. That's the kind of athlete he was. With the numbers and the things he was doing, someone would've drafted him. If he was 19, someone would've drafted him. Normally, for guys that were 22 or 23, they would be playing in Double-A or Triple-A."

For Vince Cangelosi, it was unfortunate. John Cangelosi feels his brother could have made it as a star in baseball had he stuck to it as a teenager. It just wasn't meant to be.

Back then, John Cangelosi couldn't help his brother. There was nothing that he could have done for Vince. Now, having played Major League Baseball and having acquired invaluable baseball knowledge at the big-league level, he knows he can make a difference in the lives of other kids—and he wants to help kids in the Chicago area to pursue their baseball dream. "You know," Cangelosi says matter-of-factly, "I shouldn't have played in the big leagues. I was supposed to have been too short to play Major League Baseball. But I made it. I never gave up. I feel that my story is something that can be inspiring to kids out there. Kids who have the talent to get to the next level... I wanna do something to help inspire them to get the most out of their ability. I wanna instill in these kids' minds that if you really believe in yourself—in your ability—you create a routine and you're gonna be successful in something. I mean, not just in baseball, but in life."

And if there are kids possessing Vince-like athletic talents, John wants to help further develop their skills. Hey, maybe those kids will have a shot at getting drafted—or getting recruited by colleges and someday get drafted. The way he sees it, making an impact on those young athletes and helping them change outcomes in their own lives is his passion.

It all started in 2008, when Cangelosi and his business partner, Jim Thompson, approached former MLB and NFL star Bo Jackson about a baseball training facility dedicated to developing young athletes. Athletes in the Midwest, Cangelosi believed, were at a major disadvantage to other athletes across the country due to weather conditions that prevented them from training year-round. So, an indoor training facility would allow those athletes to train even during the winter months. "About 10 years ago, I brought this concept, a dome, to my business partner, Jim Thompson," Cangelosi said in 2018. "I told him, 'I'd like to bring a baseball academy, an indoor training facility, to the Midwest area because a lot of the kids, they play outside only three-and-a-half months out of the year. Then, the rest of the time, they are inside. And they have a small batting cage, and that's pretty much it.' I wanted to create a vision, an indoor place [with] no obstruction [where] they could get a full workout. A one-stop shop where it's a rehab facility, a strength-and-conditioning facility, a hitting [and] fielding [facility]... all of it. They go there and they can have a three-and-a-half or four-hour experience and they don't have to go anywhere else. It's a state-of-the-art facility." The idea was to change young athletes' mindsets, to make them realize if they wanted to compete in a sport like baseball, they had to train year-round. Inside such a dome, where the weather wouldn't be an issue, it was easier to embrace that mindset.

"Once I had it planned, I brought it to Bo Jackson, who's a friend of mine. I said, 'Look, this is what I plan on doing. I'd like for you to be involved with this however you choose to.' He liked it so much that we're all equal partners, moving forward." And soon after, Bo Jackson's Elite Sports (BJES), a training facility dedicated to developing athletes, was opened in the Chicago suburb of Lockport, Illinois.

Home to Cangelosi Baseball, which provides private one-on-one lessons and baseball instruction, and Bo Jackson Football, BJES operates out of an indoor sports complex offering 88,000 square feet of training space for athletes. The facility includes two Major

League Baseball-sized infields with un-obstructive playing surfaces for all ages, 18 batting cages with pitching machines, a multi-purpose field with netting, and baseball video pitching simulator machines that deliver Major League-quality pitches thrown to multiple positions both within and outside the strike zone at speeds between 60 and 100 mph. It was exactly what Cangelosi had envisioned. Young athletes could take batting practice, study their swings on video, and establish their routines—just like how players do it in the big leagues. Cangelosi even brought in former big leaguers Dan Pasqua, Kevin Sefcik and Erik Pappas— all of whom had ties to the Chicago area—to provide hitting, fielding, and pitching instruction at the academy. "Then, we brought it to Nike. We have Nike sponsorship. We have Gatorade sponsorship. We just opened our second one in [the Columbus suburb of] Hilliard, Ohio, in 2017. I love what I do. I love giving back. That's my daily job."

Everyone, of course, knows Bo. The only athlete in history to be named an All-Star in both baseball and football, Jackson is widely considered one of the greatest athletes of all-time. As for Cangelosi? "I remember watching John Cangelosi play," a long-time sports editor says with little enthusiasm when Cangy's name is brought up, "and recall that one of my friends was something of a fan." Then, there's the next generation of sports fans, those same kids who are receiving hitting instruction at Cangelosi Baseball. They may not know John Cangelosi the ex-Major League Baseball player. After all, his big-league playing career ended before those kids were even born! But do their parents know who John Cangelosi is? "[Let me tell you about] the clientele there," Cangelosi says with a laugh. "One thing about the Midwest and the Chicagoland area, they're very educated sports fans. They know who I am. I'm well respected because I'm a little guy from the South Side who shouldn't have played college ball, let alone pro ball. I ended up playing 13 years and winning a World Series. I'm well respected in that arena. It's not just my name and face on the building. When I put my name behind something, I'm actually there working. People appreciate that. Parents appreciate that."

As far as he is concerned, it's all about the kids. That's why he is there at the academy all the time, coaching those young athletes. He cares about these young kids. One year around Christmas—long before Cangelosi Baseball was launched—he even talked baseball on the phone with a kid, a complete stranger, because he cared. That's just how he is.

What happened was, in the early 2000s, a 10-year-old baseball fan named Alec Cangelosi from the Chicago suburb of Burr Ridge—no relation to John Cangelosi—wanted to contact Cangy because it was pretty cool to share the same last name with a Major League Baseball player. At the time, Cangy had already retired, but he was still a hero to Alec. Alas, phone calls and letters to Cangy's former teams led nowhere—until one of Alec's relatives came up with a possible phone number.

One morning, just a few days before Christmas, the boy's mother tried the number but got an answering machine and hung up without leaving a voice message. Unbeknownst to her, John Cangelosi had Caller ID and saw that the phone line was in the name "Cangelosi." A few minutes later, the phone rang and Alec answered. It was none other than Cangy, who began the conversation with, "Hi, this is John Cangelosi. Did you call me?" What an unforgettable early Christmas gift for Alec—a phone call from his baseball hero!

John and Alec chatted baseball, and Cangy even invited the boy to his baseball clinic. "Well, why wouldn't I take time to talk to him," John Cangelosi said at the time when a local reporter ran that story in the *Chicago Tribune*, "and make a kid happy? It's kind of cool that someone has the same last name."

Parents who send their kids to Cangelosi's baseball school aren't surprised by Cangy's gesture. "Cangy's all about the kids. He's very positive with them. Just a tremendous resource for them," says lawyer and baseball memorabilia collector Michael McCormick, whose son Matt has regular private lessons with John. "A wonderful role model for kids." Bobby Valentine, Cangelosi's former manager in Texas, believes those kids are in good hands because of the passion and knowledge their coach possesses. "Now that he's working with kids," says Valentine, "I hope that not only his knowledge of the game but also his love and enthusiasm for the game could be transmitted into the next generations of baseball players—because John Cangelosi was good for the game."

"For many years, I would use Johnny Cangelosi as an example that baseball is a sport that gives an opportunity to everybody," adds Paul Mainieri, Head Baseball Coach at Louisiana State University. "You don't have to be the biggest guy. As long as you can play, people will recognize that. But of course, with the players I have today, they don't know his name as well as some of the other [current Major League Baseball players]. Now, I use examples like Dustin

Pedroia, you know, little guys like that. But for many years while I was coaching, I would use Johnny as an example for players in different schools that I was at."

Terry Collins, who managed the New York Mets for seven seasons during the 2010s, acknowledges now that it was easy for him to bring up the name Cangelosi as an example even for major-leaguers who weren't all that familiar with Cangy. "It was easy," Collins says. "I told a couple of my pinch-hitters in New York about John Cangelosi. I would tell them about a guy I had in Houston who, when he was up there, was gonna grind out every at-bat. He knew his job was to get on base, and he had a successful major-league career. John Cangelosi was the kind of guy you wanted on your team if you were gonna be successful and win a lot of games. The two years I had him in Houston, we won games because of him."

And John Cangelosi, as those who know him or played with or coached him will tell you, was good for the game of baseball. Cangelosi, they will tell you, was a blue-collar guy who worked hard and didn't quit even when people told him he wasn't going to make it. Despite a definite height disadvantage, he did make it to the big leagues and set an American League rookie base-stealing record. He was a World Series champion—and perhaps it was fitting that he won his ring with a team based in South Florida, as he grew up in nearby Hialeah. And even after he was done playing, he's not done in the game of baseball; he still inspires kids every day with his passion in the batting cage in Lockport, Illinois, where he can be heard yelling, "Practice with a purpose! Do you understand that?"

Appendix:
John Cangelosi Statistics
Major League Baseball
Hitting Statistics—Regular Season

John Cangelosi Statistics
Major League Baseball
Hitting Statistics—Regular Season

Year	Team	G	AB	R	H	2B	3B	HR	RBI	SB	CS	BB	SO	BA	OBP
1985	White Sox (A.L.)	5	2	2	0	0	0	0		0	0	0	1	.600	.333
1986	White Sox (A.L.)	137	438	65	103	16	3	2	32	50	17	71	61	.235	.349
1987	Pirates (N.L.)	104	182	44	50	8	1	0	18	21	6	71	33	.275	.427
1988	Pirates (N.L.)	75	118	18	30	4	1	0	9	9	4	17	16	.264	.353
1989	Pirates (N.L.)	112	160	18	33	4	0	0	9	11	4	35	20	.219	.365
1990	Pirates (N.L.)	58	76	13	15	2	0	0		7	2	11	12	.197	.307
1991									Did not play in the majors						
1992	Rangers (A.L.)	75	85	12	16	2	0	1	6	6	3	18	16	.188	.330
1993									Did not play in the majors						
1994	Mets (N.L.)	62	111	14	28	4	0	0	6	5	5	19	20	.252	.371
1995	Astros (N.L.)	90	201	46	64	4	3	2	18	21	7	48	42	.318	.457
1996	Astros (N.L.)	106	262	49	69	9	4	2	16	17	9	44	41	.263	.378
1997	Marlins (N.L.)	103	190	47	47	8	0	1	12	3	3	19	33	.243	.323
1998	Marlins (N.L.)	104	177	43	43	8	1	0	10	2	3	30	23	.251	.365
1999	Rockies (N.L.)	7	6	1	1	1	0	0	0	0	1	0	4	.167	.167
14 seasons		2004		73		15			154			798	322	.259	.370

Hitting Statistics: Postseason

Year	Team	Series (Opponent)	G	AB	R	H	2B	3B	HR	RBI	SB	CS	BB	SO	BA	OBP
1997	Marlins	NLDS (vs. Giants)	1	1	0	0	0	0	0	0	0	0	0	0	.000	.000
1997	Marlins	NLCS (vs. Braves)	3	5	0	1	1	0	0	0	0	0	0	1	.200	.333
1997	Marlins	WS (vs. Indians)	3	3	0	1	0	0	0	0	0	0	2	2	.333	.333
	7		9		2									222	.360

Hitting Legend:

G = Games • AB = At-Bats • R = Runs Scored • H = Hits • 2B = Doubles • 3B = Triples • HR = Home Runs • RBI = Runs Batted In • SB = Stolen Bases • CS = Caught Stealing • BB = Bases on Balls • SO = Strikeouts • BA = Batting Average • OBP = On-base Percentage

Pitching Statistics

Year	Team	W	L	ERA	G	GS	CG	SHO	SV	IP	H	R	ER	HR	BB	SO	GP
1988	Pirates (N.L.)	0	0	0.00	1					2.0	2	0	0	0	0	0	0
1993	Astros (N.L.)	0	0	0.00	1					1.0	1	0	0	0	0	0	0
1997	Marlins (N.L.)	0	0	0.00	1					1.0	0	0	0	0	1	2	0
	0		0	0.00	3					4.0	3	0	0	0	1	2	0

Pitching Legend:

W = Wins • L = Losses • ERA = Earned Run Average • G = Games • IP = Innings Pitched • H = Hits Allowed • R = Runs Allowed • ER = Earned Runs Allowed • HR = Home Runs Allowed • BB = Bases on Balls Allowed • SO = Strikeouts

Major League Baseball
Hitting Statistics

Year	Team (Level)	G	AB	R	H	2B	3B	HR	RBI	SB	CS	BB	SO	BA	OBP
1982	Niagara Falls (A-)	76	277	60	80	15	4	5	38	45	7	56	51	.289	.415
1983	Appleton (A)	128	439	87	124	12	4	1	48	87	33	99	81	.282	.421
1984	Glens Falls (AA)	138	464	91	135	17	1		36	65	16	101	88	.291	.416
1985	Kansas City (AAA)	61													.355	
1986	Buffalo (AAA)	78	244	34	58	8	3		21	14	7	46	32	.238	.358
1988	Buffalo (AAA)	37	143	23	48	6	1	0	10	14	2	19	19	.331	.410
1990	Buffalo (AAA)	24	89	17	31	2	2	0	7	15	4	12	8	.348	.431
1991	Vancouver (AAA)	36	102	15	25	1	1	0	10	9	2	11	8	.245	.324
1992	Denver (AAA)	83	303	69	89	29	3	3	25	26	13	39	29	.294	.412
1993	Toledo (AAA)	27	74	9	20	3	0	0	6	10	7	7	13	.270	.365
1995	Toledo (AAA)	113	439	75	126	23	6	4	42	56	18	56	59	.292	.376
1999	Tampa (AAA)	96	108	18	39	4	4	2	9	11	3	19	31	.368	.464
1999	Colorado Springs (AAA)	29	109	36	36	7	0	1	13	4	5	24	16	.330	.452

Pitching Statistics

Year	Team (Level)	W	L	ERA	G	GS	CG	SHO	SV	IP	H	R	ER	HR	BB	SO	GP
1991	Denver (AAA)	0	0	2.45	2					3.2	3	1	1	0	2	1	0
1995	Toledo (AAA)	0	0	81.00	1					0.2	7	7	6		1	0	

Bibliography

Feinstein, John. *Where Nobody Knows Your Name: Life In the Minor Leagues of Baseball*, Doubleday, February 2014.

Gamboa, Tom and David Russell. *Tom Gamboa: My Life in Baseball*, McFarland & Co., December 2017.

Morgan, Joe with Richard Lally. *Long Balls, No Strikes: What Baseball Must Do to Keep the Good Times Rolling*, Crown, September 1999.

Neyer, Rob. *Rob Neyer's Big Book of Baseball Lineups: A Complete Guide to the Best, Worst, and Most Memorable Players to Ever Grace the Major Leagues*, Simon and Schuster, 2003.

Wedge, Doug and Charlie O'Brien. *The Cy Young Catcher*, Texas A&M University Press, March 2015.

Newspapers / Magazines

(Arlington Heights, IL) Daily Herald
Baseball America
The Boston Herald
Chicago Sun-Times
Chicago Tribune
The Dallas Morning News
The Denver Post

(Denver, CO) Rocky Mountain News
Fort Worth (Texas) Star-Telegram
The (Greenville, Ohio) Daily Advocate
Houston Chronicle
The Kansas City Star
Los Angeles Times
The Miami Herald
(Minneapolis, MN) Star Tribune
The (New Jersey) Record
The New York Times
The Palm Beach Post
Pittsburgh Post-Gazette
South Florida Sun Sentinel
The (Vancouver, WA) Columbian

Websites

Baseball-Reference.com
ESPN.com
Retrosheet.org
SBNation.com
SI.com/vault

List of Interviews

Terry Collins. Thursday, February 8, 2018.
Paul Mainieri. Monday, February 12, 2018.
Tommy Sandt. Monday, February 12, 2018.
Shelly Dunkel. Thursday, February 22, 2018.
John Boles. Thursday, February 22, 2018.
Harold Baines. Thursday, February 22, 2018.
Bobby Valentine. Thursday, August 9, 2018.

About the Author

K. P. Wee is the author of several sports books, including *Tom Candiotti: A Life of Knuckleballs* (2014); *The End of the Montreal Jinx: Boston's Short-Lived Glory in the Historic Bruins-Canadiens Rivalry* (2015); *Don't Blame the Knuckleballer: Baseball Legends, Myths, and Stories* (2015); and *The 1988 Dodgers: Reliving the Championship Season* (2018). He has appeared regularly as an in-studio guest on "Vancouver Canadians Game Day" on TSN1040 Radio (Vancouver, Canada).

Other Riverdale Avenue Books
You Might Enjoy

The 50 Greatest Red Sox Games
By Cecilia Tan and Bill Nowlin

The 50 Greatest Dodger Games of All Time
By J.P. Hornstra

Bronx Bummers:
An Unofficial History of the New York Yankees'
Bad Boys, Blunders and Brawls

By Robert Dominguez and David Hinckley

Bases Loaded: Baseball Erotica
Edited by F. Leonora Solomon

The Hot Streak: A Baseball Romance
By Cecilia Tan